MOPAR
Small-Block Engines

How to Build
Max Performance

Larry Shepard

CarTech®

CarTech®

CarTech®, Inc.
838 Lake Street South
Forest Lake, MN 55025
Phone: 651-277-1200 or 800-551-4754
Fax: 651-277-1203
www.cartechbooks.com

© 2016 by Larry Shepard

All rights reserved. No part of this publication may be reproduced or utilized in any form or by any means, electronic or mechanical, including photocopying, recording, or by any information storage and retrieval system, without prior permission from the Publisher. All text, photographs, and artwork are the property of the Author unless otherwise noted or credited.

The information in this work is true and complete to the best of our knowledge. However, all information is presented without any guarantee on the part of the Author or Publisher, who also disclaim any liability incurred in connection with the use of the information and any implied warranties of merchantability or fitness for a particular purpose. Readers are responsible for taking suitable and appropriate safety measures when performing any of the operations or activities described in this work.

All trademarks, trade names, model names and numbers, and other product designations referred to herein are the property of their respective owners and are used solely for identification purposes. This work is a publication of CarTech, Inc., and has not been licensed, approved, sponsored, or endorsed by any other person or entity. The Publisher is not associated with any product, service, or vendor mentioned in this book, and does not endorse the products or services of any vendor mentioned in this book.

Edit by Paul Johnson
Layout by Monica Seiberlich

ISBN 978-1-61325-549-0
Item No. SA377P

Library of Congress Cataloging-in-Publication Data
Names: Shepard, Larry, author.
Title: Mopar small-block engines : how to build max performance / Larry Shepard.
Description: Forest Lake, MN : CarTech, [2016]
Identifiers: LCCN 2016007881 | ISBN 9781613252802
Subjects: LCSH: Automobiles--Motors--Modification. | Chrysler automobile--Motors--Modification.
Classification: LCC TL210 .S465 2016 | DDC 629.25/04--dc23
LC record available at https://lccn.loc.gov/2016007881

Written, edited, and designed in the U.S.A.
Printed in the U.S.A.
10 9 8 7 6 5 4 3 2

Front Cover:
Producing 500 ft-lbs of torque at 4,000 rpm and 515 hp at 5,500 rpm, this LA 427-ci small-block is built for street driving and road racing. The foundation is a Mopar Performance block with a 4.125-inch-stroke crankshaft and a bore of 4.060 inches. It also features CNC-ported Edelbrock heads with a solid roller camshaft. (Photo Courtesy Andy Finkbeiner)

Title Page:
The first Mopar crate engine was based on the 360 production engine but had some performance parts added to increase its output to 360 hp. A few years later, Mopar added the 6-barrel crate engine (still a 360) to the lineup.

Back Cover Photos

Top Left:
The stock Mopar small-block has a secondary oil feed from the main bearing shell to the cam bearings. When building an engine for high performance or rebuild, always be sure these passages are not blocked or restricted.

Top Right:
The A-engine and Magnum are fitted with either hydraulic or mechanical rockers. Production A-engine and Magnum valvetrains look similar because they are both hydraulic and center on stamped steel rocker arms. This A-engine with adjustable mechanical rockers has aluminum roller-tip rockers.

Middle:
The cast-iron Indy A-engine cylinder head uses both exhaust manifold–attaching patterns. The stock one is close to the ports and the wide one was used on the W2 original heads. As a precaution, I recommend plugging the holes that you do not use on the W2 with small Allen screws.

Bottom:
Many Holley-based carburetors have two float bowls and two fuel entrances. With this configuration, you should use a fuel-line setup similar to this. Several kits are available for these Holleys that make the extra plumbing easy to organize.

CONTENTS

Acknowledgments 4
Introduction 4

Chapter 1: Blocks 9
Block Design 9
Identification 10
Basic Features 15
Block Oiling 17
Motor Mounts 18
Core Shift 18
Machining 19
Main Caps 23
Special Features and Operations ... 25

Chapter 2: Crankshafts and Connecting Rods 26
Production Cranks 26
High-Performance Street Cranks .. 28
Race Cranks 29
Material 29
Full-Radius Journals 31
Crank Prep 31
Bearings 33
Vibration Dampeners 33
Connecting Rods 34

Chapter 3: Pistons and Rings 39
Production Pistons 39
Aftermarket Pistons 40
Piston Profile 41
Compression Ratio 42
Piston Design 42
Piston Pins 47
Piston Rings 48

Chapter 4: Camshaft, Lifters and Cam Drive 51
Production Cams 51
Aftermarket Cams 52
Camshaft Technology 52
High-Performance and Race Cams 56
Cam Selection Process 57
Cam Installation 61
Tappets 63
Cam Drive 63
Timing Sets 65
Oil Pump Drive 65

Chapter 5: Cylinder Heads 66
Identification 66
Production Cylinder Heads 68
Head Spec Comparison 71
Aluminum Heads 73
Cast-Iron Heads 75
Bare Heads 76
Cylinder Head Selection and Prep .. 76
High-Performance Valve Job 79
Special Head Considerations 81
Valves 82
Head Gaskets 85

Chapter 6: Valvetrain 86
Oiling System 87
Pushrods 88
Rocker Arms 89
Valvesprings 94
Valvetrain Parts 97

Chapter 7: Intake Manifolds 98
Production Intakes 98
Aftermarket Intakes 101
Fuel Distribution 103
Manifold Selection 104
Manifold Prep 105
Porting Matching 105
Carburetors 105
Throttle Body 108
Fuel Pump 108
Fuel Injection 109
Nitrous 109
Superchargers and Turbos 109
Final Installation and Prep 109

Chapter 8: Oiling System 110
Oiling Hardware 110
Oil Pump 112
Breathers and the PCV 113
Oil 113
Oil Filter 114
Windage Tray 114
Oil Pan 114
Oil Pump Drive 116
Dry Sump 117

Chapter 9: Ignition System 118
Spark Advance 118
Distributors 119
Aftermarket Ignition Systems ... 122
Advance Curve 123
Ignition Timing 123
Spark Plugs 124
Distributor Drive 125
Coil and Ballast Resistor 125
The ECU/ECM 125
Wiring 126

Chapter 10: Fuel System and Tuning 127
4-Barrel Carb System 127
Fuel Injection System 128
Fuel 129
Magnum MPI 130
Fuel Injectors 130
Fuel Lines 131
Airflow 131
Carb Tuning 131
Magnum MPI Upgrade 132
A-Engine MPI Conversion 133
Nitrous Oxide 133
Supercharger 134

Chapter 11: Exhaust System 135
Manifold 135
Header 136
Flanges 141
Merge Collectors 141
Oxygen Sensor 141
Installation Clearance 141
Coatings 141
Pipe Crossovers 142
Mufflers and Catalytic Converters 142
Cat-Back Systems 143
Tailpipes 143
Gaskets 143

Source Guide 144

ACKNOWLEDGMENTS

The Chrysler/Mopar small-block V-8 engine was in production for almost 40 years and was raced in many different categories and configurations during this time. Chrysler built millions of these engines with so many racing variations that the history alone could easily fill a book. Quick references and focusing on availability kept it within the covers. So hats off to Indy Heads (cast iron and aluminum), Edelbrock (aluminum), and B1 (aluminum) for maintaining key performance parts for the small-block.

The small-block program had many ups and downs, many parts programs that came and went, and too many racers who helped with these competitive efforts to name individually, but thanks to all! I owe a lot to the many contractors and Chrysler engineers: Ted Flack, Al Nichols, Tom Hoover, Pat Baer, Bill Hancock, Tim Zuehlke, and Jim Szilagyi, with special thanks to John Wehrly. They taught me well! I also want to thank the many manufacturers that display their new hardware at events and shows such as PRI & SEMA; their representatives are always willing to answer questions and discuss the latest hardware.

I thank Rob Cunningham of Mancini Racing and Bob McSwain and Rob Miela of Godfather Racing for their help. Plus a big "thanks" to Gary Stanton, Ron Keselowski, and Larry Henry for helping me with history data conflicts.

The writing and photography required for an engine book is a lot of work but not anywhere near the amount of work that went into the design and development of the parts originally. Extra thanks to Scott Koffel, Dave Koffel, Leonard Lawson, and Greg Charney for helping with the photographs and their leading-edge creations, along with Frank Parker for the real heavy work.

I owe the most thanks of all to machinist Richard Koffel, and engine builder Dan Parker, and the 340 engine's owner, Charlie Henry. I couldn't have done it without them! They all put in lots of time to help me put photos and words together.

Perhaps most of all, I must thank my editor, Paul Johnson, for his patience, guidance, and foresight. He took a tremendous number of words and photos on small-blocks and made it fit into this book and be readable.

I would like to give extra special thanks to my wife, Linda, for her steady hand in keeping our household going during this project and accepting the huge piles of research material and photographs that I used to create this manuscript.

INTRODUCTION

Any discussion of the Chrysler/Mopar small-block V-8 engine has to start with the introduction of its ancestor, the A-engine, in 1956, but the original engine was relatively bulky and heavy. By 1962–1963 it was obvious that the compacts needed more power, so the LA-engine was created. The A-Body was the compact-size cars produced by Chrysler called Valiants and Lancers.

Equally important in the engine's design was having less weight; after all, it was going to be installed into smaller, lighter vehicles.

A Bit of History

The new engine went into production in 1964 as the 273 LA-engine. Its name, "LA," comes from one of its three major design parameters, lightweight A. The new engine was designed and developed under the engineering code of A828.

1965

In 1965, the 273 engine was upgraded to 235 hp with the addition of a 4-barrel carb, high-performance cam, higher compression ratio (10.5:1), and black-painted valvecovers. This high-performance package was developed under the A861 engineering code. Next was the 318 with

INTRODUCTION

The old-style 318 or the original A-engine, also called the polysphere engine, shares the same displacement number (318) with the new LA-engine, but the old engine's valvecover is held on by only two screws: one on each end.

a bigger bore (3.91). The new 318 also had hydraulic tappets and cam and stamped steel rocker arms, and it was rated at 230 hp.

The new V-8 engine was originally referred to as the A-engine. The A-engine was the older version introduced in 1956. Over the 30 years of production, this distinction has been lost and all 1964 and newer small-blocks are now referred to as A-engines.

1968

In 1968, the performance version of the A-engine was introduced as the 340. The 340 engineering code is A105 and it features a big bore (4.04 inches), bigger valves (2.02/1.60 inches), high-flow, bigger-port cylinder heads, heavy-duty forged steel rods, beefed-up block and mains, bigger hydraulic cam, high-rise intake manifold with larger runners, high-flow exhaust manifolds, viscous fan, and windage tray. The result of all this hardware was a 275-hp rating with 340 ft-lbs of torque.

1970

The 340 6-barrel engine (called the A340) was added in 1970 in the Trans-Am cars (called Challenger T/A and AAR Cuda), which were intended for SCCA Trans-Am road racing. The 340 6-barrel engine package featured three 2-barrel Holley carbs, an aluminum high-rise intake manifold, modified cylinder heads, adjustable valve gear, and heavy-duty 340 block bulkheads for potential four-bolt mains. The engine was rated at 290 hp and 345 ft-lbs of torque. The 340 6-barrel was only produced in 1970.

1971

The final production A-engine displacement increase was introduced in 1971 as the 360 engine. The 1971 360 was built only as a 2-barrel

The 1964–1967 273 LA-engine looked small, but it is actually the same size as the 340 and 360. The bigger engines got bigger air cleaners and high-rise intake manifolds that make them look bigger.

The 340 was Chrysler's standard high-performance engine for many years. The basic parts of the 340 package were very good performance parts.

INTRODUCTION

One of the higher-output crate engines, and certainly one of the largest small-blocks, was the 408-ci version with aluminum heads.

A unique crate engine was the Magnum MPI version (360 or 5.9L) with the high-flow intake manifold.

carburetor, which continued for the first three years of production. It was introduced just prior to the new federal emissions laws of 1972, which required the use of low-octane fuel, which required lower compression ratios. The engine was originally built in Chrysler's Windsor, Canada, engine plant.

The new 360 engine featured a longer stroke (3.58 inches) at the stock deck height (no raised block), 4.00-inch bore, smaller intake valve (1.88 inches), external-balance weights at each end of the crankshaft, and cast crank with larger main bearing diameters (2.81 inches). It also included block core holes similar to the 340 lined up on the halfway point between the adjacent bores, which allows steel shot to have better aim and access to the water-jacket in the cleaning process to clean out core-sand. In addition, the main bolt spacing was increased by .31 inch. With an 8.7:1 compression ratio, the result was a 255-hp rating.

1974

From a performance standpoint, 1974 was a milestone date because the 360 replaced the 340 as the small-block performance engine. It was generally called the E58 engine option and used the 1972–1973 340 Thermo-Quad carb, 360 heads with the 1.88-inch intake valves, bigger 340 hydraulic cam, and 340 high-performance valvesprings, which resulted in a 245-hp rating with 320 ft-lbs of torque. This change took place during the first 1974–1975 gas crisis, which introduced fuel economy concerns.

1978–1985

The first 318 4-barrel engine was introduced in 1978; it used the Thermo-Quad carb. In 1981, the 318 was introduced with fuel injection in the Imperial only. This option continued through 1983. In 1985, the 318 engines were introduced with hydraulic roller tappets and roller cam with higher compression and a 140-hp (up from 130) rating.

1992–1993

The new Magnum 5.2L V-8 engine package replaced the 318 LA-engine (commonly called the A-engine) in 1992.

The new Magnum 5.9L V-8 replaced the 360 in 1993. These engines were originally placed in Dodge pickup trucks then Jeeps; rear-wheel-drive cars were added at a later date. Magnum engines had high-tech electronic fuel injection or multi-point fuel injection, hydrau-

INTRODUCTION

lic roller cams, revised valve gear for an oil-through-the-pushrod oiling system, and revised heads and valve sizes (1.92/1.625 inches).

Today

From the introduction of the LA-engine in 1964 through the end of production in the early 2000s, small-block engines were installed in many special cars, such as the 1970 Trans-Am E-Bodies, the 1978–1979 *Little Red Express* truck, the 1970 340 Duster/Demon, the 1974–1976 360 Dusters, the 1978 Street Kit car and Super Coupe, the 1993 and newer Dakota R/T 360, and the 1966 D-Dart.

Racing Highlights

For this book, I wanted to organize the various racing highlights into something that made sense, but I couldn't come up with a title for each category until I settled on "Phase." My five categories (covering 40 years!) start and stop, but there is much overlap.

Phase One

The first phase began in 1964 with the introduction of the 273 V-8 and ran through the end of 1969. During this period of time, Chrysler was heavily involved in racing big-blocks, both Hemis and wedges. The first competition for the small-block V-8 was the 1964 Mobil Gas Economy Run.

The small-block cars had many first-place finishes in A- and B-Body cars. Small-block engines continued to compete successfully in this series that ran through 1968. The engine also competed successfully in the Union Pure Race Trials. In 1966, in the inaugural SCCA Trans-Am road racing series, Bob Tullius (in a 1966 Dodge Dart) and Scott Harvey (driving Team Starfish's 1966 Plymouth Barracuda Formula S) both competed with the 273 V-8. With the introduction of the 340 in 1968, the A-engine competed in NHRA/AHRA drag racing classes, mainly within Stock eliminator.

In 1969, Chrysler launched the P69 program, an Indy racing program that allowed a stock-block engine to compete with the racing-specific engine. The P69 program used the LA-engine block at 318 to 330 ci. Two cylinder heads were used: a modified wedge head for short tracks and a raised-port special head for speedways.

Phase Two

This could be considered the first push in small-block performance, and it begins roughly in 1970 and ends in 1971–1972. With the introduction of the 340 Duster in 1970, racing in the NHRA/AHRA Stock and Super Stock classes became more popular, led by Ed Hamburger.

In 1970, Chrysler returned to the SCCA Trans-Am series with Dan Gurney's AAR Barracuda and Ray Caldwell's Challenger, both with 305-ci A-engines with a Holley 4-barrel carburetor. These specs (engine size and carburetor) were dictated by the SCCA. Chrysler's Pete Hutchinson led the Trans-Am program.

Phase Three

This phase could be titled "the refocus era" because Chrysler shifted attention in performance from big-blocks to the small-block. This was a major adjustment. This refocus started in about 1972 and went until the Loan Guarantees in 1979–1980. During this era, sanctioning bodies such as NASCAR and NHRA began handicapping the big-block engines. At first it was factoring or adding weight and restrictor plates, but it grew into actual banning of specific engines by displacement or design.

The rules adjustments led to Richard Petty and other Chrysler racers switching from big-blocks to a 355-ci small-block A-engine. Petty won NASCAR championships in 1974 and 1975 using the race-developed 355 A-engine.

These NASCAR racers originally used 340 Trans-Am blocks but an even better X-block was developed for this program, along with the W2 cast-iron oval-port high-flow cylinder head that featured oval intake ports, high-flow exhaust ports, offset intake rocker arms, rocker shaft stands and modified pedestals, and no heat crossover. Chrysler's John Wehrly and his team developed the 355 small-block; it made more than 600 hp with a 4-barrel carburetor in the mid-1970s!

In 1974, Chrysler production switched its performance engine from the 340 4-barrel to the 360 4-barrel. To promote this new engine package, Chrysler raced 360 4-barrel A-and E-Bodies in NHRA Super Stock led by Ted Flack and Judy Lilly. These new SS cars and engines were very competitive.

In 1975, Chrysler, through the Direct Connection program, introduced a circle-track race car parts program called the Kit Car Program. A racer could buy a complete short-track race car from Chrysler in kit form, which meant you had to put it together. The engine, drivetrain, and sheet metal all came disassembled. The frame and roll cage were welded together, but everything else had to be assembled.

Although the Kit Car featured the small-block, there were many variations. The sheet metal was originally

INTRODUCTION

based on E-Body cars (Challenger/Barracuda), then on A-Body cars (Dart/Duster), and finally on F-Body cars (Aspen/Volare). Chrysler's Larry Rathgeb and Bill Hancock led the Kit Car Program. Many races were won across the country.

With the success of the NHRA Super Stock program, in 1976, Chrysler moved into NHRA Modified and Gasser classes in drag racing with the W2 head and generally destroked 340s, which were slightly smaller than the earlier 305 Trans-Am package, in the 288- to 295-ci area. These classes allowed two 4-barrel carburetors on tunnel ram intake manifolds.

Also in 1976, the A-engine small-block was used in the Formula 5000 and in the 1977–1978 Can-Am series with the UOP Shadow team. Engine development was led by Bob Tarozzi.

The NHRA Modified and Gasser successes, both in horsepower and durability, led Chrysler to support a 1978 340 Arrow in NHRA Pro Stock. The 340 Arrow was built and driven by Bob Glidden and coordinated by Chrysler's Dave Koffel. Of the nine NHRA national events in 1978, the 340 won seven of them; Glidden won the championship.

Chrysler's Tom Hoover and John Wehrly led much of the small-block engine development in this era. Everything ended in 1979–1980 with the loan guarantees.

Phase Four

For the next 5 to 10 years, not much new happened in Chrysler's performance arena. Therefore, it is probably correct to label this phase as "the reawakening era." It had very humble re-beginnings, and you could say that it evolved into "the return" era.

It started very slowly in about 1988, with sprint cars and short-track circle-track racing and continued to about 1994–1995. Even before this phase started, drag racing Stock and Super Stock class activity had continued but was somewhat below the radar. In the late 1980s, Mopar Performance (the revised and renamed Direct Connection program) began working on USAC Sprint Cars and ARCA circle-track cars as hard parts development programs for the small-block.

Chrysler/Mopar's Larry Henry and Mark Reynolds led these programs, which featured racers including Jerry Churchill, Gary Stanton, and Bob Keselowski. Gary Stanton's USAC Sprint Car won the Silver Crown championships in 1994 and 1996, driven by Jimmy Sills. Bob Keselowski in a Chrysler LeBaron with a small-block finished second in 1992 and third in 1993 in the ARCA championships.

Dodge and Mopar Performance returned to the Trans-Am series in 1992 with the Archer Brothers with Joey Arrington engines. Mopar Performance entered the World of Outlaws winged sprint car series in early 1997, which led to Mark Kinser and the all-aluminum Mopar small-block winning the World of Outlaws championship in 1999. Engine builder Gary Stanton and Chrysler's Lee Carducci led this sprint car engine program.

Phase Five

Chrysler returned to NASCAR racing and entered the Craftsman Truck series in 1996. Chrysler and Mopar Performance raced in this truck series consistently using Arrington small-block engines and won the championship with Bobby Hamilton in 2004 and with Ted Musgrave in 2005. The development programs to support this racing series were led by Chrysler's John Wehrly and Ted Flack.

In about 1998, the NHRA launched the new Pro Stock Truck class that was limited to small-blocks. Mopar's small-block was heavily involved.

The big news came in 2001, when Dodge and Chrysler returned to NASCAR Sprint Cup racing with several teams, led by Ray Evernham and his number-one driver, Bill Elliott. Team Penske ended up winning the 2012 NASCAR championship, with driver Brad Keselowski.

To race, you have to have parts. In about 2005, Mopar Performance had about 23 small-block blocks and around 30 small-block cylinder heads to service the needs of all the Mopar A-engine small-block racers and the various racing categories in which they competed. Mopar Performance/Chrysler designed and manufactured all of these hard parts; this did not include parts made by Edelbrock, Indy Heads, or B1/Brodix.

Mopar Performance had always made hard parts for off-road use. However, beginning in 1996, Mopar Performance began developing high-performance parts for the Magnum small-block engines used in Ram and Dakota trucks that were emissions–exempt as certified by the California Air Resources Board (CARB). Therefore, it was legal to sell and install them on street vehicles.

The Mopar small-block had been so successful in various sprint car racing venues that Mopar Performance developed a 4-cylinder race engine (half of the Mopar small-block) for use in midgets. Jim Szilagyi coordinated this Mopar midget engine program. It was very successful in the early 2000s with several series championships using one A-engine head. It continues today through Gary Stanton Racing Engines.

CHAPTER 1

BLOCKS

The engine's cylinder block is the basic foundation for virtually everything in an engine project, and as such, it affects almost every part in the engine, either directly or indirectly. Improved performance is the typical goal of an engine project, and to accomplish this basic goal, all parts used in the engine must work together.

All parts need to be compatible, but they should also be complementary. You may take the engine apart and put it back together several times before you arrive at the final assembly steps to complete the engine. As you begin building your foundation, use a notebook to keep track of everything that you see and do, from casting numbers to bore sizes, etc., for every part that you use. Once the engine is together, it can be very difficult to gain this information and it may be helpful for any troubleshooting that is required.

Block Design

Basic block design could be considered similar to architecture because it defines how the block is laid out. An engine family such as the LA-engine and the Magnum extension tend to share many

Once the block is disassembled or the new block is obtained, it is usually mounted to the engine stand. It is typically mounted upside down or crank-side up because that section is where you are going to start.

The bare block, no plugs, is the first step in preparation for sending the block to the machine shop. In this common position, the block is upside down and the passenger's side is toward the left, which can be confusing. If this were a Chrysler race block (cast-iron versions), the large "X" or "R" would be located on the passenger-side face of the block, which is also the passenger-side face as installed in the car. It is on the front of the number-2 cylinder, above the dipstick holes and the core plug.

CHAPTER 1

Both A-engine and Magnum blocks share the same 10-bolt head bolt pattern, or 4 bolts around each cylinder, but some of the race blocks add 2 more (for a total of 6) per cylinder, and this is covered later in this chapter.

features that define them. The LA-engine small-block family is a basic 90-degree V-8. This angle is best for dynamic balance considerations and also makes for a very rigid block.

Cylinder numbering begins with the driver-side front cylinder; number-2 is the passenger-side front cylinder. The A-engine has a production deck height of 9.60 inches; the Magnum group uses 9.585 inches. Small-block race blocks have deck heights as low as 9.0 inches. Both groups of small-blocks share the 4.46-inch cylinder bore centers and the 6.125-inch camshaft centerline height. The LA-engine block is lighter than the original A-engine block and weighs about 160 pounds. The newer 1973–1974 thinwall cast versions are about 4 to 8 pounds lighter, which carries over to the Magnum blocks.

Identification

Although there are four different cylinder bore sizes, Chrysler made two basic blocks. One is the 273, 318, and 5.2L block; the other is the 340, 360, and 5.9L block. Most A-engines use a motor-mount design that attaches to the sides of the block close to the front, and the mount ears and bolts are parallel to the cam centerline. The 273 and 318 share the same arrangement.

However, the 340 and 360 share the same driver's side configuration, but the passenger's side has the three-bolt pattern reversed.

The Magnum engine, originally used in trucks, had a three-bolt pattern on each side, and these mounts bolted into the side of the block itself. This bolt pattern is located in the center of the block starting just above the pan rail. In addition, these Magnum blocks had the ears cast in and machined for the earlier system.

Both groups of blocks have three core plugs per side; the 318 group has them wide-spaced, and the 340–360 group has each core plug aligned with the center of the water jacket between two cylinders.

The easiest way to identify a small-block Mopar is to compare the casting numbers. Each casting is unique. In other words, you can't machine out the 273 bores to make a 318. You also can't make a 340 out of a 318.

These rules don't apply to 340 and 360 blocks. You could probably bore out the 360 block to the 340 stock bore size of 4.04 inches, but the 360 has a large main bearing diameter crank. The large main bearing diameter makes the long-stroke 360 (3.58 inches) much stiffer. In addition, the 340 oil pan's front and rear

Engine Block Specifications					
	318	*340*	*360*	*5.2L*	*5.9L*
Years	1967–1991	1968–1973	1971–1992	1992–2002	1993–2005
Weight (pounds)	158	160	158	152	154
1976–1992 thinwall blocks	152	na	154	n/a	n/a
Cylinder bore spacing (inches)	4.46	4.46	4.46	4.46	4.46
Main bearing bore diameter (inches)	2.6925/ 2.6930	2.6925/ 2.6930	3.0025/ 3.0030	2.6925/ 2.6930	3.0025/ 3.0030
Approx. block height (inches)	9.60	9.60	9.60	9.58	9.58
Tappet bore diameter (inches)	.9050– .9059	.9050– .9059	.9050– .9059	.9050– .9059	.9050– .9059
Tappet boss centerline (degrees)	59	59	59	59	59
Cam centerline height (inches)	6.125	6.125	6.125	6.125	6.125

sealing surfaces are the same as the 318's; the 360's are smaller.

The 1970 340 T/A is the trick block for racing applications because it has thick bulkheads on the number-2, -3, and -4 main bearing bulkheads. The added thickness allows for vertical four-bolt main caps to be added to these center mains. None of the Magnum blocks have this thick bulkhead.

In the mid-1970s, Chrysler offered a four-bolt main race block known as the X-block (it had a large "X" on the passenger-side front wall of the casting). In the mid-1990s, Mopar Performance and Chrysler revised this race block and offered the R1 through R4 race blocks. These were generally called the R-blocks and all featured four-bolt mains.

When you are selecting a block for your particular build, remember that for all five of my performance packages, the standard 340/360 or Magnum block can be used as long as the bore size is limited to .020/.030 overbore for the last two packages. An R-block is not required as long as the blocks are limited in overbore. If a big-bore engine is desired, an R-block

The 340 T/A block is very difficult to find; it's even more difficult to find someone willing to give one up for a performance project. The 340 resto block, by Mopar Performance, is more readily available. It uses the 340 T/A casting number and the 340 displacement number after it, followed by an "M," all the way to the right after "340."

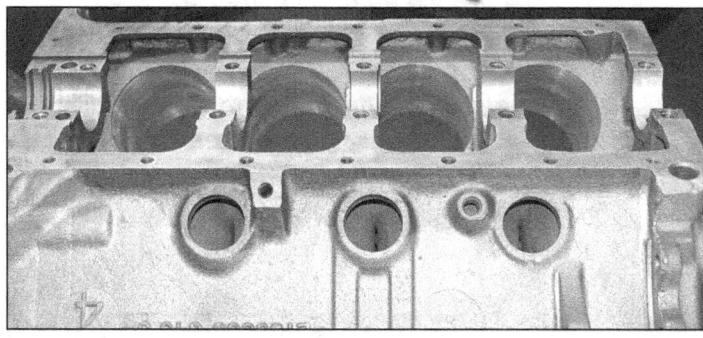

The 318/5.2L and the 360/5.9L are the two groups of small-blocks. You can identify them easily by quickly looking at the core plugs located in the sides of the blocks. There are three in each side. In the 340 and 360/5.9L group, the core plugs line up with the three center bulkheads, and if the plugs are removed, you can see the water-jacket gap between adjacent cylinders.

On the 318 and 5.2L blocks, the core plugs are spaced farther apart and don't line up with the bulkheads, except the center one is close to the number-3 main. The R-block will support the most power, then the X-blocks and then the T/A and then all stock blocks. Magnum blocks are slightly stronger than the standard A-engine blocks. The stock blocks with 0 to .020/.030 overbore have done over 550 with no problem (good bolts and good main caps) but the upper limit is unknown. Most members of the 700-hp club use some version of the race block. The race blocks make more horsepower.

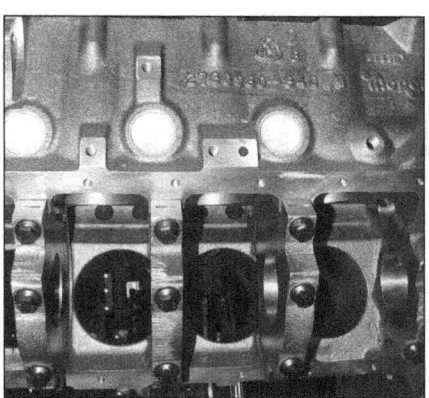

Around 2000, Mopar Performance started offering a 340 restoration block that not only had the thick bulkheads of the 1970 T/A block, but also had actual four-bolt mains on the center three mains. It used the same casting number as the original 340 T/A with a 340-M added, but the siamesed-bore block is no longer offered. This stout non-siamesed bore block can support at least 1,000 hp, but availability is limited. The R3 race block is an excellent block for 700-hp street builds, but these can be expensive and difficult to obtain so other choices are offered.

CHAPTER 1

The large round hole with a plug in the center is the cam's rear plug. The threaded square-drive plugs on either side of the cam plug are the oil galley plugs. These allow the oil galleys to be drilled and then sealed. The main oil feed galley is the one on the right.

The 318 Magnum block is tipped over to the driver's side so the passenger-side deck is horizontal. The oil galley plugs are in the middle toward the bottom. The distributor bore is at the left and the china wall runs up toward the right from the large distributor bore. The rear intake gasket seal is just ahead of this surface. At the upper end of this machined surface is another oil hole typically used for oil pressure senders. It is important to know where this hole is for future discussions in this chapter.

The bare front face of the block has lots of holes. The core plugs are the two at the bottom; one is on the right while the other is on the left. At the top right and left are the block's two water feed holes. The cam bore is in the center. The oil galley holes are on each side of the cam bore. The cam retainer is attached by the four smaller holes: two below and two above. The two larger holes above the cam retainer attaching bolt holes are vents from the tappet chamber to the front cover.

Cylinder Block Casting Numbers

Years	Engine	Casting Number	Stock Cylinder Bore (inches)	Main Bearing Bore Diameter (inches)
1964–1966	273	2465330	3.63	2.6925
1965	273	2536130	3.63	2.6925
1965–1969	273	2806130	3.63	2.6925
1967–1975	318	2536030	3.91	2.6925
1976–1979	318	4006730	3.91	2.6925
1980–1984	318	4104230	3.91	2.6925
1985–1991	318	4387530	3.91	2.6925
1968–1973	340	2780930	4.04	2.6925
1970	340 T/A	3577130	4.04	2.6925
1971–1974	360	3418496	4.00	3.0025
1975	360	3870230	4.00	3.0025
1976–1986	360	4006830	4.00	3.0025
1987–1992	360	4315830	4.00	3.0025
1992–2004	5.2L	53006714	3.91	2.6925
1993–2005	5.9L	53020006AB	4.00	3.0025

BLOCKS

With the main bearing shell removed, you can see the two oil passages intersect just above the hole. The white welding rod is in the main oil feed from the main oil galley (hole to the right of the cam plug hole). The oil comes from the main oil galley down to the main bearings and then up to the camshaft through this Junction.

is required, and the siamesed-bore version allows the largest bores. The 340 resto block is a version of the R-block. If your 340 or 360 block is already overbored too far, sleeve the bore back to 4.020 inches (360) or 4.04 inches (340).

Race Blocks

The original race block for Mopar small-blocks was the 340 T/A in 1970. It was produced for only one year. When NASCAR began handicapping the big-blocks, both Hemi-head and wedge-head designs in the early 1970s, the NASCAR teams began using the T/A blocks, but they had to remove them from actual Trans-Am cars. This was a lot of extra work! To solve this problem, Chrysler introduced the X-block, which had all the features of the T/A block plus a few more. This X-block was readily available to racers and was very successful.

When the government issued the loan guarantee to keep Chrysler operating, the X-block tooling was lost during the confusion it created. In the late 1980s, the demand for a race block began to build, so Mopar Performance introduced the new "R1" block, which replaced the X-block. Then came the R2, R3, and R4. Each one has its name cast into the passenger-side front wall of the block.

Block Height Calculation

The block height, or deck height, is defined as the distance from the center of the crankshaft to the top of the block's deck surface, measured along the cylinder bore's centerline. The small-block Mopar's production block height is 9.58 to 9.60 inches, but blocks are commonly milled or decked at each rebuild, so do not depend on this number as an absolute. You don't always know the block's history. However, you can calculate the block height using the following simple equation:

$$BH = S \div 2 + RL + CH + DH$$

Where:
BH = block height
S = stroke
RL = rod length, center to center
CH = compression height of piston, measured on the actual piston
DH = deck height of piston, measured in the actual block

For example, on a 318 (or 5.2L) engine, the stroke is 3.31 inches, rod length is 6.123 inches, stock piston's compression height is 1.74 inches, and the piston's deck height is .082 inch below the deck. Using the formula, you find that block height is 9.6 inches (1.655 + 6.123 + 1.74 + .082).

If this engine's deck height measures .062 inch (instead of .082 inch), it indicates that the block has been decked .020 inch.

Deck height is often confusing because it sounds similar to block height. However, it is defined as the distance from the top (flat) of the piston at top dead center (TDC) to the top of the block's deck surface. Typically, it is measured with a dial indicator or a bridge, which includes a dial indicator. If you have a dished or domed piston, the top of the piston is the flat part at the outside edge that is not part of the dome or dish. ■

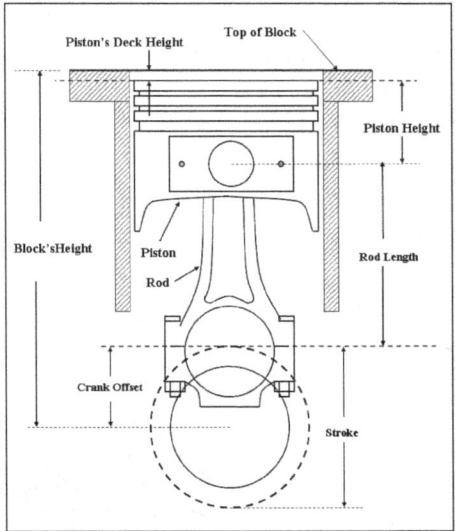

This drawing shows the relationship of the various block specs required for the block height calculation. The key spec is the piston's deck height because it is used in the compression ratio calculation, which is very important for max-performance engines.

CHAPTER 1

The standard production small-block tappet angle is 59 degrees (shown), but the R-block family has the capability for using 48-degree tappets. The 48-degree angle was selected based on installing a race W cylinder head and race adjustable rocker arm onto the block (in the computer) and drawing a straight line from the center of the camshaft to the center of the rocker's pushrod pivot. The resulting tappet angle was 48 degrees. While the R-block casting is made to use both the tappet angles, once the block is machined for one tappet angle, it can't be converted to the other tappet angle!

The 59-degree tappets are so close to the tappet wall that the wall has a relief machined in for each tappet/pushrod on the Magnum blocks. The 48-degree tappet blocks have the tappet bosses much farther away from the tappet wall with no reliefs required.

Magnum tappet bores are machined at the top to provide space for the yoke to sit around the hydraulic roller tappets. The yoke sits in the relief and is held in place by the spider.

Some of these R-blocks are cast with siamesed-bores, which means that the bore walls of adjoining cylinder bores are merged together, with no gap. This siamesed situation exists at three places per side (cylinder bank). This siamesed-bore alignment generally allows the actual cylinder bores to be larger because there is no water-jacket between the cylinders.

R-blocks can be converted to a six-bolt cylinder head by adding two more head bolts to the stock four-bolt pattern. This is a critical upgrade for super-high compression ratios, such as 13:1. A study showed that four-bolt heads were bending the head over the gasket's sealing ring. The two extra head bolts keep the gasket material farther away from the bore. The bolts and gasket support help maintain a flat deck surface with high clamping loads.

One boss was added straight up in the tappet chamber and one was added straight down on the outside of the block. In some cases these bosses are left unmachined or are machined off if not desired. If they are machined, they do not have to be used. If you use them, you must use a six-bolt–style head gasket. All of these race blocks (X and R versions) are cast-iron blocks made with high-nickel-alloy cast iron.

Most LA-engine small-blocks were built at the Mound Road Engine plant in Detroit, then added to the Windsor engine plant in Canada, and later the Toluca plant in Mexico. Many A-engine blocks were cast at Chrysler's Indianapolis, Indiana, foundry, which was closely involved in the early stages of the R-family of blocks.

Aluminum Blocks

Mopar Performance began offering aluminum small-blocks designed for racing in the early 1990s. They are designed and built for the serious Sprint Car and drag racer who competes in classes that allow aluminum blocks. The latest version weighs approximately 95 to 100 pounds,

The Mopar aluminum small-block shown comes in basic deck heights: stock-style height of 9.56 inches and the short-deck version at 9.00 inches; it can support more than 1,000 hp. The block features a fully skirted low end, similar to the 426 Hemi.

BLOCKS

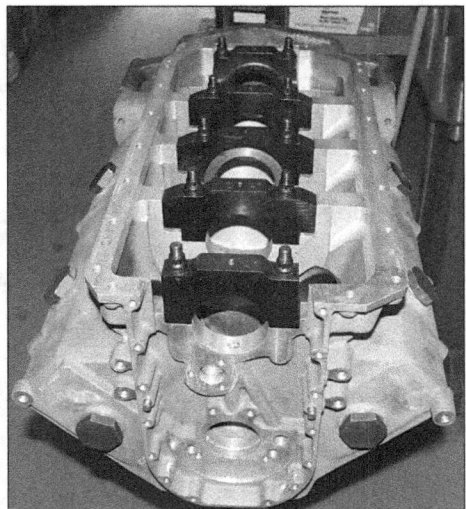

Only two core plugs are installed per side in the aluminum block. There is also one large one in the front face. Notice that the center three mains are cross-bolted for maximum strength, similar to the 426 Hemi. Each center cap (number-2, -3, and -4) is cross-bolted similar to the 426 Hemi in Top Fuel. Therefore, it's much stronger and stiffer than any four-bolt cap, but the cast-iron blocks do not have the skirt on the block for anchoring.

The aluminum block uses steel main caps, and the center three are cross-bolted. Moreover, they use studs rather than bolts for greater strength. The unique front cover does not match the A-engine or Magnum engines.

The deck surface shows the sleeves pressed in each cylinder. The standard four-bolt small-block head bolt pattern sits around each bore with the added top and bottom bolts showing the six-bolt race pattern. The four-bolt head gaskets and four-bolt head works without the two extra bolts if that is desired. Note how far the tappet bores (48 degree) are from the centerline of the cylinders, even with the six-bolt in the tappet chamber.

The aluminum block does not use either style of motor mounts and is designed for use with motor plates. The block is much lighter without all the motor-mount bosses.

a weight savings of more than 25 pounds over the previous version. These blocks were offered in two basic deck heights, 9.00/9.10 and 9.56 inches. They are shipped with one of several options in bore size.

Basic Features

By about 2005, Mopar Performance offered more than 20 different blocks for the small-block. All were designed for racing; many options were available for virtually any engine project.

Mopar Performance Aluminum Block Features
- Ductile iron dry cylinder liners
- 48-degree tappet angle for almost ideal valvetrain geometry
- Six-bolt head bolt pattern for superior head gasket sealing
- Full skirted block design, similar to 426 Hemi for increased strength and rigidity
- Cross-bolted main caps for added strength
- High-strength A1 studs, bolts, etc.
- 50-mm roller cam bearings designed to reduce friction

A new block will come with new cam bearings but all others will have to have the cam bearings replaced. The block is upside down and the cam bearing oil hole is shown at the top and points down toward the main bearings. The oil holes in the bearing shell must line up with the holes machined into the block. In some cases you must use a small mirror to see if this is true.

CHAPTER 1

The standard water jacket extends down to just above the block's pan rail. The core plugs are at the bottom of the water jacket. a threaded plug is also there that allows draining of the block. These threaded plugs are difficult to use after time. Installing a block drain allows you to drain the block fully and easily.

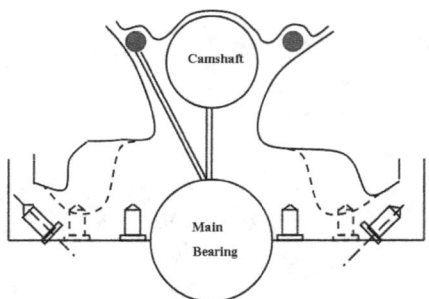

The main bulkheads must have enough material and strength to support four-bolt caps with vertical outers. Thus, there must be enough material between the main cap bolt of the two-bolt design and the outer wall below the pan rail. In this drawing, the dotted line represents the standard block casting. The solid line above it is closer to the performance blocks, such as the 340 T/A and the X and R block families. The vertical outer bolts break through in the standard casting. The main reason for splayed outer bolts is to put the bolt into solid material. This drawing is not to scale.

Bore

The amount of overbore depends on the block itself and when the block was built. Early 273 and 318 blocks (pre-1973–1974) can generally be overbored about .060 inch. Early 340 blocks can be overbored about .040 inch, or 4.080-inch actual bore size. The 360 is a gray area, but I use the 340 as a guide and limit overbore to .040 inch, or an actual bore size of 4.04 inches. All newer blocks, A-engines, and Magnums are thinwall casting designs, and overbore should be limited to .020 to .030 inch.

All race blocks can be overbored more than production blocks. You can overbore the resto block to 4.08 inches with the siamesed-bore versions able to be overbored the most (approximately 4.22-inch max for the siamesed-bore versions). When pushing the boundary of bore size and overboring, it is best to sonic-test the block before you begin any boring operation.

Most race blocks are bored or rough bored to approximately 4.00 inches. There are many reasons to use a race block even if the bore size is less than 4.00 inches (such as the 318's 3.91 inches). If you plan to race a small-bore engine, such as 3.91 inches or even 3.63 inches, you should not use the production block. It is a better package to use the race block with the proper-size sleeves.

Mains

The two basic main sizes are the 273/318/340 and 5.2L engines. The 360 and 5.9L use a larger main. The 360 has a large 3.00-inch main; the other group is small at 2.69 inches. The main cap bolt spacing on the 360/5.9L is also wider, or spread. Magnum engines have a small dowel that locates the number-5 main cap. Magnums also use smaller main cap bolts in the number-5 cap. Typically the main caps are made of high-nickel cast iron. If the main caps have been replaced or damaged, or if they bind during crank rotation, the mains should be align-bored, which is a machine shop operation.

Height

Most A-engine blocks were built at 9.60-inch block height; Magnum engines were built at 9.58 inches. Race blocks can be about 9.00- to 9.10-inch block height. Do not try to mill a production block to this height. Deck milling on production blocks should be limited to about .060 inch.

You need to determine if the engine was rebuilt or repaired in the past and whether the block was decked .060 inch at that time. If the block has been decked by .060, the actual deck now is 9.54 inches. You should not take off another .060 inch because the deck becomes too thin and causes head gasket sealing problems that you will not be able to fix. This is one reason that it is so important to measure the block's actual height before you start machining.

Stroke

The A-engine/Magnum engine can generally accept long-stroke cranks. Most of them use a 3.31-inch stroke; the 360/5.9L uses a longer 3.58-inch stroke. The performance aftermarket offers 4.00-inch strokes that are easy fits. Because the camshaft sits so high above the crank, long-strokes do not cause the connecting rods to hit the camshaft lobes. The pan rail and the bottom of the cylinder bore (pulling the skirt too far out the bottom) are still concerns with strokes longer than 4.00 inches.

BLOCKS

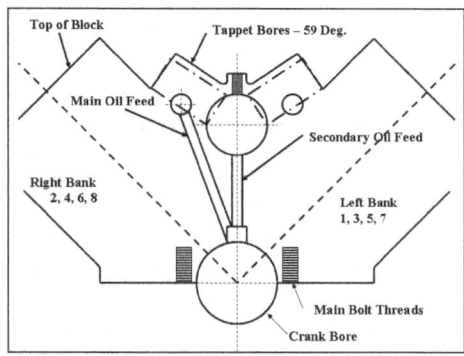

Oil routes from the pump to the oil filter on the side of the block, and then back into the block and up to the right side (next to cylinders -2, -4, -6, and -8) main oil feed galley. The right oil galley runs from the rear of the engine to the front, and it feeds down to the main bearings. As can be seen, the tappets are oiled directly since the tappet bores intersect with the galley. Then the oil goes up to the cam bearings.

Block Oiling

A-engine and Magnum blocks oil in basically the same way. The difference comes in oiling the head and valvetrain. The A-engine oils the valvetrain and head through the head; Magnum engines oil the valvetrain and head through the pushrods.

Basically, the oil pump feeds the oil filter and then pushes oil to the passenger-side main oil galley. From the main oil galley, the oil feeds the passenger-side tappets and the main bearings. Then it crosses to the driver-side oil galley and oils the driver-side tappets. Then, from the mains, the oil goes to the camshaft bearing.

On the A-engine, the oil goes to the rockers and the head from the cam bearing and through passages in the block and head to the rocker shaft. On Magnum engines, the oil goes to the head and rockers through the pushrods from each tappet.

Block Plug Verification

All A-engine and Magnum blocks have a special plug at the rear of the block pressed into a vertical passage in the block. The first priority is to check that it is there. The second priority is to see if it is properly installed because it is vital to the proper function of the oiling system.

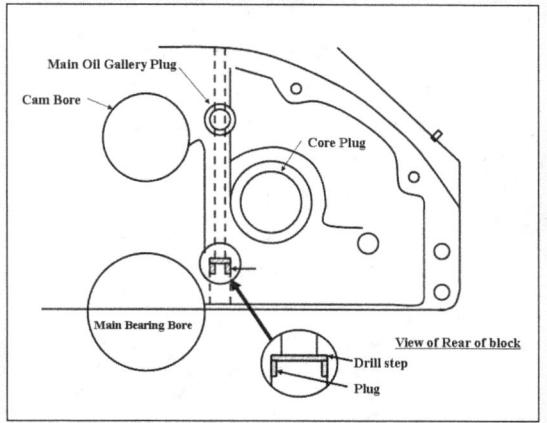

All small-blocks use a small, pressed-in plug at the rear of the block. This plug is not visible once it is installed. It is installed in a vertically drilled passage and divides the oil passages into "to-oil-filter" and "from-oil-filter" sections; both are drilled horizontally inward from the oil filter mounting area. This plug should sit at 7½ inches to 7¹¹⁄₁₆ below the rear china wall and 2⅛ to 2⅜ inches above the parting line for the number-5 cap. If the plug is too low, use a flat dowel to tap upward into position.

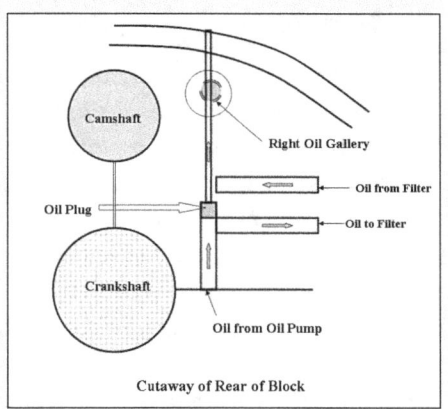

The special plug is very important to the engine's oiling system. It blocks the oil from the oil pump from going straight up and forces it to go out to the oil filter. Once it passes through the filter it returns to the block above the plug and goes directly to the main oil galley. If the plug is missing or not installed properly, it could cause erratic, low, or no oil pressure.

With the main cap off, you can check the height of the special oiling plug, which is pressed up inside the passage covered by the number-5 cap; a white welding rod can be used to measure. The correct height should be 2⅛ to 2⅜ inches.

CHAPTER 1

Motor Mounts

The aftermarket (specifically Schumacher Creative Services) makes mounts/brackets to use with either the 340/360 or 273/318 ears. Race blocks use the 340–360 ears but are often machined off to lighten the engine. Aluminum blocks are designed for mounting by motor plates.

The backsides of the motor mount ears are machined to hold tolerance on mount location and thicknesses. The three ears form a sort of box with one corner missing. The change from 340/360 to 318/273 on one side is that the missing corner ear switches location, so the mounts are not interchangeable. The aftermarket mounts (from Schumacher) make a full box bracket and include all four holes to fit either engine.

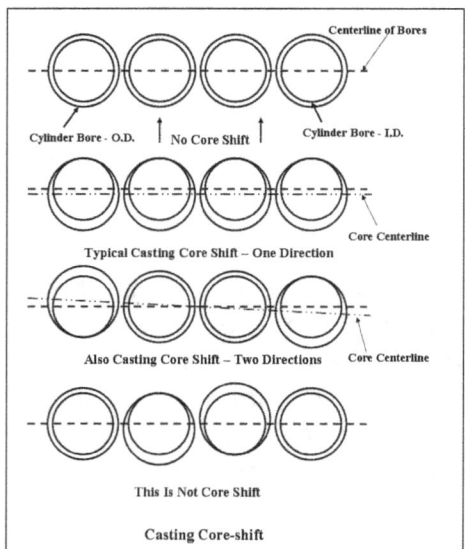

Magnum blocks may have both styles as shown. This Magnum block (5.2L) has the four ears, machined on the rear, and the bolts into the side of the block (only two are showing) so it could be used with either style of mount.

The Magnum engine uses bolts (three per side) directly into bosses in the middle of each side of the block. The three bolts are spaced around the right core plug: one to the bottom, one to the upper left, and one to the upper right, both just below the pan rail. Remember, the block is upside down.

Core shift occurs when a core such as the water-jacket core moves or shifts relative to the cylinder bores or if the core breaks, which allows the ends to shift. If the core shifts, thin sections will be on one side of the bore and thick sections will be on other sides of the bore. Remember that the core is a solid piece so if it shifted, then all sides will be shifted in the same direction. For example, if cylinder number-1 has the core shifted upward and cylinder number-3 has it shifted downward, then it probably isn't a core shift!

Core Shift

Cores are used to make all cast parts, including cylinder blocks. A core is typically made of hardened sand and is used to make an internal passage or relief such as the water jacket. A special bonding agent holds together the hard sand. Cores don't typically bend but they do break.

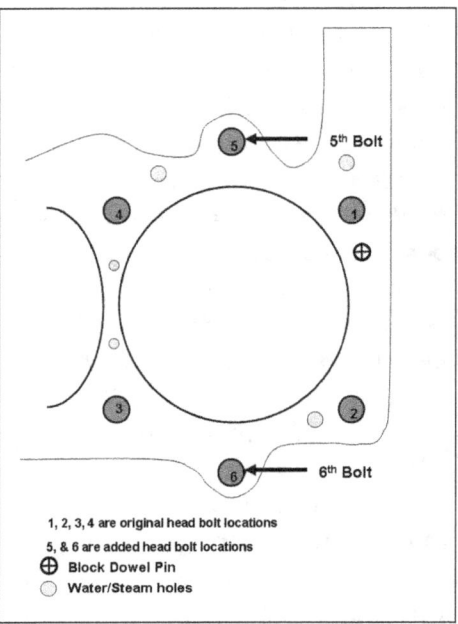

All production small-block engines use the same ten-bolt-per-bank head bolt pattern, which is four bolts around each chamber for exceptional clamping strength. Some race blocks use the eighteen-bolt-per-bank head bolt pattern, which has six bolts around each chamber. If you have a six-bolt race block and your application does not require the two extra head bolts, you can use four-bolt heads and four-bolt gaskets and not install bolts on the two extra holes per cylinder. All high-performance packages that I put together use 11.5 CR max, and the current MLS gaskets from Fel-Pro or Cometic will easily seal this with the standard four-bolt system. The six-bolt system is not required for street/strip.

MOPAR SMALL-BLOCK ENGINES: HOW TO BUILD MAX PERFORMANCE

BLOCKS

Although the Magnum group and A-engine water pumps look similar when installed on the engine, they are not because the Magnum group does not have an attachment hole in the right side of the cover for the mechanical fuel pump (all MPI) and the A-engine cover has a hole with two attaching bolts for the mechanical pump. In addition, the two water pumps run in opposite directions and the vanes that direct the water into the pump that are cast into the cover are tipped in opposite directions.

All Magnum engines have a two-bolt crank sensor mount at the right rear of the block next to the bellhousing face. The bosses are machined for a two-bolt attachment and the sensor itself can look directly at the ring gear wheel. This sensor would not be used if you do not use fuel injection (MPI) but is mandatory if you plan on using Multi-Point Injection. If you want to add the Magnum-style fuel injection to an A-engine, consider duplicating this boss, location, and basic setup.

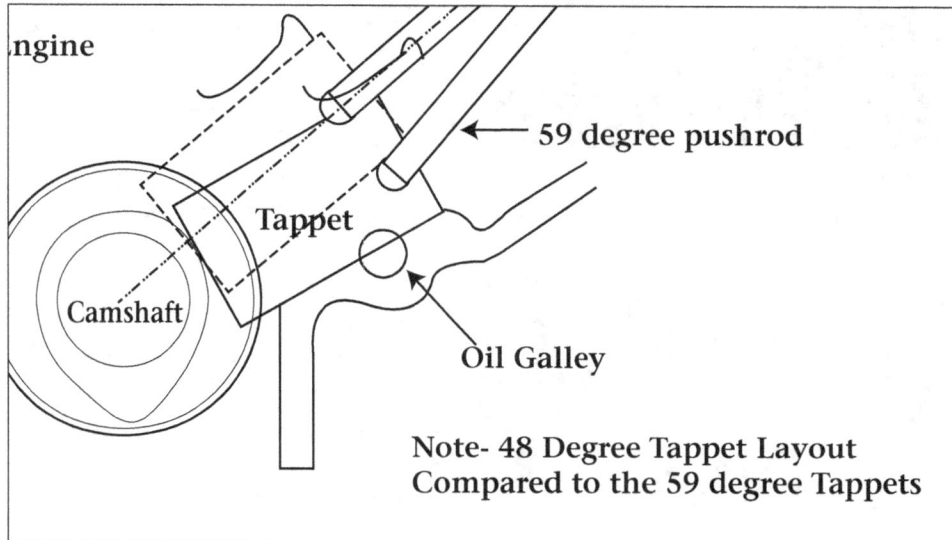

The 48-degree tappets were created to offer the perfect valvetrain. The race blocks can be machined with either the standard 59-degree tappets or the 48-degree tappets. Once machined, they can't be changed. Similar to the 50- and 60-mm cam bearings, the biggest advantage for the 48-degree tappets comes about with high cam lifts, high valvespring loads, and high engine RPM.

Once you decide to deck the block, be sure to address the head dowel pins, two per bank. They are pressed into the deck surface and must be removed before the milling machine can deck the block. They should be installed after the milling is complete. I recommend new ones. If they are being replaced, check the height before removing and set the new ones to the same height.

And when cores break, the broken pieces usually tear large holes and/or create solid chunks where they aren't supposed to be, and then the block has to be scrapped.

Today, block castings are machined on CNC-machines, and this precision machining process centers the actual machining on the cylinder bore and centers the wall thickness. This centering process tends to reduce or cancel out the effects of any core shift. In addition, foundries today try to design the cores so that they are locked in place and can't move once assembled. The foundry uses sonic testing to help find any broken or damaged core blocks and keep them from getting into the machining process.

Machining

Find a machine shop that has a history of machining Mopar engines and that engine builders recommend highly. As such, a machine shop familiar with the A-engine small-block design will perform the best job. This basic process actually starts with a close inspection followed by many accurate measurements. The measuring process usually starts with a thorough cleaning of the various parts. With new parts you tend to know more about them when you bring them to the machine shop; in some cases you may have purchased them already machined. Race blocks are often shipped rough-bored so your machine shop can finish them to your specifications.

Honing plates should always be used when boring and honing the cylinder block. These put the cylinder head stresses into the cylinders, so that it simulates what the cylinder walls do with the head installed. During this process the cylinder bore's diameter is measured with a dial-bore gauge. The machine shop leaves about .001 to .002 inch of material for the final honing operation.

Decking/Milling

Once cleaned, the machine shop can tell how flat the deck surface is and if there is any damage (scratches, etc.) that needs to be fixed. You probably don't need to deck a new block. The decking process tends to remove

You can make many measurements on the block, such as bore size (diameter in inches) or center-to-center distance (4.46 inches on small-blocks) and many others. The dial vernier is the quick and easy way to get rough ideas of what you are dealing with. The machine shop will use a dial bore gauge for the fine-tuning measurements. This is usually the preliminary step to boring/honing the block.

The honing stones work on the cylinder wall, and the result is a cross-hatch and roughness in the finish. The typical cross-hatch angle is about 45 degrees. The roughness you could describe as very smooth, but you generally do not want to mirror finish.

With a new block, you select the bore size based on the block's overbore capability, but you typically leave yourself room for at least one rebuild. With a used block, once cleaned and measured, the machine shop gives you some numbers: what is takes to fix the wear that is observed, which will be something around .010 to .020 inch (and you know the maximum the block should be overbored); on today's thinwall blocks, the overbore number is about .020 to .030 inch. Older blocks (1972 or earlier) can do .040 to .060 inch, but the old 340 blocks should still be limited to 4.08-inch max!

Honing Plates

Honing locations for A-engine and Magnum engines are reasonably common. A honing plate is a 1- to 2-inch-thick steel or cast-iron flat plate with all head bolt holes and cylinder bores. The heavy plate attaches to the cylinder block and uses the actual head bolts, which are torqued to the same specifications as the heads.

A honing plate is designed to simulate the stresses, distortions, and wall movements that are normally caused by the installed and fully torqued cylinder head.

It is generally recommended that the main caps be installed and properly torqued during this honing operation.

The machine shop tends to have the honing plate and will have the special head bolts to attach it with. To do the best job, the thread engagement with the honing plate should match the thread engagement used for the cylinder head. (Photo Courtesy R. Koffel)

BLOCKS

Milling Calculation

Precisely fitting all engine parts together requires extremely accurate machining. When you mill or deck any part of the engine (with the most important being the block and head), consider milling all three surfaces so everything lines up again as the engineers planned. It is too late when you find that the manifold does not fit to the head at final assembly. This is not just a concern for the block. Take the amount that you plan to machine off the block's deck surface and add that to the amount that you plan to machine off the head's deck surface.

For example, if you take .030 inch off the head and .020 inch off the block, it makes a total of .050 inch. The intake manifold face cut could be made to the intake manifold, but I recommend that it be done to the intake face on the head. That way all manifolds fit, rather than having to specially machine all manifolds for this engine. If the china wall front and rear aren't shorted the proper amount, they tend to hold the intake manifold up, and it won't seal to the head. This is probably not required for small amounts such as .010 inch.

You can assume that new heads are machined to fit like a production head with zero milling. New heads might be milled to change the combustion chambers to a specific size. ■

Amount to be Removed		
Total From Head/Block (inch)	From Intake Manifold Face (inch)	From Front and Rear China Wall (inch)
.005	.00475	.0072
.010	.00950	.0144
.020	.01900	.0288
.030	.02850	.0432
.040	.03800	.0576
.050	.04750	.0720
.060	.05700	.0864

.010 to .020 inch, unless a special amount is requested. Typically, production blocks can have up to .060 inch milled off without causing problems.

Align-Boring

Sometimes a used block has distorted or damaged main bearing caps and saddles. If you've measured the caps and saddles and determined that they need honing or boring, a machine shop needs to perform this service. Align-boring trues them so the crankshaft performs at its best and does not bind.

Align-boring is required if the block's main caps have been replaced (one or all), and upgrading to steel main caps provides additional strength. To align-bore the block, a very small amount of material is removed (milled) from the main cap's parting line surface of each main cap. (Photo Courtesy R. Koffel)

Stress Relieving

Manufacturers stress relieve all new blocks; a used block is seasoned, so it has been stress relieved through repeated thermal cycles. Stress relieving removes the stresses that were introduced into the block during the casting process. Once the block has been stress relieved, it is best to take your time machining it so that you don't introduce any more stresses into the block. Take two cuts, not just one. Take three cuts instead of two. Try boring the block in the cylinder sequence of (driver-side bank) number-3, -7, -1, -5.

High-Performance Gasket Options

In the past, high-horsepower A-engines used very high compression ratios (12:1 or higher), and it made cylinder sealing difficult. New O-ring designs made running these high compression ratios for racing feasible. Then the aftermarket made head gaskets with the O-ring built in (Fel-Pro, for example). Next, the aftermarket (Fel-Pro and Cometic, plus others) introduced the multi-layered-steel (MLS) version, which was the best of both worlds. Then Mopar Performance introduced the six-bolt block (versus the standard four-bolt block) and the problems have disappeared. Note: Four or six bolts around each cylinder.

If you want to use an O-ring, however, they are generally used with copper head gaskets. You use a .032-inch-thick stainless steel wire. The machine shop must cut a groove around each bore that is .032-inch wide and .017-inch deep. The round wire sticks above the deck surface and with the proper gasket (copper), they work very well. In practice, it is more common to O-ring the cylinder head (rather than the block). Do not O-ring both.

On used blocks, you need to replace the pressed-in distributor bushing. On a new block, check that it has a bushing pressed in properly. It is poorly oiled and takes a lot of abuse in performance applications so it is best to replace it in any used block. If it is worn, it affects the ignition timing and allows the camshaft a walk. This movement changes the cam events that you try so hard to control.

You can use the intermediate shaft and gear to test the distributor bushing. Lower the gear into position just above the cam where the gear is not engaged. This position is about 1 to 1.5 inches raised above the gear's seated position. Try to wiggle the shaft in different directions.

You can also practice the gear install. To lower the shaft and gear into position, the gear rotates. The slot in the gear is supposed to be pointing at the first intake-attaching bolt on the driver's side once it gets into position. This takes some practice to get this to occur.

Generally, the last step in the engine disassembly process is to spin the crank once the rod-and-piston assemblies are removed. The engine builder tends to notice a tight spot during the general disassembly, but the final spin is confirmation. If no tight spot is observed during the disassembly process, the align-boring operation is not required. It is required if the block has been welded upon or suffered a major failure.

Sonic Testing

Sonic testing uses sound waves to determine the cylinder wall thickness around the bore. Thus it tells you how thick the bores actually are and if there is any core shift, and if there is core shirt, which direction it is in. If you are building many engines, buy a high-quality sonic tester; otherwise have your machine shop sonically test the block. The major thrust area on the driver's side of each bank should be tested.

By determining bore thickness, you can figure out how much overbore is safe and where to stop. If you have two or more blocks, it tells you which one is best. Always sonic test before you start the overboring process. If a cylinder is found to be too thin, re-sleeve the cylinder or use a different block.

Sleeving

You can use sleeving as a repair or as a bore change.

Once the block is cleaned, the machine shop may tell you that one or two of the block's cylinder bores are damaged and need to be fixed. Basic wear and/or scoring in the bore are the most common causes. No matter the reason, sleeving by a machine shop should fix it. If the process is executed properly, the rebuilt engine should be as good as new.

There are no 318 race blocks and the smallest 340/360 race block bore is 4.00 inches. The 318 block cannot be bored out to a 4.00-inch bore (3.97 inches on pre-1973 blocks but only 3.94–3.95 on 1973 and newer thin-wall cast blocks). Perhaps your current race engine is worn-out; its last rebuild was at the maximum bore size for this block and it is time for another rebuild. Do you scrap the block? Sleeving all eight cylinders is one solution.

BLOCKS

As the open loads went past 500 pounds, the friction went up and the racers wanted to use 50-mm roller cam bearings. With the 50-mm roller cam bearing, all the bearings are the same size and the inside diameter of the bearing itself is about the same, but the roller bearing is larger in outside diameter and this means the block must be machined for bigger bearing diameters. Most stock production blocks do not have enough material in this area to allow this to occur. This feature was added to all R-blocks. (Photo Courtesy R. Koffel)

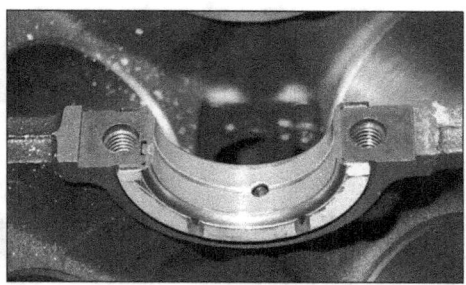

The first step in building up a short block is to install the main bearings. Actually, you install the upper shell, which has the oil hole in the center and the groove around the face from side to side. It is very important that each oil hole line up with the hole in the block. The groove helps spread the oil and oil pressure around the crank journal. The other shell goes in the cap itself and does not have the hole and usually does not have the groove.

The production main caps are cast all together and then cut apart. They are rough machined and then installed onto the block for final machining. The number-5 cap (on right) is the most obvious. The other four caps look very similar.

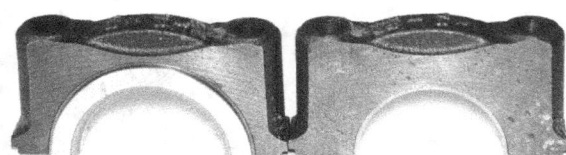

The number-3 cap takes the crank's thrust, so it is machined differently than the -1, -2, and -4 caps. The number-3 cap on the left has the front and rear faces machined to accept the flanged thrust bearing. On the number-1, -2, and -4 caps (cap on right), there is no relief for the thrust bearing flanges.

The number-5 cap is the most complicated. The rear oil pan seal installs across the top at the bottom. The crank flange is below this surface and not part of the cap. The main cap bolts are toward the top left and middle right. The oil pump bolts to the two threaded holes (center top and middle left) and the oil passes through the hole between these two attaching holes.

What if you want a race block with a bore of 3.97 inches (a .060-inch 318)? For small bores or worn bores, sleeving is a reasonable approach. For example, if you want to build a 310-ci A-engine with the readily available 3.31-inch stroker based on the 360/5.9L block (original 4.00-inch bores), you need a 3.86-inch bore. Sleeving is the only way to accomplish this bore size.

Main Caps

The typical main cap is made of cast iron (high-nickel alloy), similar to the block. Most race blocks use four-bolt caps, which may be steel or ductile iron. The number-3 cap is specially machined to accept the thrust bearing on the front and rear faces. The most complicated cap is the number-5.

Heavy-Duty Main Caps

All production blocks have cast-iron main caps with a tensile

CHAPTER 1

The tricky part with the mains caps is that they must stay in order: number-1 cap on the number-1 main bulkhead, etc. Cap numbers-3 and -5 are easy, but the other three all look alike. The production engineers had the caps' number cast into the top of the cap, 1, 2, etc. Since the mid-1980s, the caps have two numbers on them: one for the V-8 version and one for the V-6 version ("4" on V-4s and "3" on V-6s). Without cast numbers, you would have to stamp the main number onto the cap once installed. The cast numbers on the caps are fuzzy and difficult to read.

strength of approximately 241,000 psi. The tensile strength of ductile cast iron is about 413,000 psi, or more than 70 percent higher. Making main caps out of ductile cast iron results in a big strength gain.

Most R-family race blocks use special upgraded heavy-duty caps (ductile iron or steel). Also, the 360 and 5.9L engines, which have the larger main diameters, should also have the main cap bolts spread .31 inch farther

The main cap bolts are 1/2-13. The Magnum uses a slightly smaller head on the number-5 cap bolts (at the top). The most unique main cap bolts are the ones used on the number-2 and -4 mains on the 340/360 engines when the windage tray is used. The head of these bolts is thicker and is machined to accept to small screw that is used to hold the windage tray in position.

Splayed Main Caps

Many years ago, the splayed cap was used to add the four-bolt main caps to stock-style blocks. The angle was designed to go to the outer wall of the block, below the pan rail where there was enough material to hold this size of bolt. In these blocks, the bulkhead did not have enough material for four vertical bolts.

At one time, the X and R race blocks were readily available with the added thickness in the bulkhead and the vertical four-bolt main caps, but the splayed cap is rarely used today.

Neither approach works on the Magnum blocks because there is not enough material below the pan rail in the outer wall to support the 1/2-inch bolt. However, Chrysler/Mopar has tested the two-bolt Magnum blocks at very high outputs without problems (in the range of 500 to 550 hp).

You can convert your two-bolt main caps to four-bolt caps. To do so, the two outer holes are drilled at 7.06-inch centers and centered on the main bearing bore. Drill the 27/64-inch hole, 1.32-inch deep and then tap with a 1/2-inch-13 tap, 1.19-inch deep. At the top, or parting line surface, add a counterbore .52 inch in diameter, .12-inch deep (T/A and X+R blocks only).

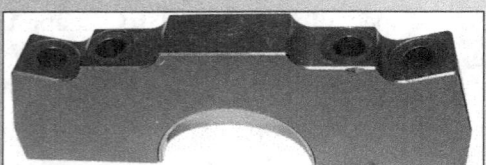

A splayed main cap is a style of four-bolt main cap, and it has the two outer bolts angled or machined at a different angle than the two inner bolts. With a splayed-style cap the outer two bolts also tend to be shorter so that the cap itself has a down-step from the standard height inner bolts. This step gives the splayed cap a unique appearance.

apart than other engines.

Heavy-duty main caps, such as those offered by ProGram Engineering, should be used on nitrous and supercharged applications. For naturally aspirated engines, the switch is related to RPM and stroke length. Install heavy-duty main caps if mechanical roller cams are used or if the valve lift is more than .600 inch.

Four-Bolt Main Caps, Vertical

The key to installing or using a four-bolt main cap is to have the material added to the main bulkhead to allow this modification. Only the 340 T/A block and the new X- and R-block have the added material on main bulkheads number-2, -3, and -4. The majority of R-blocks come with four-bolt caps.

Special Features and Operations

The A-engine small-block started production in 1964 and the Magnum engine's production ended in about 2003. That's almost 40 years of production. Over such a long period of time, some problems inevitably pop up, and they may only apply to a few engines.

Cam Bearings

When race cams became much bigger, valvespring open loads went from 750 to 1,000 pounds. And this creates two problems. First, the cam's nose must fit through the inside diameter of the cam bearing, but bigger cams have bigger and thus higher-lift cam lobes. To gain the higher lift, using the standard or 50-mm bearings, the cam lobe's base circle has to be ground down. Obviously with less material, the cam becomes weaker.

Rear Main Seal

The neoprene or rubber rear main seal replaced the rope seal that was installed on A-engines during the first few years of production. No one services the rope seal in gasket sets anymore. The rubber seal has a lip and must be installed in the proper direction. The rubber seal is better (with one exception).

Little grooves are machined into the rear-seal groove-sealing surface on the crank (see Chapter 2). Grooves are not commonly found on a used crank. However, if you have a brand-new crank, there is a chance that these little grooves are cut too deep, too long, or have too sharp of an edge. In this situation, the rubber seal leaks. The solution is to install a rope seal. Contact Best Gaskets in California; they still offer rope seals.

Second, the higher spring loads caused deflections, and that inhibits engine performance. So racers went to 60-mm roller cam bearings, and an R3 race block was required. The large bearing diameter allows the lobe to become larger without grinding down the base circle. This bigger base circle makes the cam stiffer and stronger.

Standard cam bearings from manufacturers such as Clevite, Speed-Pro, and Dura-Bond work fine for all street/strip applications. Although not required, you should replace the cam bearings in used blocks. Roller cam bearings are not required for the street or street/strip engines but need to be used in race engines with mechanical roller cams with valve lifts more than .650 inch.

Block Drain

A small, threaded, solid plug is at the bottom of the water jacket, near the pan rail, on each side of the block. They are only removed when the block is cleaned or hot-tanked. If the engine is to be raced, consider replacing this solid plug with a block drain, available at any standard auto parts store.

Siamesed Bores

A few blocks are cast with the bore walls joined. These special blocks are called siamese-bored blocks. The bore walls of adjacent cylinders are joined solid. This allows for slightly larger bores. It also makes the cylinder bores somewhat stiffer. The negative thing is that they cut off water flow around the cylinders, especially on the two center cylinders on each bank.

Fasteners

Bolts hold the Magnum engine; race heads use main cap bolts that are longer than the standard long bolts in production A-engine heads. ARP, A1, and other aftermarket companies sell studs that replace these bolts, and provide higher clamping force.

The studs' biggest advantage comes into play if you race the engine and normally pull the caps to check the bearings or pull the head to check seats or guides or to modify it. Typical street or dual-purpose engines are assembled and run for many thousands of miles over a long time. Because the engines tend to be disassembled infrequently, there is very little wear and tear on the threads by the bolts.

CHAPTER 2

CRANKSHAFTS AND CONNECTING RODS

A crankshaft's main function is to change the pistons' up-and-down motion into rotational motion, which can be measured as torque and horsepower. Each small-block crank has five main bearings and four journals with two rods per journal.

The crankshaft is another engine part that you should take to a machine shop for inspection. A machine shop can repair almost any crankshaft if it is still in one piece. The most common problem is that small pieces of dirt pass through the engine over time and the dirt scratches the journals. The machine shop or crank grinder can typically repair this damage by carefully grinding the crank journals undersize. A common amount for this operation is .020 inch. The crank is then referred to as a 20-20 crank meaning the mains and rod journals are both .020-inch undersized. You use .020-inch undersize bearings with it.

Production Cranks

The stroke measurement is often used to categorize small-block cranks. Mopar A and Magnum cranks fall into one of two groups. The 3.31-inch stroke for the 273, 318, 340, and 5.2L is one group; the 3.58-inch stroke for the 360 and 5.9L is the other.

The 3.31-inch-stroke crank weighs about 54 pounds; the 3.58-inch-stroke crank weighs about 58 pounds. Cast cranks are generally lighter than forged cranks. The long-stroke 360 crank also has larger diameter mains by .310 inch. The radiused, sealing surface on the end of the number-5 main is smaller on the large-main 360 oil pan.

Small-block cranks become complicated in relation to external balancing. All 360/5.9L cranks are externally balanced, but the 5.9L uses less weight than the 360. The 318 is not externally balanced in either A-engine or Magnum versions. The forged-crank 340 (1968–1971) is not externally balanced, but the cast-crank 340 (1972–1973) is externally balanced.

When building an engine, consider your performance targets. Production crankshafts are suitable for up to about 600 hp for a high-performance street build. If you're planning to build a race engine, start with a race block and use a performance crank (typically forged or billet).

Both forged and cast crankshafts are internally balanced and have been installed in 318 production engines.

Only a few production crankshafts are offered for the Magnum and A-engine. This cast 3.31-stroke crank has a casting number on the second counterweight on the left. All street and street/strip packages use the 3.31 stroke crank, and it can typically support 500 to 600 hp. But chances are if you plan on building this much power, you would want at least a 3.58-inch stroke.

Common Crankshaft Specifications

	273/318/340	360	5.2L	5.9L
Stroke (inches)	3.31	3.58	3.31	3.58
Crank pin diameter (inches)	2.124/2.125	2.124/2.125	2.124/2.125	2.124/2.125
Main journal diameter (inches)	2.50	2.81	2.50	2.81

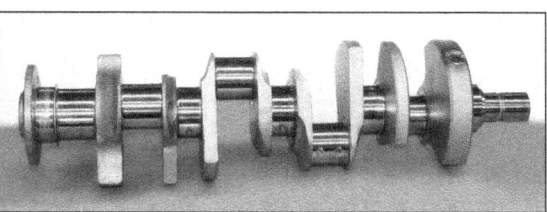

An Eagle forged crankshaft is ideal for performance applications. This 3.31-inch-stroke crank should be good for any street or street/strip package. Customers that want the high-RPM, high-output model probably would want a longer stroke, at least 3.58 inches. The key for cranks, after the stroke, is if the journals are full radiused. Production cranks are under-cut and performance cranks often are fully radiused, and the full radius requires the bearings to be clearanced on the sides, offered by Sealed Power.

When a crankshaft is externally balanced, non-symmetrical weights have been added to the vibration dampener and the flywheel/torque converter/flexplate. The A-engine generally added weight to the torque converter face; the Magnum family adds the weight to the flexplate. In manual transmission cases, the weight is removed by drilling holes in the engine side of the flywheel.

It is very difficult to differentiate between a forged crank and a cast crank. If you have a cast crank and it has a casting number on one of the counterweights, you are in good shape. Forged cranks generally do not have 5-, 6-, or 7-digit numbers on the counterweight that can be used for identification. The basic forging

External Balancing

Vibration and unwanted harmonics are the enemy of any engine, and if left unresolved, they lead to catastrophic engine failure. Thus, any engine, particularly high-performance engines, must be properly balanced. For a max-performance or race engine, I recommend internal balancing performed by a machine shop.

My main reason for recommending internal balance for max-performance engines is that flywheels and converters are often swapped or replaced for performance reasons. Therefore, each time, it must be externally re-balanced. With Magnum engines, external weight is added to balance the flexplate, so converters can be swapped (tested) easily without adding weights to each converter.

With many max-performance applications, SFI dampeners are required. There are SFI externally balanced dampeners, but the choice tends to be limited. Most of these racing applications need lighter-weight dampeners and the external weight limits this approach.

Max-performance engines equipped with manual transmissions present another challenge. These often use a clutch with an aluminum flywheel; it's very difficult to use aluminum flywheels with any external-balance setups. The drilled holes in the flywheels are used to create the proper amount of external weight, but it assumes that the hole is drilled in steel or cast iron. Because aluminum is so much lighter than cast iron or steel, the balance holes need to be very large.

Solutions are possible, but they are expensive. One solution is to add steel weights to the engine side of the flywheel, but they must be machined into a relief so they do not hit the block. They are then screwed into the flywheel, which makes it expensive.

To explain why some small-blocks are externally balanced and some are not, you have to look at the engines in more detail. The size of the production counterweights on the crankshaft is designed for the production piston, rod, and stock stroke of 3.31 inches in standard forged steel.

Cast iron is slightly lighter than forged steel. When the Chrysler 340 switched from forged steel to cast iron in 1972–1973, the counterweight lost weight and the balance was lost. A small amount of weight was added externally to put the engine assembly back in balance. With a longer stroke, the counterweight has to become larger (heavier).

Space inside the crankcase is also a limiting factor. The long-stroke 360 needed a lot of weight, so it was added externally. When the Magnum 5.9L was introduced, it had much lighter pistons; therefore, the amount of external weight was reduced. ■

CHAPTER 2

Crankshaft Specifications

Engine	Years	Material	Stroke	Main Journal Diameter (inches)	Rod Journal Diameter (inches)
273	1964–1967	forged	3.31	2.50	2.125
318	1967	forged	3.31	2.50	2.125
318	1968–1991	cast	3.31	2.50	2.125
340	1968–1971	forged	3.31	2.50	2.125
340	1972–1973	cast	3.31	2.50	2.125
360	1971–1992	cast	3.58	2.81	2.125
5.2L	1992–2004	cast	3.31	2.50	2.125
5.9L	1993–2005	cast	3.58	2.81	2.125

The number-5 main journal is the widest journal on the crank, and therefore it is the least loaded on a load-per-area basis. It is also where the rear seal is located. It is to the left of the bearing surface. The bearing surface is smooth, while the rear seal surface has oiling slots cut at an angle, at approximately 45 degrees. The rear seal groove is the trapezoid-shaped area cut into the block below the seal surface. It is wider at the top and narrower at the bottom. The rear seal sits in this area. If the new crank has these oiling slots cut too deeply or the edges are left too sharp, the neoprene (rubber) seal will leak. This requires a rope seal, which fits in the same groove.

The crank journal oiling holes are in every journal, several per journal in most cases. The crank gets oil from the main oil galley down to the main journals. From there the crank gets the oil out to the rod journals. There are typically two holes per journal, one for each rod. Each one of those holes comes from one of the mains. The production cranks basically let the machining enter the journal and then add a small radius. The aftermarket cranks take this a step further and taper the entrance in the rotation directions (left and right as shown). This helps get oil into the bearings.

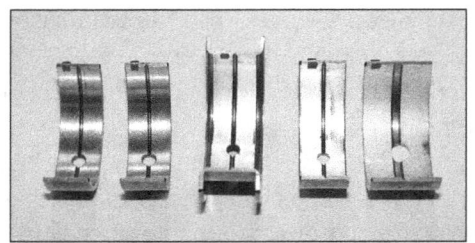

These are the top half of the main bearing shells. The top shells get the oiling hole and the groove that helps spread the oil around the bearing. Grooving the crank weakens the crank. Most of the bearing loads are on the bottom shell because the pistons are trying to push the crank out the bottom, so the top shell, the one in the block, is loaded lightly, relatively speaking. This means that the groove doesn't really weaken the bearing and is very important to getting oil around the bearing. Sealed Power and Clevite are two good choices.

process tends to wipe away any number, so they are very rounded and difficult to read. Cast cranks tend to have sharp edges, whereas forged cranks do not.

To tell a 360 crank from the 3.31-stroke group, measuring the main bearing diameter and looking for 2.81 inches is probably easier than measuring the 3.58-inch stroke.

High-Performance Street Cranks

An aftermarket performance crank's most important attribute is that it often has more stroke, so you can create a stroker package and thus add more cubic inches in the engine. Another advantage is having a version that is not otherwise available, such as a 360 crank (3.58-inch stroke) with small mains (318/340 size).

Most production cranks are cast, but forged cranks are stronger and take more abuse. Cast iron is lighter than steel if all specifications are the same. Performance cast cranks from manufacturers such as Scat and Eagle weighs about 54 to 56 pounds. Forged cranks with these same strokes from Scat, Eagle, K1, and Callies weigh about 58 to 60 pounds.

The problem is that all of these crank manufacturers offer lightweight and super lightweight forged crank options; however, they do not list weight specifications for these options. The weight is removed from the crank by machining. If you plan on running a high-RPM engine (more than 7,000), you should consider a lighter forged crank.

Race Cranks

Actual race cranks for the small-block come in all sizes and styles. Although most race cranks tend to be forged or billet, the aftermarket does make cast crank versions because they are much less expensive to build.

Early in small-block racing, race cranks were made with an eight-bolt crank flange, similar to the Hemi racing block. This adds complexity to the customers' overall engine package, so in later years, six-bolt cranks were also used in max-performance applications.

Flywheels and flexplates are available for either flange. Most max-performance or racing cranks use a special stroke to achieve a certain displacement. The 2.96-inch stroke was designed to give the 340 engine a displacement of 305 ci, which was required by the Trans-Am sanctioning body. This is what the 1970 305 Trans-Am racing engine used.

The second race crank consideration is inertia, or rotating weight. The forged race crank can be made at less weight and less inertia.

The cast crank is slightly lighter because of the material but not as strong as the forged crank. In general,

Every rod must have an oiling hole and that hole must be connected to a main journal. These holes are drilled at an angle that has to be calculated by the manufacturer to start and end up in the correct places.

the amount of stroke is more important than the amount of horsepower. With the 3.58-inch stroke, more than 600 hp might mean a forged crank, but you probably have selected the forged crank earlier because it is lighter. Be sure to balance any new and lighter crank.

Material

Production forged cranks made from 1050 or 1053 heavy-duty alloy of mild steel are strong and easy to machine in very large quantities. The aftermarket developed a special alloy forging steel and it offered a 65-percent increase in strength over mild steel. When racing RPM and output went up, strength needed to increase.

To fill this need a special alloy steel called 5140 was introduced for cranks that offered a 6.5-percent gain in strength over the 1050 steel baseline. Then the aftermarket moved on to 4340 material that offered around a 75-percent gain over the 1050 baseline. These high-carbon steels (5140 and 4340) offer more strength but are more difficult to machine and they wear out tools fast, which makes them suited

Note that on the rod journal that is just below the pan rail, with only one rod and rod cap on it, next to the main cap, the journal does not have a groove (undercut) next to the side of the crank. It transitions from the rod journal to the side of the crank in a smooth radius, which is called a full-radius crank. This style of crank is made for racing and generally very popular in the aftermarket because it is stronger than using the undercut. With full-radius cranks, you have to radius the bearing shells.

to low-volume performance/racing applications.

Most engine builders have opted for 4130 (125,000 psi) or 4340 (145,000 psi) forged cranks because of their toughness and longevity. The 4340 crankshafts have supported up to 1,500 hp, so unless you need a billet crank, a 4340 forged crankshaft is suitable for extreme and racing builds. Strength numbers are based on SAE tensile-strength data.

Billet Cranks

A billet crank starts out as a large round log of steel (an ingot) and then a CNC mill fully machines it into the desired dimensions. This process makes it very easy to change the stroke; therefore, you can produce a special one-off crankshaft that has the exact dimensions you need.

With a forged crank, small adjustments can be made, but these

Measuring the width of the rod journal on the crank with a dial vernier is quite easy and the width will come in handy to estimate rod side clearance. It is difficult to measure rod side clearance directly until the engine is being final assembled, which might be too late to fix any potential problem.

changes are very limited by the forging. If you are looking for a special stroke length, such as 2.88 or 4.25 inches, you might be looking at a billet crank.

A billet crank can be used for a high-horsepower street/strip engine, but these are expensive cranks used for their high strength in race engines. Weight considerations must be taken into account if a lighter crank is desired in a race engine. Moldex is one of the premier billet crank manufacturers but has a limited website; Winberg, Callies, K1, and Scat have more information posted on their websites. They can make almost any variation of the Mopar small-block crank.

For example, the Trans-Am engine used a 4.04-inch bore (stock 340) and a 2.96-inch stroke. Assume that you want to build a 295-ci engine out of the basic Trans-Am package; the stroke has to be 2.88 inches and that length is not readily available. If you want to duplicate it, you must purchase a billet crank. Longer stokes than offered by readily available forgings are more likely, such as 4.050 inches or longer.

Opinions differ about whether or not a billet crankshaft is stronger than a forged crank. One thing is certain, billet crankshafts are stronger than cast and, in most cases, support up to 1,500 hp. But it can cost up to $3,000 to build a billet crankshaft.

Displacement					
Stroke (inches)	Bore (inches)	Displacement (ci)	Stroke (inches)	Bore (inches)	Displacement (ci)
3.31	3.63	274	3.79	3.91	364
3.31	3.66	279	3.79	3.94	370
3.31	3.91	318	3.79	4.00	381
3.31	3.94	323	3.79	4.04	389
3.31	3.97	328	3.79	4.07	394
3.31	4.04	339	4.00	3.91	384
3.31	4.07	345	4.00	3.94	390
3.58	4.00	360	4.00	4.00	402
3.58	4.03	365	4.00	4.04	410
3.58	4.04	367	4.00	4.07	416
3.58	4.07	373			

Notes:
- The 340 block has thin cylinder walls and it cannot be overbored more than .030 inch. Sonic-test before boring to be sure proper thickness is available.
- The .030-inch oversize is a common aftermarket piston and ring size for these engines.
- The 3.79-inch stock was a common performance crank/stroke in the 1980s and 1990s before the 4.00-inch cranks were readily available.
- Race blocks allow bigger bores than 4.07 inch.
- Most cranks that increase the amount of stroke over the engine's standard stroke are generally called stroker cranks. Stroker cranks are an easy way to increase the engine's displacement for increased torque and horsepower. A stroker crank must be used with other parts that work together as a team. The easy one is a stroker crank and a special piston that adjusts for the extra stroke length by moving the pin up in the piston and using the stock rods. In some cases both the rods and pistons are changed.

Crankshafts for Your Application

In an effort to tie all engine hardware together into performance packages, I created five packages that vary from 350 hp to over 700 hp, and all are intended for street/strip applications.

Package	Best Crank	Rod
No. 1	Stock, cast or forged	Stock with good bolts
No. 2	Stock, cast or forged	Stock with good bolts
No. 3	Aftermarket cast or forged	Above or HP I-beam
No. 4	Forged	HP I-beam or H-beam
No. 5	Forged	HP I-beam or H-beam

Note: Any one of these packages could use a lightweight forged crank. But neither a lightweight forged crank nor a billet crank is required.

quick check on the crank's end play by installing the number-1, -5, and -3 thrust bearings and lowering the crank into place, torqueing the three main caps, and checking the end play with a dial indicator.

In most cases, a new crank comes polished. In some cases, a used crank can be polished to remove very light scratches and normal wear; then reinstalled.

Repair

If the wear is high and/or there are

Unless you need to construct a billet crankshaft for a special application, you are probably better off with a forged crankshaft. The biggest advantage of a billet crank is being able to build an engine with a unique stroke.

Full-Radius Journals

Almost all race cranks use full-radius journals on the cranks; all production cranks, both cast and forged, use undercut journals. The full-radius journal makes the crank much stronger. Undercut-radius cranks make it easier to assemble the engine, which is very important when you are building 50 engines per hour or 1,500 engines per day. The bearings must take a full radius into account either by radiusing the bearing individually or by obtaining bearing manufacturer information for full-radius journals.

Crank Prep

When you buy a new crankshaft, you don't have much prep work before you install it, but you should carefully inspect it for nicks, scratches, and any damage. You also need to verify a few measurements. I recommend doing a

A technician uses a special machine to balance your crank, rods, pistons, and dampener and flexplate/flywheel. You need to balance the assembly and you can't change pieces after the balance numbers are set. Sometimes the dampener (at far right) and flexplate/flywheel (about in the center) are optional. If you can provide all of the weights needed, the manufacturer can balance the crank. With a used crank, if the rods are staying the same, and the pistons are made to service weight, then balancing may be optional. However, many performance pistons are lighter and you might want to rebalance for the lighter hardware.

A machine shop might put the crank in V-blocks to measure the stroke. However, if you want to measure it yourself, it is most easily done in the engine. With one piston-and-rod assembly installed (rings optional), rotate the piston to BDC (bottom dead center) and use a dial vernier to measure from the top of the block to the top of the piston. Use a straight edge at the top of the block to help keep the vernier straight. Rotate the piston up to TDC and measure from the top of the piston to the top of the block (piston's deck height). Subtract the two numbers for the stroke. (Photo Courtesy R. Koffel)

scratches that are too deep to polish out, the crank is typically sent out for repair, which means to grind it undersize. This might be .020 inch. It is common to grind the crank .020/.020-inch undersize and then use matching undersize bearings.

If the crank needs more serious repair and the amount of undersize grinding is .040 or .060 inch, you should consider having the crank re-heat-treated by a process called nitrating. Grinding the crank more than .020 or .030 inch grinds much of the crank's surface hardness away. The nitrating process can add hardness.

A qualified local machine shop should check the balance of your new crankshaft (in this case, it's an Eagle forged crank). Most cranks are ground to an assumed common package, but most engines are somewhat different, so there can be problems that your local shop will find because they have the actual hardware. If extra-light pistons were assumed and only light pistons are being used, the crank's counterweight may have a lightening hole that is not needed. The shop will press in a cast iron/steel plug, cut to size, and then weld it in (the dark spot at the top left of the first counterweight). Aftermarket manufacturers usually use the stamped numbers on the front face on forged cranks for identification purposes.

Lubrication Grooves

The rear main seal surface, just before the crank flange, contains small grooves cut at an angle to the centerline of the crank. Almost all production cranks have these grooves. Aftermarket cranks may or may not have these grooves. Chrysler replaced the original rope seal in the late 1960s, and the newer rubber (neoprene) seal with the lip design that must point at the center of the engine does not require these grooves. If you find a new crank that has the grooves and they have sharp edges, the grooves should be polished to help protect the rear seal from damage.

On a new crank, if the grooves are cut too deep or the edges of the grooves are too sharp, the rubber rear main seal may not seal and the engine leaks oil. The solution is to use a rope seal, but they are difficult to find. It has been so long since rope seals were used that most manufacturers just put the rubber seal in the various gasket kits. You can obtain a new rope seal from Best Gaskets, among other suppliers.

Crank Mods

Crank manufacturers offer special modifications. Some modifications offer advantages in windage and rotating inertia, but they can be very expensive. When it comes to making the crank lighter, I prefer to cut down the counterweights' diameter because it gets the most weight off.

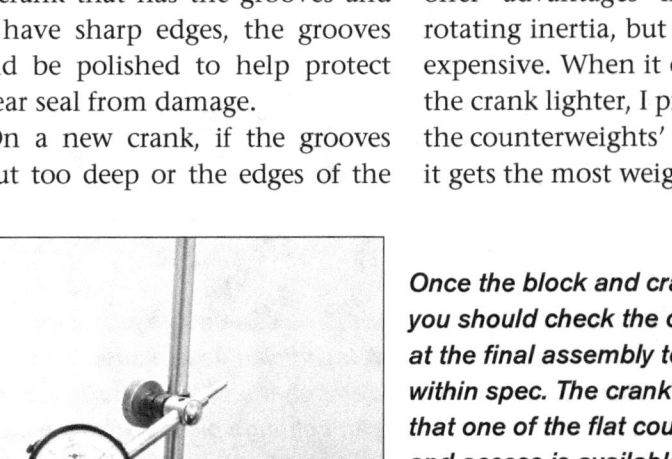

Once the block and crank are prepped, you should check the crank's endplay at the final assembly to make sure it's within spec. The crank is rotated so that one of the flat counterweights is up and access is available. Set up the dial indicator with the pointer parallel to the crank centerline and the pointer on the flat surface of the counterweight. Use a large screwdriver between the counterweight and the bulkhead and lever the crank rearward. Zero the indicator and then lever the crank forward. The reading on the indicator is the crank endplay.

The main cap just to the right of center has the special cap screws used with the windage tray. If a windage tray is going to be used, these special headed bolts are required. If you are planning on using a stroker (long-stroke crank) then you may have to clearance the rotating assembly to the windage tray. This holds true for special aftermarket scrapers and windage trays by companies such as Milodon.

Knife-edging also makes a crank lighter. For this approach to be helpful, you have to include high RPM in the equation. For most people, knife edging isn't worth the expense, but a lighter crank at a competitive price is worth it!

Bearings

Only two bearing sizes are offered for the small-block: the standard 273-318-340 and the large main 360. Bearings have been made of tri-metal, aluminum, or babbit, but tri-metal is the most popular today. Clevite, Sealed Power, Mahle, King, and Dura-Bond make bearings for the Mopar small-block.

Most make a version of a tri-metal bearing (copper-lead mix typical), but several manufacturers offer an aluminum mix. Mahle offers a moly-graphite coating, which may provide a wear benefit.

Some bearing companies offer bearings that have been radiused for use with full-radius cranks. Most bearing companies offer various under-size bearings for the repaired cranks (.020-inch undersize is common).

Vibration Dampeners

The basic dampener design has a steel/cast iron outer ring that is mounted to the hub by a rubber isolator (thin strip). As the engine vibrates, the outer ring absorbs these vibrations and basically cancels them out. You should always select a vibration dampener suited for the specific engine, in this case a Mopar A or Magnum. Although not required, SFI dampeners are best; these include versions from ATI, TCI, or BHJ.

I recommend staying away from aluminum dampeners (solid) or any one-piece dampeners. If an SFI dampener is not available for your engine, stick with the production dampener for street use. A street engine or street/strip engine must have a dampener, and many options are available. Any street/strip manual transmission should have an SFI dampener, and any engine using 7,000 rpm or higher should have an SFI dampener. The leading manufacturers are ATI, TCI, BHJ, Pro/Race, and Fluidampr. Each unit is unique.

Race engines need lightweight dampeners, but street or street/strip engines do not require a low-mass dampener. The TCI Rattler weighs just over 8 pounds and features a unique construction.

The Pro/Race offerings are more traditional with a steel outer ring construction and a production-type weight of more than 11 pounds.

The BHJ dampener is also built with the outer-ring-style construction (similar to production) and weighs just under 8 pounds with a combo option at just over 6 pounds.

ATI has the most models that feature two or three discs/rings mounted inside of a shell. The shell can be made of steel (8.75 pounds) or aluminum (6.25 pounds). Both are three-ring versions plus there are two-ring versions at 7 and 5.45 pounds, respectively. I do not recommend the two-ring versions for street use.

The Fluidampr is distinctly different from others and is around the production weight.

Dampeners need to be tuned for specific engine hardware: stroke, engine RPM, etc. I feel the Fluidampr is best for non-standard engine hardware, unique stroke length, or unique cubic inches, etc. Several dampener manufacturers solve the external balance issues of the 360 and 5.9L engines (they are not the same) by adding small weights in the hub area.

The non-symmetrical 360 dampener is basically round but has an offset weight. The weight is placed in the wide flange on the front of the dampener, which only extends for about 200 to 250 degrees, or in a trough cast into the front face of the outer ring for less than 180 degrees.

These non-symmetrical dampeners are also somewhat thicker than the standard 318/340 dampener. The

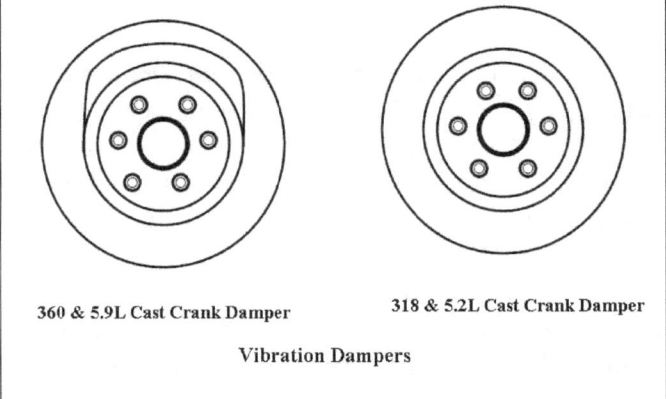

The 318 dampener (on the right) is symmetrical; basically a round disc. There is the timing mark on the outer ring and the six bolts that allow the front pulley to be attached. The 273 and 340 forged crank dampeners are basically the same as the 318. The original Magnum 5.2L engines used a similar dampener but newer versions went to a one-piece dampener and front pulley assembly, which is very heavy and difficult to work with. The 360 external balance dampener is on the left with the weight added toward the top of the dampener.

CHAPTER 2

The 360/5.9 external balance dampener can have the external weight removed from the opposite-side weight (see page 33). The trough in the face of the dampener from about one o'clock to about seven o'clock removes weight that balances the engine just like adding weight to the dampener at four o'clock.

original 5.9L Magnum used a dampener similar to that of the 5.2L. Newer versions used a large, one-piece dampener and front pulley.

Connecting Rods

The connecting rods are a critical part of the rotating assembly. The rod's weight (in grams), material (steel, titanium or aluminum), alloy (forged steel or high-carbon steel for the steel versions), style (I- or H-beam), and pin retention (pressed or floating) are all important.

Production Versions

There is not much to pick from in the production small-block connecting rod area because they are all made of forged steel and are 6.123 inches long. The tricks come with the 318 rod being lighter and the 340 rod having a bushing in the small end to accept a floating pin. All production rods use 3/8-inch bolts and nuts to attach the cap to the rod's beam.

All race dampeners are SFI-approved and these dampeners can be used on externally balanced engines. Race dampeners were made much lighter, but lighter weight tends to place more stress on bearings. In some very popular engine packages, the manufacturers actually develop (or tune) the dampener to the specific engine package and RPM range that the engine is currently using.

For high-performance applications, use ARP bolts in place of the stock rod bolts in any production rod. With good bolts, the stock rod is fine. High RPM will cause problems for pressed pins, but stock rods typically hold up well.

Aftermarket High-Performance Rods

Selecting the correct connecting rod is one of the most important decisions you make when building your engine. Mopar connecting rods are offered in I- and H-beam design and in forged or billet constructions. Cast rods (not used in Mopar small-blocks) are adequate for base high-performance street engines up to 500 hp, but beyond that you need to consider a forged connecting rod. Billet rods are typically used for 800-hp race builds. Aluminum

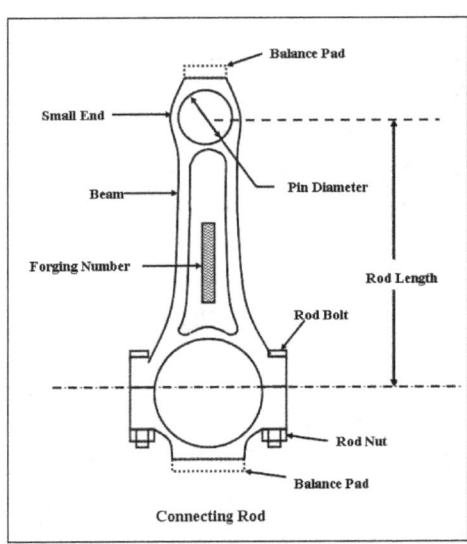

Connecting rods are detailed parts. Because all production rods have the same length (6.123 inches) you can use the forging number for identification or you can weigh the assembly and compare weights.

rods are also forged and are used on supercharged engines but not required in the street/strip versions. They are limited to race engines. Another player is titanium, but these are also race-only parts.

For engines built to rev more than 7,500 rpm, I recommend a high-performance rod from Eagle, Scat, K1, Carrillo, or Manley. You must not mix and match rods; they need to be installed as sets. My first choice is the 585-g Scat I-beam with 7/16-inch bolts and cap screws; it provides adequate strength for any street/strip build package. All production rods use 3/8-inch bolts, except K1 rods, which use 7/16-inch bolts for greater strength. However, these bolts add weight to the rod assembly.

In some cases, the I-beam rod is slightly lighter than the race-designed H-beam style. The Eagle I-beam rod weighs 605 grams; the H-beam version weighs 680 grams. The standard Manley I-beam rod weighs 555 grams

CRANKSHAFTS AND CONNECTING RODS

Connecting Rod Specifications

	273/318	340/360	5.2L	5.9L
Center-to-center length (inches)	6.123	6.123	6.123	6.123
Weight (grams)	726	758	758	758
Bolt	3/8 x 24	3/8 x 24	3/8 x 24	3/8 x 24
Journal width (inches)	.9295–.9315	.9295–.9315	.9295–.9315	.9295–.9315
Bearing bore inside diameter (inches)	2.2505	2.2505	2.2505	2.2505
Pin outside diameter (inches)				
Pressed	.9832	.9832	.9832	.9832
Floating	Not used	.9845	Not used	Not used
Pin bore length (inches)	1.20	1.20	1.20	1.20

Note: Only the 340 used floating pins. Connecting rod weights: big end, 500 grams; small end, 226 grams.

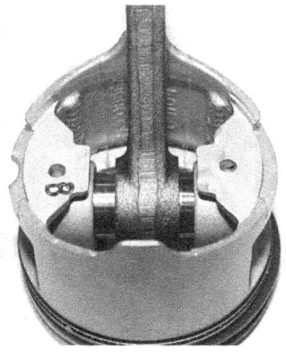

When mounted to the connecting rod, the piston must have clearance between the two-piston pin towers (one on each side). This production-based piston has 1/4 inch on each side. With performance or racing pistons, this clearance tends to get much smaller and, in some cases, may have to be checked. This is not really required for production or service packages. Note the round hole in each pin tower for pin oiling. Each manufacturer uses a different method to oil the pins.

The big end of the rod holds the rod bearing shells and bolts hold the cap on to the beam, which in turn holds the rod to the crank. The key to all of that happening correctly is the rod bolt and nut (toward left). Production-based rods use the rod bolt and nut attachment method. Note the forging number on the beam (at right). It has eight digits so it is probably a Magnum rod. The A-engine used seven-digit forging numbers.

The 340 forging is the only A-engine connecting rod that has a bushing for use with a floating pin. It is difficult to see the bushing after it is installed but you can see the small step in the machining at the pin bore, which is just the end of the bushing. This bushing cannot be added to the standard forging used in 273/318 engines because there is not enough material around the small end to support the bushing machining.

but is limited to 550 hp; the "Pro" I-beam rod (a heavier forging) weighs 670 grams and is rated at 700 hp.

The H is actually a heavy-duty rod designed for extreme performance and racing. Keep in mind that Scat and Carrillo do not publish weights for their H-beam rods. The K1 H-beam rods weigh 656 grams with 7/16-inch bolts. However, I don't think 7/16-inch bolts are required for these street applications, but they are a nice plus if they don't add weight as does the lightweight Scat design.

Dyers and other billet rod manufacturers offer H-beam rods in four categories: light (585 grams), ultra light (575 grams), super light (540 grams), and heavy (600 grams). Billet rods are best suited to special-application engines, such as race 305 engines with 2.96-inch stroke.

A standard 6.123-inch rod with that stroke makes the piston very heavy; therefore, you use a longer billet rod, which allows you to use a light piston. In general, aluminum rods are used in supercharged race engines. They could be considered for other race engines that are rebuilt frequently as part of the normal maintenance routine. If you want to spend your money on lighter rods, several light steel rods are available that are better choices.

Today's steel alloy rods are made of 8640, 5140, or 4340 steel; the 4340 rod has established itself as the strongest and most popular. Changing the steel alloy only doesn't change the overall weight. However, in many cases, using stronger material allows you to use a lighter forging and that removes weight.

For example, the 273/318 rod was a light forging and Chrysler engineers went to a heavier forging (thicker) with the introduction of the 340 engine because it made more power and was expected to run at higher RPM.

About 15 years ago, Mopar Performance made max-performance rods using high-strength 4340 steel; they were offered in the light forging style (273/318) and the heavy forging style (340/360), which is about 6-percent heavier than the standard forging, so let's assume that it is 12- to 20-percent stronger than the light forging. The 4340 material offers strength increases of 65 percent, which means that the 4340 light forging could be 45-percent stronger than the stock heavy forging. These were great rods for Stock and Super Stock race cars.

The 4340 rods are great rods, which were available for 5 to 10 years but are difficult to find today. If you didn't purchase them new, you can use aftermarket rods such as those from Eagle and Carrillo.

Race Rods

Although only two small-block rods are in production today many aftermarket rods are available: aluminum, titanium, and billet. Steel rods are made of high-carbon steels, such as 8640, 5140, and 4340, and many variations of the 1050 family. Most of these materials are forged into rods first before they are final machined. Billet rods are different because they use a different material and machining process. Although all production rods are based on the basic I-beam design, race rods also use an H-beam style.

Rod Weight

Most aftermarket manufacturers publish the weights of their rods. Machining .050 inch off each side of an aftermarket I-beam rod makes the rod lighter. It also makes the rod weaker. This means that you have to be very careful with lighter rods. Manufacturers have been through most of these scenarios before and can provide reliable guidelines.

Rod Length

The small-block rod is 6.123 inches long. Shorter rods (6.00 inches) are lighter and longer rods (6.25 inches) are heavier. Longer rods tend to make more power and shorter rods tend to favor torque. For example, on the 2.96-inch-stroke crank used in the Trans-Am engine, you could have used a 6.00-inch rod. The rod would have been lighter, but the piston would have to be longer to connect to the shorter rod, and the longer piston would have been heavier.

Carrillo aluminum rods appear bulky at first because they have a large, thick beam. The aluminum material allows them to have the thick area without the weight that it would bring if it were steel. Supercharged engines push down very hard on the connecting rod, and the cross-sectional area (thick beam) helps keep the rods together in this extreme application.

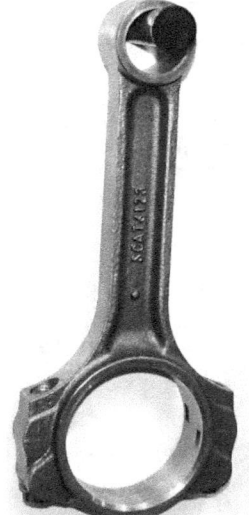

Scat and other aftermarket manufacturers offer race rods made to service specifications except for weight. The rod has a bushing in the small end while the big end uses a bolt threaded into the end of the beam rather than a bolt and nut. In addition, neither end of the rod has balance pads.

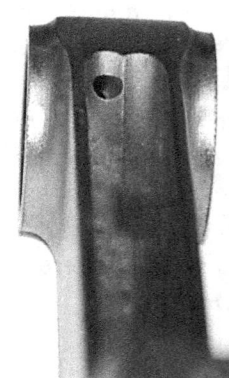

The H-beam rod has the ridge to the left and to the right, which make up the H-beam. This style of rod typically uses a small, drilled hole just below the pin boss at about four o'clock to help get oil to the floating pin.

To date, all common Mopar small-block strokers, including 3.31, 3.58, 3.72, and 4.00 inches, use the same 6.123-inch rod because piston height is adjusted to accommodate the particular rod. Thus, only a new set of

CRANKSHAFTS AND CONNECTING RODS

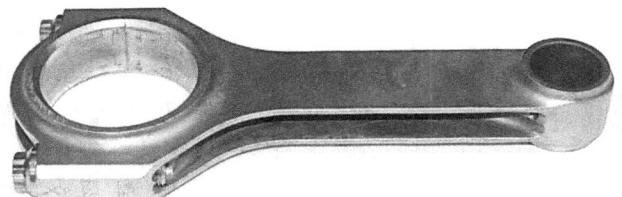

The typical H-beam rods (from Carrillo, Scat, K1, Eagle) are common in racing. They have a slot or trough on each side and a flat face up and down. The big end uses a bolt into the beam–style of cap attachment.

The production rod cap features a location notch and oiling provision. At the left side parting line surface, a small, tapered notch locates the bearing shell. On the opposite side, there is a small trough (notch) cut all the way across the surface through the bolt hole. The hole is important because it helps oil the cylinder walls. Race rods may not have this feature because of the higher RPM expected and the much higher windage that goes with the increased RPM.

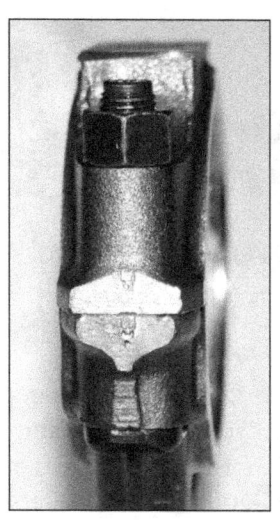

All production rods have an identification mark at the parting line for the cap and the cylinder they are installed in. These numbers or marks are stamped into the machined flat surface. However, newer engines use rods with symbols rather than actual numbers. The two symbols should match and you should write down which symbol goes in which cylinder or you should stamp a number on the cap to tell you what cylinder it goes in.

pistons is required for most builds and it's a much less expensive approach.

A 4.00-inch stroke yields a rod ratio of 1.53, which is still acceptable. If the stroke is increased to 4.25 or so, you still use the 6.123 rod length and a shorter piston (1.46-inch compression height down to approximately 1.33 inches). Race engines probably change both rod length and piston compression height, but it is not required for street engines.

Cap Retention

The obvious approach is to use a rod bolt and nut. However, with performance rods and racing rods, it is much more popular to use a bolt that threads directly into the beam of the rod; no nuts. Typically when this is done, the hole is drilled through. The attaching bolts are also 12-point.

Rod Ratios

The rod's center-to-center distance divided by the crank's stroke is the engine's rod ratio. There are many opinions and theories about what the rod ratio should be for any given application. The best answer is that there is no ideal rod ratio for all types of racing. The 318/340 and 5.2L engines share the same 1.85:1 rod ratio. The 360 and 5.9L engines have a lower 1.71:1 rod ratio. The 4.00-inch-stroke small-block using the stock rod length comes in at 1.53.

Application	Ratio (:1)
Street or street/strip	1.40–2.00
Short oval track	1.50–1.75
Long oval track	1.70–1.80
Drag racing (unlimited)	1.75–1.85
Drag racing (limited)	1.50–1.85
Road racing	1.50–1.75

This chart assumes that it is legal to change the rod ratio in the class that you plan to compete in. To summarize, the lower the rod ratio (smaller number), the more torque the engine makes. The opposite also tends to be true: the higher the rod ratio, the more power the engine makes and the peaking RPM increases.

It can be expensive to change both the rods and the pistons to obtain a new rod ratio.

Do your calculating on a computer before you actually spend any money on new parts. The rod ratio is just an equation and the engine's hardware may limit your rod ratio selection. If this is true, change your cam's lobe center by 2 or 4 degrees to help offset the rod ratio limitation. Cams are much easier to adjust than rod ratios and probably less expensive also.

If you need a lower rod ratio in the engine, you can have the cam manufacturer grind the cam's lobe centers closer together by 2 to 4 degrees to help gain the desired performance. ■

CHAPTER 2

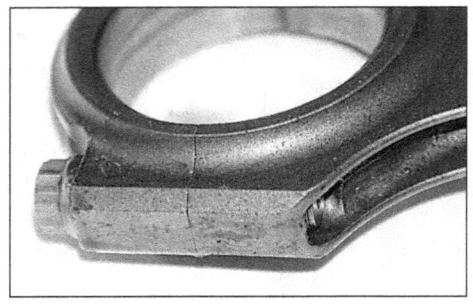

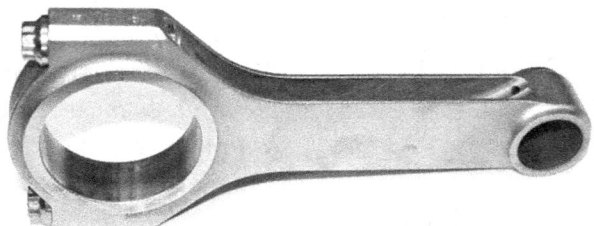

Steel rods, such as the H-beam rod, may use the 12-point bolt threaded into the beam. The typical machining goes through the rod, but it is not always tapped through.

Connecting Rod Prep and Bolts

New rods come already prepared for installation. Your machine shop may check a few things such as the big- and small-end diameters, the rod's length, and perhaps the rod's width. Most connecting rod prep comes into play when you plan on re-using stock rods.

Always replace the stock bolts in any rod that is going to be re-used. Rod bolts lose their tensile strength, and once stretched, clamping force is reduced. When bolts fail, so does the engine. A new rod is sold with new bolts so this does not apply.

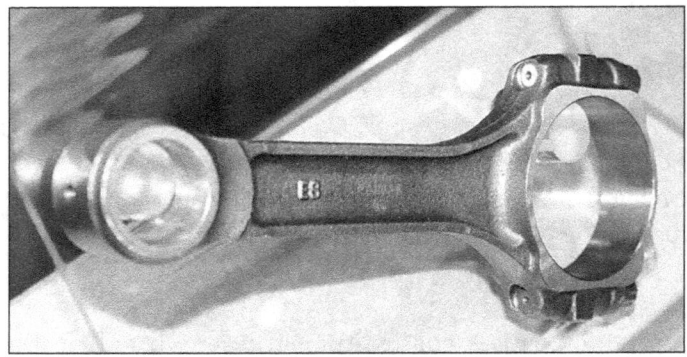

Aftermarket rods typically accept a bushing for floating pins on the small end. The I-beam style of performance rod is designed for use with floating pins; it tends to oil the pin with a small hole drilled in the top of the rod (far left end), as shown on this Eagle rod.

High-strength rod bolts are available from several sources, such as ARP, and also come in several grades, including Hi-Perf 8740, Hi-Perf Wave 8740, and ProWave ARP2000. The Hi-Perf 8740 should be more than adequate for street builds.

Rod Length Measurement

The rod length, or center-to-center distance, is easy to see and you can estimate it with a ruler. All small-blocks use a rod length of 6.123 inches. Although it is easy to see, it is very difficult to measure accurately. The problem is that other rods might be 6.00 or 6.25 inches, so to determine which one is which, accuracy is very important. The accuracy issue comes into play trying to estimate the centers of the big end and the small end by eye. Here's the formula to determine your rod length:

RL = (PD ÷ 2) + (BD ÷ 2) + BL
RL = rod length (center-to-center distance)
PD = pin bore diameter
BD = big-end bore diameter
BL = beam length (top of bearing bore to bottom of pin bore)

For example, let's assume that your measurements are as follows: pin bore diameter of .9830 inch, big-end bore diameter of 2.2502 inches, and beam length of 4.5063

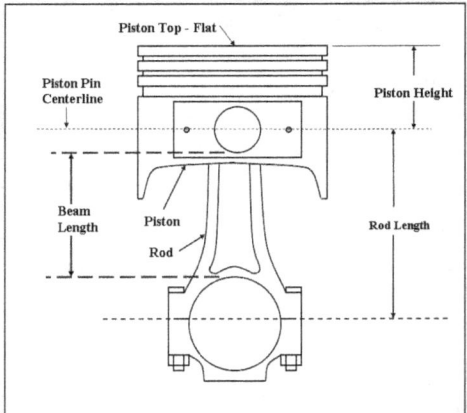

To measure as accurately as possible, use a snap gauge and then a micrometer to measure the piston pin hole diameter and then measure the big-end diameter (without bearing). Then, using a dial vernier, measure the length of the beam from the bottom of the pin hole to the top of the big-end bore.

inches. Using the formula, your rod length is 6.123 inches [(.9832 ÷ 2) + (2.2502 ÷ 2) + 4.5063 = .4916 + 1.1251 + 4.5063]. ■

CHAPTER 3

PISTONS AND RINGS

When building a high-performance engine or Magnum engine, you need to choose between hypereutectic and forged pistons. OEM-type cast pistons can only withstand about 400 hp, and thus should only be used for a stock rebuild.

Piston selection is based on the performance targets and application of the engine. For high-performance street builds, hypereutectic and forged pistons provide suitable strength and durability. When building a street/strip or full race engine, most builders select a forged piston for common displacements. If it's a special application engine, billet pistons are often selected. When aftermarket manufacturers change aluminum alloy and add some silicon, you have a hypereutectic piston, which is part cast and part forged. The bore of the piston is the most common specification but the piston's weight is the hidden performance edge.

The typical cast production pistons come in a wide range of sizes, from 3.63 to 4.04 inches. These cast pistons can support a 400-hp build and can rev up to about 6,500 rpm. Increase revs, increase horsepower, or use forced induction, and you're risking an engine failure. So as you can see, these are not suited for a max-performance build.

The Magnum 5.9L piston is the lightest small-block piston at 470 grams. It took a lot of technology and engineering expertise to accomplish this weight reduction with a piston this large.

Forged pistons are more expensive and the hypereutectic pistons are in the middle. Hypereutectic and forged versions are typically lighter in weight and offer more options and features. The lighter weight is typically the deciding factor for performance applications. The exception is the 5.9L Magnum piston at 470 grams (light) and 4.00 inches but very limited in options.

Production Pistons

Every engine rebuild typically requires new pistons with a large bore size. In a used engine, the mileage wears on the cylinder bores. Once the machine shop measures them, they must be bored and honed to a larger size, such as .020-inch oversize. This much change in the cylinder bore requires pistons that are also .020-inch oversize.

When building a high-performance engine, you need to replace the pistons. Most engine builders select a forged or hypereutectic piston from Keith Black, Icon, Sealed Power, Scat, or another manufacturer. The top of the piston could be flat, dished (shown), or domed. The block dictates the bore size (.020 or .030 oversize). The skirt could be standard or coated (hypereutectic shown). The rings could be standard or special. The crank's stroke and the block height along with rod length generally dictate the piston pin height.

Piston Specifications						
	273	318	340	360	5.2L	5.9L
Nominal bore size (inches)	3.63	3.91	4.04	4.00	3.91	4.00
Piston weight (grams)	547	592	719	584	594	470
Compression height (inches)	1.82	1.77	1.84	1.57	1.77	1.57
Pin bore diameter (inch)	.9845	.9845	.9845	.9845	.9845	.9845

The thickness, angle, and orientation of the reinforcing struts inside the piston allow the piston manufacturer to fine-tune the stiffness and expansion characteristics of the piston so it can handle tighter piston-to-cylinder clearances for improved sealing and more power. Tighter piston clearances also reduce piston rock, which in turn reduces piston rattle and cylinder wear when the engine is cold.

Aftermarket Pistons

When building an engine for high-performance street use, you need to choose between hypereutectic and forged pistons. The horsepower target, application, and budget determine the piston choice, but that choice must be considered in the context of the overall engine package. Your piston selection must be compatible with your rod, crankshaft, head, valvetrain, and block selections.

For performance engines, you want to upgrade to lighter-weight pistons for added performance. Most manufacturers offer several levels of weight: light, lighter, and lightest; each weight reduction adds cost.

If you're building an extreme engine of 1,000 hp or more, you should use a billet piston. The exception is the 5.9L Magnum engine, which has a 470-gram piston weight. This makes it more than 100 grams lighter than the 360 A-engine piston (at the same bore size) and it is therefore an excellent piston for the 360 engine. Finding a piston that is this much lighter than the 5.9L Magnum is going to be difficult. Lesser gains might have to be accepted.

When selecting a piston, first determine bore size, hypereutectic or forged pistons, and then pin type. Your choice is between a pressed or floating pin. Rods generally dictate this choice, and only the 340 came with floating pins. If yours is a max-performance build, your engine is going to rev above 6,500 rpm and therefore it necessitates the use of floating pins. Use pressed pins for torquey, mild street builds with a rev limit of 6,500 rpm.

Most of these pistons are lighter than production versions. The lighter weight puts less stress on the rod and crank and allows the engine to rev quicker. When comparing piston weights, remember that domed pistons weigh more than flat pistons, a dish-top tends to weigh less, a big-bore piston tends to weigh more than a small-bore piston, and shorter pistons used with longer strokes tend to weigh less than tall pistons used with shorter strokes.

With a forged or hypereutectic piston, horsepower and RPM are not really concerns. The high RPM leads to floating pins and you want less piston weight if that is available at a reasonable cost.

KB offers 318, 340, and 360 pistons, hypereutectic and forged. In addition, it also offers a piston for the 4.00-inch stroke and 4.00-inch bore (basic 360, but the 340 version is covered by .060-inch-and-higher overbores).

Icon forged pistons are offered for 318 and 360, plus the 4.00-inch versions for the long-stroke 318 and the 408-inch 360. Several shapes (tops) are offered.

Other manufacturers, including Wiseco, Diamond, JE, CP, Mahle, Ross, and Speed Pro, offer hypereutectic and forged pistons.

Hypereutectic

Hypereutectic are cast pistons, but they are set apart from a standard service piston because of their alloy content. They contain about 18-percent silicon (double of production cast aluminum pistons). The silicon content provides increased heat resistance and strength, so you can build engines with 600 to 700 hp. In fact, these pistons have about 15-percent less thermal expansion than a standard service piston, and with their heat-resistance properties, they have tighter installation tolerances.

In addition, the hypereutectic has increased hardness in the pin boss and ring groove, so you have better ring sealing. Some models feature T5 or T6 heat treatments. T6 is claimed to improve strength by up to 30 percent, but not throughout its service life. Some claim that the T5 has a more consistent heat resistance.

Forged

Forged pistons are stronger than hypereutectics because the manufacturing process packs the metal molecules tightly together. These pistons withstand more heat and cool quicker than cast. However, this thermal expansion requires a greater piston gap tolerance and may produce piston slap when cold.

As a step up from hypereutectic, forged pistons are often selected for building an engine that produces more than 600 hp up to 1,500 hp.

When selecting a forged piston, the most important features are dome shape, weight, bore size, and floating pin design as well as cost and availability. For nitrous-oxide and forced-air engines, which are highly stressed, material is an important consideration. Low-silicon 2618 and 11-percent silicon 4032 aluminum alloys are often used. The 2618 pistons offer greater ductility, strength, and crack resistance, which allows it to deform and not shatter. When 4032 pistons fail, they tend to shatter, which can cause catastrophic engine failure. Use 2618 pistons in nitrous and forced-air induction engines.

Piston Profile

The application often determines the compression ratio; compression ratio and horsepower targets determine the piston profile. A street engine should typically be 10.5:1 or

Aftermarket performance pistons are hypereutectic or forged. Forged pistons (forged Speed Pro shown) have a dense molecular structure for superior strength over cast. Typically, forged pistons are offered in 2618 or 4032. The low-silicon 2618 forged pistons are suitable for extreme performance, forced air induction, and race engines, while the 4032 has a higher silicon content for high-performance engines.

less so the engine can run on pump gas. You do not want high compression ratios so you probably will not use a domed piston top. The 318/5.2L engine uses flat pistons and the 360/5.9L engines uses dished pistons.

When selecting an engine package, calculate the compression ratio to the best of your ability (see below). You only accurately measure the compression ratio when the engine is almost assembled.

Ordering the pistons is one of the early steps in the building process, so you and your machine shop must estimate some items. You need to determine the complete build plan and stick to it because all components function together as a system, and this includes pistons. Changing the heads you plan to use can affect compression ratio.

For example, if you start with an aluminum head with a max 10:1 compression ratio and then switch to a cast-iron head with a 9:1 compression ratio max, changing the piston's compression height is one of the easiest ways to drop 1.0 point in compression ratio. Remember that if you order the pistons based on the final bore size and then mill

The aftermarket pistons (forged Wiseco shown) have many benefits over a stock piston. These are stronger, and often lighter and shorter for less inertia and better acceleration. They can be coated on the top and on the side; it is usually two different coatings.

The early A-engines could use this Sealed Power domed forged piston because high-octane gas was readily available. Domed pistons tend to sit higher in the cylinder bore so they almost always have large valve notches. This dome appears to be around 1/8 to 1/4 inch, and that's common for the small-block racing engines.

When building an engine, you need the exact bore for the piston, so you need to use a micrometer to the measure across the skirt, about even with the pin. The machine shop must measure precisely, so they can bore and hone the block to the proper size. The manufacturer and the machine shop take the piston-to-wall clearance into account; this recommended clearance is provided to your shop.

the block's deck .030 inch and the head .030 inch, the total is actually .060 inch, almost one full point of ratio. Waiting to order until all the milling is complete might actually delay the project.

I recommend that the piston manufacturer cut the valve notches (for valve size, valve angle, valve lift) because it is easier than setting the pistons up a second time at the machine shop.

Using ring grooves is another option offered by piston manufacturers. Be sure that the ring size is available in the style you desire before the custom ring grooves are cut in the piston.

Calculating Compression Ratio

Before you can use the formula to calculate an engine's compression ratio, you need to know the following:

$$VBDC = VTDC + CD$$
$$VTDC = CC + HG + DH + DV$$

Where:
VBDC = volume above the piston at bottom dead center
VTDC = volume above the piston at top dead center
CD = cylinder displacement
CC = combustion chamber volume (in head)
HG = head gasket volume
DH = deck height volume
DV = piston dish volume

Compression Ratio

The piston has a large influence on the engine's compression ratio. The block, crank, rod, cylinder head, and head gasket all play a part, but the piston is the most adjustable. The piston affects the volume above the piston at TDC by changing its compression height. It can also affect this volume by having a dome or dish as part of the top's shape.

The formula to find the compression ration is quite simple:

$$CR = VBDC \div VTDC$$

For example, let's assume that you have a 360 engine that's .020-inch oversize (4.020 inches) with a 4.00-inch crank (402 ci), a 65-cc chamber head, a .040-inch-thick gasket, a .030-inch below-deck piston height (deck height), and a flat piston. One cylinder displaces 50.769 ci (831.95 cc)). The head gasket has a volume of 8.32 cc and the deck height has a volume of 6.23 cc.

Using the information above, you can calculate that the VTDC is 79.55 cc (65.0 + 8.32 + 6.23 + 0).

And you can calculate that the CR is 11.45:1 [VBDC ÷ VTDC: (831.95 + 79.55) ÷ 79.55 = 911.5 ÷ 79.55].

The last number in the VBDC is zero because the piston is flat. If the piston were dished, say 9 cc, that amount would be added to the VBDC volume, making it 88.55 cc. With this dished piston, the compression ratio would be 10.4:1 [(831.95 + 88.55) ÷ 88.55].

If the piston had a 10-cc dome on top, the dome volume would be negative and would in effect be subtracted from the VBDC, making the volume 69.55 cc. The ratio with this domed piston would be 12.9:1.

Most aftermarket piston manufacturers provide the specs for their dish or dome volumes, so you can determine the piston that's suitable for your engine build. Most max-performance pistons have valve notches because of the big cams that tend to be used.

Valve notches are like a dish in the piston, and their volumes are added to the dish volume or subtracted from the dome volume. Notch volumes vary greatly from one engine to another and therefore are generally not published. You have a couple of ways to "guess" the answer. But to actually measure it, you must use a method called the 1/2-inch-down fill volume, which is similar to cc-ing a cylinder head.

It is critical to determine the engine's actual compression ratio, and the engine must have the correct CR for the combination. Once the engine is together, it is very difficult to measure. If the CR is too high, the engine detonates; if it is too low, it runs poorly.

If you built the engine at 9:1 you can generally use pump gas (92 octane max, typically), but if the engine has a higher compression ratio, such as 10.5:1, you must run race gas, which is very expensive.

Piston Design

A typical rebuild project probably uses basic service pistons, which are designed to duplicate the original design except for the bore

Calculating Piston Compression Height

One of the ways of changing the engine's compression ratio is to move the piston up or down by changing its compression height (distance from the center of the piston pin to the top of the piston), which changes the piston's deck height. If you do not know your piston compression height, you can calculate it by adjusting the block height equation from Chapter 1:

$$CH = BH - \tfrac{1}{2}S - RL - DH$$

Where:
CH = compression height of piston
BH = block height
S = stroke
RL = rod length, center-to-center
DH = deck height of piston

From the earlier example for calculating block height, the block height is 9.60, the stroke is 3.31, the piston deck height is .080, and the rod length is 6.123. The math works out to a compression height of 1.742 inches (9.60 - 1.655 - .080 - 6.123). ∎

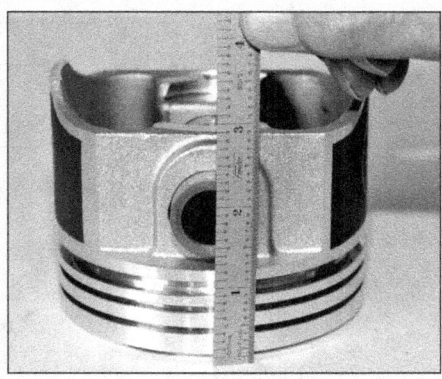

One of the key measurements in that calculation is the piston's compression height, which is center of the piston pin to the top/flat of the piston. You can estimate it using a steel scale but this is not the most accurate method.

The most accurate way to measure the piston's compression height (sometimes supplied by the manufacturer) is by measuring the diameter of the pin with a dial vernier.

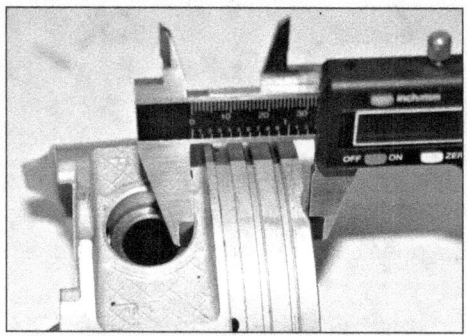

Then you use the dial vernier to measure from the top of the pin bore to the top of the piston. If the piston has a dome, then you should measure to the flat, not to the top of the dome. Half of the pin diameter added to this measurement will give you the compression height.

size (oversize because of wear on the cylinders). With a max-performance project, many more factors can enter into your equation. In most cases, the piston manufacturer can adjust for these variations, but you have to provide guidelines.

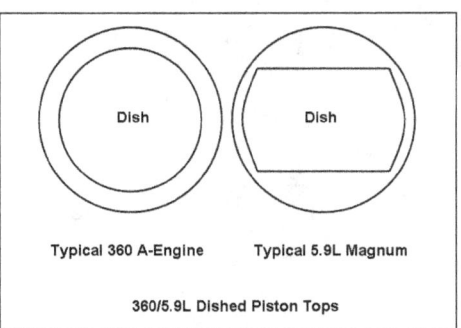

360/5.9L Dished Piston Tops

The production 360-ci A-engine used a round dish in the top of the piston. The 5.9L Magnum engines used a somewhat rectangular-shaped dish. Both dropped the engine's compression ratio. None of these engines had compression ratios as high as the 1968 340. While they were around 9:1, the early 360s were probably closer to 8 or 8.5 and slowly worked up to 9; the Magnum engines were slightly higher. It is difficult to estimate the volume of a dished piston by observation.

Valve Notches

The machine shop usually cuts the notches in the top of the pistons based on the engine's compression ratio and the size of the camshaft (lift and duration). With max-performance applications, cylinder heads are sometimes changed for increased performance. All standard cylinder heads have

Determining Fill Volume

You need to determine combustion chamber volume in order to obtain the correct compression ratio. The most accurate method is cc-ing, whether you have a dish volume, a dome volume, or valve notches. Essentially, the procedure is the same as cc-ing the cylinder head's combustion chamber.

Most small-block piston domes have a height of .125 to .40 inch so the "1/2-inch-down" was selected based on the typical height of the dome. The top of the dome must be below the deck surface.

To perform the procedure, you bring the piston to TDC, measuring with a dial indicator on the top of the piston. (Use the flat surface at the outer edge of the piston if you have a domed or dished piston.)

Once at TDC, zero the indicator, then lower the piston very carefully to .500 inch below TDC.

Next, seal the top of the piston to the cylinder bore using light grease. Wipe off any excess.

Run a thin bead of light grease around the top of the cylinder bore and press your cc-ing plate against the deck surface.

Keep the fill hole on the high side of the cylinder.

Fill the volume above the piston with cc-ing fluid.

Record the volume.

Fill Volume		
Engine	Bore (inches)	1/2-inch-Down Volume (cc)
318	3.91	98.4
	3.93	99.4
	3.94	99.9
	3.95	100.4
	3.97	101.4
360	4.00	102.9
	4.02	104.0
	4.03	104.5
	4.06	106.1
340	4.04	105.0
	4.06	106.1
	4.08	107.1
	4.10	108.2

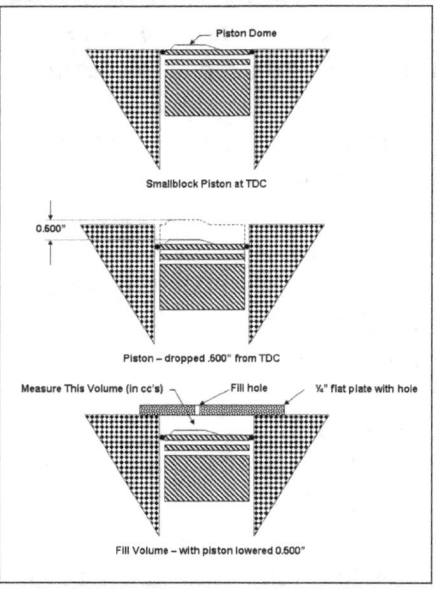

1. To determine the engine's compression, you must know certain things about the piston. The easiest method is similar to cc-ing the combustion chamber in the cylinder head. With this procedure, lower the piston exactly .500 inch and measure the volume above the piston. Since most small-block domes are in the .125- to .375-inch area, lowering the piston .500 inch assures you that the dome will be below the deck surface.

2. The first step is to bring the piston up to TDC using a dial indicator. Then zero the indicator at TDC.

3. Next, lower the piston down the cylinder bore exactly .500 inch using the dial indicator. Once there, remove the indicator and set it aside.

PISTONS AND RINGS

4 Seal the piston to the bore using light grease, such as Vaseline. Try to fill the area above the top ring. Wipe off the excess material with a paper towel.

5 Run a small bead of light grease around the top of the cylinder bore and place your cc-ing plate over the bore. Plates are usually clear plastic about 1/4-inch-thick with a hole drilled in one corner. Fill the enclosed volume with cc-ing fluid.

> *Note:* The 1/2-inch-down fill volume procedure is a function of bore size only, not of total displacement or stroke.

As an example, let's assume you have a 360 engine with a 4.02-inch bore. The perfect 1/2-inch-down volume is 104.0 cc. So if you have a piston with a 9.0-cc dish, the measured volume should be 113.0 cc.

If you have a piston with a 10-cc dome, the measured volume should be 94.0 cc.

If you have a flat piston with intake- and exhaust-valve notches that total 6 cc, the measured volume should be 110.0 cc.

The cc-ing procedure determines the volume. If you measure a dished piston's volume at 119.0 cc, you know that the dish volume plus the notch volume equals 15 cc (119.0 - 104.0); the manufacturer supplied the dish volume of 9 cc, so the notches' volume is 6 cc (15 – 9).

With a domed piston, you measure 101.2 cc. The dome plus valve-notch volume is 2.8 cc (104.0 – 101.2), so the 10-cc dome (manufacturer supplied) has 7.2-cc (10.0 – 7.2) notches. Once you subtract the volume of a perfect disc from the actual measured volume, you arrive at 2.8 cc.

According to the compression ratio equation, you see that 2.8 cc is a positive number (greater than the perfect disc) so 2.8 cc is subtracted (less than the perfect disc). You could have valve notches that are so large that they have more volume than the dome and this would be more than a 10-cc volume. ∎

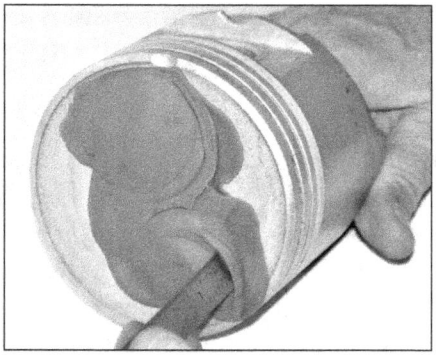

You can measure valve-to-piston clearances, but the most common method is to use modeling clay. A lump of clay is usually flattened across the top of the piston and assembled into the engine. The engine is rotated so that the clay pushes against the head and leaves an impression of the combustion chamber in the head. Too much clay, and you can't turn the crank; too little clay and it won't leave any marks.

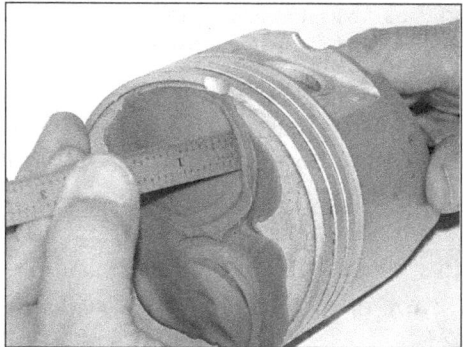

With the cam properly center-lined, and the clay properly located, turn the engine over one revolution and the valves leave imprints in the clay. Using a steel scale, you can measure how much clearance you have. If you do not install the head gasket, you must add the gasket thickness to the measured number for the actual valve-to-piston clearance.

CHAPTER 3

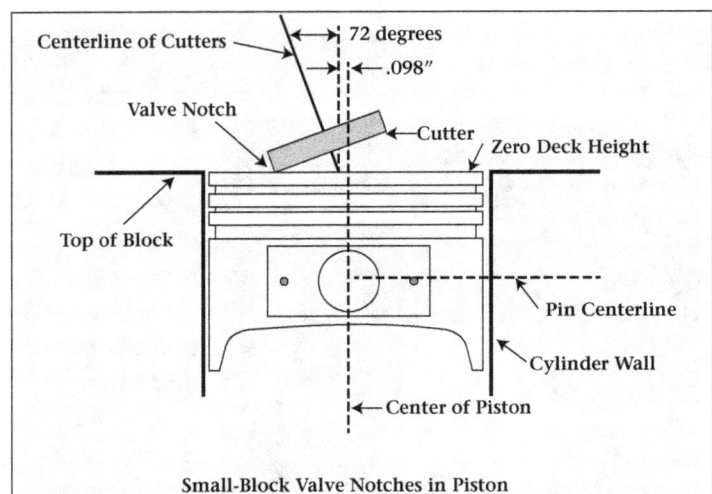

The valves in the A-engine and the Magnum engine are located in the same places and at the same angles. The 318 has small valves, the early 340 has large valves, and the newer 340 (1972–1973) and the 360 have slightly smaller intake valves. Magnum engines are in-between but unique.

This basic layout has been used for years. For max performance, some race cylinder heads use 15-degree valves. This example is based on 18-degree valves (90 - 72 = 18).

The intake cutter (and therefore the intake notch, right) is larger than the exhaust valve notch (left). The 1.87-inch valve center's dimension is common for all A-engines and Magnum engines. However, some race cylinder heads for these engines use the larger 1.935-inch valve centers to allow the use of much bigger valves.

18-degree valves. However, some W2 and W9 cylinder heads use a 15-degree valve angle; some aftermarket heads may use a valve angle other than 18 degrees. If you were to cut the valve notches in the top of the piston for 18-degree valves and then swap to 15-degree valve heads, the notches should be re-done at 15 degrees.

Another concern is the valve spacing. Standard heads use a valve spacing of 1.87 (valve centerline to valve centerline) inches. Most performance heads also use 1.87 inches, but the W9 uses 1.936 inches, which allows the use of larger valves.

Other aftermarket heads that are designed mainly for racing may also use the wide centers. Obviously if the valve notches were cut for the wrong centers, they need to be re-cut.

It is extremely important to provide the piston manufacturer or machine shop with the valve size (especially the intake), the valve angle (15 or 18 degrees), and valve centers (1.87 or 1.936 inches), along with the valve lift for notching the pistons.

Compression Height

A piston's compression height can change the compression ratio. If you assemble your street or street/strip engine and find that it has 11:1 compression ratio, you have a few alternatives. But often, the best option is to buy new pistons, and therefore the compression height is adjusted to achieve the desired ratio. It's better than running race gas or milling the pistons, which could collapse. You might consider using a dished piston in conjunction with changing the compression height.

Try to wait until after the block and head milling amounts have been decided and the head selected (material and chamber size) before finalizing the compression height decision.

Dish Top

The dish is a round shape or a D-shape, and it sits below the deck surface; it doesn't have to be clearanced to the head. The 360/5.9L engines have dished pistons, so you probably want to copy most street applications of this size engine.

Flat Top

The 318/5.2L engines use flat pistons for a 9:1 compression ratio with most heads. Flat-top pistons are probably the best choice for these displacements.

Dome Top

Once the valve notches are cut on a domed piston, many sharp edges are found on the top of the piston. The ideal dome shape is round and smooth, so you should de-burr and radius all sharp edges. The dome also has to fit inside the head's combustion chamber, so be sure that the dome selected is designed for the style of chamber of your head: open, closed, heart-shaped, and bathtub.

For street use with pump gas, you generally do not want high compression ratios (11:1 and up) so a flat piston is a better choice for this application.

Piston Skirt

Most piston skirts are the slipper type, sometimes called a TRW skirt. It has two feet that are approximately 1-inch wide and about 3/4-inch high that blend into the barrel of the piston. The skirt transfers loads to the cylinder walls as it moves up and down. If the piston is set up too tight (not enough piston to wall clearance), the piston and skirt will scuff.

Most aftermarket Mopar piston manufacturers use slipper skirts.

Ring Grooves

Typically, three ring grooves are cut into the piston, measuring 5/64 inch, 1/16 inch, 1.5 mm. If you want to use a specific ring thickness, you must tell the piston manufacturer so the correct grooves can be cut. Otherwise, when you buy pistons, you must match the rings to the grooves. In some cases, this could limit your selection.

Be sure that the ring manufacturer offers the ring style desired in the bore size required by your block *before* having the piston ring grooves cut.

Piston Pins

The piston pin is sometimes the forgotten engine part. Typically, a piston pin comes with the piston, so you don't have to purchase the pin separately. A typical small-block pin is just under 1 inch in diameter, about 3 inches long, round and

Piston Speed

For every revolution of the engine, the piston goes to the bottom of the cylinder and stops and then goes to the top of the cylinder and stops. The faster the engine turns, the higher the piston speed. Most people use piston speed to refer to the engine's mean piston speed. The equation for mean piston speed in the engine is as follows:

$$PS = 2 \times RPM \times S$$

Where:
PS = piston speed (in fpm, or feet per minute)
RPM = engine RPM
S = engine stroke (in feet)

For reference, the mean piston speed of a diesel engine is about 1,000 to 2,200 rpm. A stock passenger car engine tends to be in the 2,500- to 3,500-rpm range. A high-performance engine is closer to 4,000 rpm. A Sprint Car NASCAR engine might be as high as 5,600 rpm, while a drag race engine (Pro Stock or Super Stock) might be 6,500 rpm. These numbers change.

The piston speed is zero at TDC and BDC, which means that the maximum velocity or speed occurs about halfway between these two end points. Peak velocity is 1.6 times the mean velocity. ■

Pin Specifications

	273, 318, 340, 360	5.2L/5.9L
Pin outside diameter (inch)	.9841 to .9843	.9841 to .9843
Length (inches)	2.99 to 3.00	2.99 to 3.00
Weight (grams)	154.6	154.6

This forged and coated Wiseco short piston (long stroke) has a short compression height. A forged, dished, or flat-top piston, such as this, is suitable for any street or street-strip package except nitrous/supercharged engines. This piston has horizontal gas ports (top surface of top ring), which extend to the rear of groove. These holes must be drilled before the ring grooves are cut.

A pin for floating piston use looks just like a pin for pressed-pin use; the difference is in the rod.

Pin Oiling

You should always know how the piston tower is designed to oil the travel to be sure there are no blockages. Pistons that use an angled hole drilled from the pin tower to intersect with one drilled back from the oil ring groove must be checked extra closely because the intersection point could have a chip or burr blocking the passage.

Pin Locks

True-Arc, Spiralock, round wire lock, and several other versions of floating pins are available. True-Arc provides excellent pin retention and is the choice of many max-performance engine builders. Spiralock pin locks are suitable for mid-level high-performance engines.

The piston retention grooves must be cut to match the locks. Pin locks can be difficult to install and even more difficult to remove. Generally, you install one lock in the piston without the pin, and then install the pin through the piston tower and the rod, and then into the second tower. Finally, you install the second lock.

Material

Most pins are made of mild steel. Race pins are made of very high-strength steel, and are often used on max-performance builds. The extra strength of the material allows for thinner wall thickness.

Piston Rings

New rings are mandatory. The finished bore size and the ring groove width in your pistons dictates what rings you buy. If your piston is cut for 1/16-inch-wide rings, you must install 1/16-inch rings. By starting your search for parts at the ring design, you can find the rings that you want and then ask the piston manufacturer to cut the ring grooves in the piston to match the rings.

Sealed Power, Total Seal, Hastings, and Mahle offer a variety of rings. Sealed Power and Total Seal offer the biggest selection. Ring sizes for A-engines are 5/64 inch, 1/16 inch, 1.5 mm, 1.2 mm, and .043 inch.

Mahle offers both standard and low-tension options in 5/6 inch, 1/16 inch, .043 inch, .031 inch, 1.5 mm, and 1.2 mm in the typical 4.00-inch bore to about 4.100-inch bore. For street/strip use, I recommend either 1/16 inch or 1.5 mm, if allowed by the piston.

Aftermarket pistons, including this hypereutectic piston, have many different approaches to getting oil to the piston pin in the pin towers. This piston uses slots on the side of the pin bore. Most of the forces in the pin area are toward the top or bottom of the pin bore.

Many production-based pistons use 5/64-inch ring grooves. Hastings offers 1.5-mm compression rings and 4-mm oil rings for the 1992 and newer Magnum engines.

Your first choice is whether or not to use file-fit rings. On a street engine or street/strip application, I recommend using non-file-fit rings. Save the file-fit rings for all-out race engines. The difference is only a few thousandths, maybe .005 to .010 inch, and it saves a lot of time that you can use in other areas.

Dykes and Headland rings also have an L shape to their cross-sectional area. In addition, gapless rings are available, and they are offered in a number of thicknesses. Dykes rings and Headland rings require special ring grooves in the piston and should generally be considered race-only rings. The .043-inch rings are generally used with gas ports and should also be considered race-only rings.

That leaves the other four sizes. For performance applications, you should not use the OEM 5/64–style ring unless you have no alternative. The 1/16-inch rings are good for almost everything. The 1.5-mm is only a few thousandths thinner than the 1/16, so it is equally good but somewhat more difficult to find. The 1.2-mm is just slightly thicker than the .043-inch, so it could also be considered a ring for gas port use, but it is fairly new and not as readily available. For engines planned for performance use you should consider using the 1/16-inch or 1.5-mm rings with low tension. The top ring is often coated with a special coating, such as moly (low friction), on the face. The second ring may not have the same coating. Gapless rings can

The production rings are spaced a reasonable distance apart. They are also dropped below the chamber or top of the block/piston. The rings that are being used dictate the width of the ring groove. The wide ring groove at the bottom (actually toward the right) is for the oil ring (the three-piece assembly), the top ring is to the left, and the second ring is in the middle.

PISTONS AND RINGS

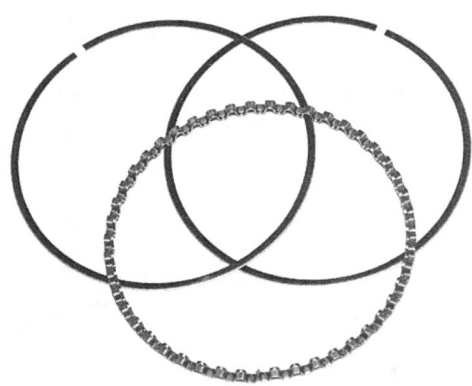

The oil ring is the most complicated ring; it's three pieces. I suggest using non-gapping rings because they are easy to install. A moly coating is good for both top rings.

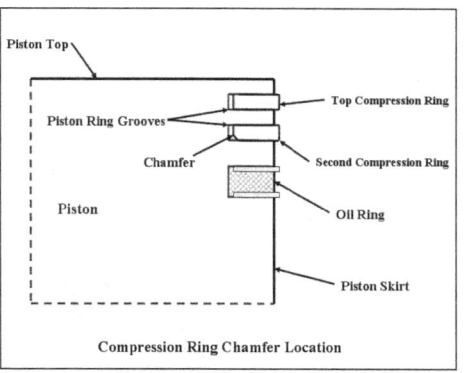

Each ring manufacturer has its own system but in general rings follow these basics. The top ring, or number-1, has a dot on the top surface. The oil ring is the bottom ring and most obvious because it is three pieces. The second (middle) ring uses an inner chamfer on the bottom as shown.

It is common to gap the rings for racing engines. The rings are ordered and require the ends to be ground or gapped. Before you can gap the rings, you must know the ring's gap in your block's cylinder bores. Use a feeler gauge to measure and move it vertically through the gap.

be used in the second groove. Race rings are typically thin with low tension, a moly-coated top ring, and the file-fit configuration. The thin (1/16 inch or 1.5 mm or less) ones help reduce the weight.

Ring Height

The general height of the piston relates to the compression height of the piston. Racing and performance pistons push the ring package closer to the top of the piston, but there are limits to this approach. You can cut the ring grooves closer together, but this approach also has its limits. You can put the pin bore inside the ring package (race only).

These changes in how the performance piston is made and the resulting ring package are the main force behind changing the ring gap recommendations over the past few years.

Ring Grooves

The top two grooves are generally the same width. The third (or bottom) ring groove is much wider than the first two; a 3/16-inch ring is generally used, but a 4-mm and a 1.5-mm can be installed together. Over the years, two rings have been tried in racing very unsuccessfully.

End Gap Guidelines for Rings

If you select file-fit rings, you have to decide what gap to file them to. The non-file-fit rings probably come in around .025-inch gap, while the file-fits are much closer so you can file on the ends of the rings to obtain the gap that you want in your specific bore size. Sometimes these gaps are given as a "per inch" but most of the small-blocks are around 4 inches so it seems easy to just list the gap.

The above numbers are for the top ring only. Years ago, gapping the second ring to the same gap as the top ring was the general approach. Then the low-gap approach (top .015–.017, second .010–.012, or 65 to 70 percent of the top ring gap) was the basic recommendation. The strategy today is to use the wide-gap approach for the second ring (same as top ring up to perhaps .004-inch larger). ∎

Application	Specification (inch)
Street and street/strip	.018–.024
Drag/oval racing engine	.018–.020
Nitrous street engine	.020–.022
Nitrous drag engine	.028–.030
Supercharged/turbocharged engine	.024–.026

CHAPTER 3

Gas Ports

Gas ports in the top of the piston flow gas pressure and push the ring against the cylinder wall for better sealing and high speed. Gas ports are generally used with thin, light rings such as the .043-inch or the 1.2-mm. The gas ports themselves are 14 equally spaced small holes drilled vertically from the piston top into the ring groove. These small holes are .040 to .045 inch; they should be drilled by a machine shop or by the manufacturer.

Gas ports work, but you should be aware that the high cylinder loading causes rapid cylinder bore wear.

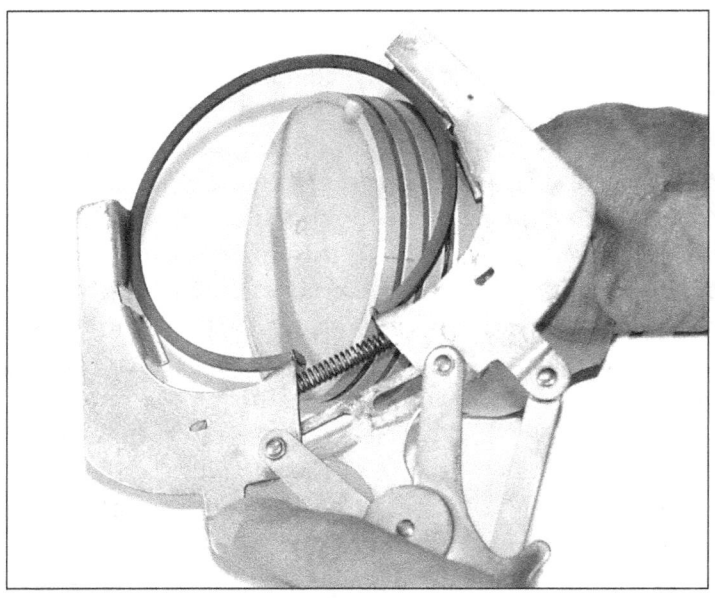
You don't necessarily install the ring into the piston grooves until final assembly. However, any time that you place a ring onto the piston, use an ring expander to enlarge it enough to get it over the top and into position.

To do this, the ring is installed in the bore and the height in the cylinder bore is set. In this case, a micrometer is used. Try to pick a height that is about where the ring would run at TDC.

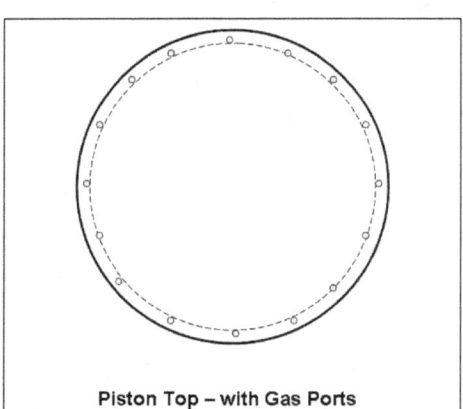
Pistons with gas ports are only used for racing and use a thin ring, usually .043 inch, or 1.2 mm. They have 12 to 16 small holes drilled from the top of the piston straight down to the back side of the top ring groove. This allows combustion pressure to push the ring hard against the cylinder wall for better sealing at high RPM and high loads.

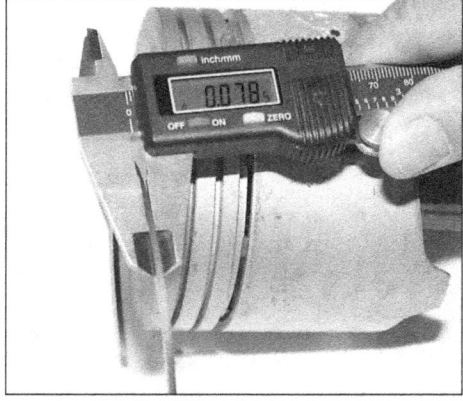
Ring thickness must match the grooves in the piston. It is often helpful to know the actual thickness of the rings that you are using. Rings are usually discussed in numbers such as 1/16 inch, .078 inch (the same as 5/64 inch), and 1.5 mm. The piston shown is a stock, cast piston.

The actual gas ports in a gas port piston are very difficult to see unless you look closely. This piston shows a different type of gas port. These are drilled horizontally at the top of the top ring groove. The small holes must be drilled before the manufacturer machines the ring grooves.

CHAPTER 4

Camshaft, Lifters and Cam Drive

Selecting a camshaft is one of the most important decisions you make when building a max-performance engine because the cam controls crucial timing events. And those events need to occur at the proper time in the engine's cycle and in conjunction with the engine's other component operations. If these events do not occur at the correct time, the engine does not reach its performance potential.

Once you decide to change the cam, you are faced with a vast selection of manufacturers, profiles, designs, and options. The cam dictates most of the valvetrain specs and should work with the amount of air that the cylinder head can flow and with the intake manifold/induction system. The camshaft is part of the engine's short block, so cranks, pistons, rods, and valvetrain need to be considered.

On the other hand, cylinder heads are very popular. With the Magnum versions, installing a cam and tappets should be done before the heads are installed because after the heads are installed, it is very difficult to install the tall, hydraulic tappets under the edge of the head.

Production Cams

Of the major parts within the short block, the camshaft is substantially different between A-engines and Magnum engines. The A-engine has a long nose at the front of the cam; the Magnum engine has a short nose. This difference is because the A-engine has a mechanical fuel pump eccentric-mounted on the nose and the Magnum engine does not use a mechanical fuel pump.

A few Mopar Performance crate engines, however, were based on the Magnum engine, and they were designed for use with a cam that had a long nose and a mechanical fuel pump.

A-engine and Magnum cams look similar because the difference in overall length is only about 1/4 inch. The distributor drive gear is located at the rear of the cam along with a small number-5 bearing journal. The other four journals are basically the same size (just under 2 inches). Cams are made of cast iron or steel. Most aftermarket cams are stamped with profile numbers or manufacturer numbers, but production cams have no actual stamped or cast numbers.

Production cams were mechanical (1964–1967), hydraulic (1967–1985 and 1991), and hydraulic roller (1992–2003). It is not easy to differentiate them.

If you have a small-block cam but don't know which one, you use cam

Cam selection is crucial for any engine build, and correct cam selection is critical for a max-performance engine because these timing events largely dictate the performance potential. Most cams look alike; it is very difficult to tell a hydraulic from a mechanical cam and even a hydraulic roller doesn't stand out. The exception is the mechanical roller because the lobes are so large; the high lift and long duration make the lobes almost look square.

CHAPTER 4

The main function of the camshaft is to open the valves. The tappet is the first part that helps transfer the cam movement toward the valves; the pushrods are the next part in the valvetrain. This chapter covers the cam and tappets; the pushrods are covered with the rest of the valvetrain in Chapter 7.

Cams are often sold as cam kits that include the tappets. The hydraulic roller tappet can give you clues about the cam because the mechanical roller tappet looks different. (See the hydraulic roller chart in Chapter 4.) There are three levels and two specific cams per level (listed by profile number). You can't get any more specific than that.

A mechanical cam requires adjustable rocker arms. The hydraulic cam does not require adjustable rockers. The stamped rockers shown can only be used with hydraulic cams. What isn't as easily seen is that the A-engine oils the valvetrain up through the block and heads to the rocker shaft (shown), which distributes it to the rockers and valves. These stamped rockers are used on most 318s, 340s, and 360s but not on the 273 or the 340 T/A.

lift to help identify it. (Measure lift at the tappet, if possible, and multiply by 1.5 to use the chart on page 52.)

If you have tappets that operate with the cam, identifying your cam style is easier.

The lift number can also help identify aftermarket profiles if no stamped identification numbers are visible.

Aftermarket Cams

Comp, Crane, Isky, Bullet, Edelbrock, and other cam manufacturers offer a wide range of profiles for flat tappets, hydraulic rollers, mechanical rollers, etc. Assuming that the cylinder head is matched to the cam, the more valve lift you put in, the more power the engine makes. However, remember that higher lifts create longer durations, and long durations can cause serious problems with street engines and drivability.

As the valve lift increases, you need to select the appropriate cam. A base performance cam is hydraulic, and then you move to hydraulic roller cams, to mechanical cams, and to mechanical roller cams. Billet cams tend to focus on the racing end of the cam scale.

Camshaft Technology

All small-blocks are four-stroke engines, which have four phases to the engine cycle: intake, compression, power, and exhaust. Each phase is 180 crankshaft degrees. This means that the full engine cycle takes two full revolutions of the crank (360 degrees makes one complete revolution). Because the cycle takes two revolutions, the camshaft runs at half-crank speed and the cam sprocket is twice as large as the crank sprocket.

Common Factory Camshaft Specs

	318	340	360	5.2L	5.9L
Lift (inch)	.373/.400	.429/.444	.410/.410	.432/.432	.410/.417
Duration (degrees)	240/248	268/276	252/252	251/264	249/269
Overlap	26	44	33	31	49
Centerline cam (degrees)	112	114	109	113	109
Centerline installed (degrees)	110	114	108	115	117
Type	Hydraulic flat tappet	Hydraulic flat tappet	Hydraulic flat tappet	Hydraulic roller	Hydraulic roller

CAMSHAFT, LIFTERS AND CAM DRIVE

Cam Specs by Manufacturer

It is very difficult to compare cam manufacturers, but I will try to keep it as straightforward as possible.

For the street, Crane is the best choice because its cams have the widest centerline (at 112 degrees). Other than that it's pretty close. They all have bigger cams and smaller cams so it is difficult to pin this down.

You could ask Comp Cams to grind a cam at 114 degrees and you would have a winner. Custom centerlines cost more, but I believe they are worth it for street use.

Edelbrock offers mainly hydraulic cams. Edelbrock includes one cam in a package that is rated at 417 hp. It has a .488-inch valve lift, 234-degree duration at .050 inch, and uses a larger exhaust lobe, similar to many high-performance production cams such as the 340. Its specifications compare well with similar profiles from Comp Cams and Crane.

The main reason that I lean toward Crane and Comp Cams is that they have more profiles from which to select. Besides 284-degree-duration cams, these two companies offer cams at 286 or 288, as well as 280 and 278.

Cam	Valve Lift (inch)	Duration (degrees)	Duration at .050 inch (degrees)	Centerline (degrees)
Isky	.485	280	232	108
Crane	.480	284	228	112
Comp Cams	.485	280	230	110

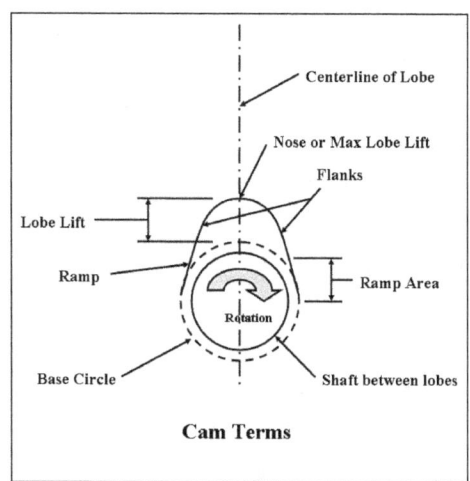

Match the cam's lift and duration to combustion chamber capacity, head port size, exhaust system design, and other aspects of the engine. There are many more aspects to the cam than lift and duration, but these two are important. Remember that the nose of the cam or max lobe lift must fit through the cam bearing's inside diameter. This means that in a given engine, if you want a cam with more lift, the manufacturer must grind down the base circle to gain lift or lobe lift.

Lift

The cam lift, or lobe lift, is the distance that the tappet moves upward in the tappet bore. However, it is more common to discuss valve lift, which is the distance that the valve moves off the valveseat. These two types of lift are influenced by the rocker arm ratio (typically 1.5 or 1.6). Valve lift tends to be the most popular lift number, and it is also the easiest to measure directly.

Duration

Duration is defined as the number of crank degrees that the intake and exhaust valves are open off their seat. Advertised duration is the most popular and probably the most common. It is loosely defined as the point at which the tappet is approximately .012 to .017 inch off the seat (zero position), but some aftermarket companies use a tighter tolerance, maybe .005 inch.

The second type of duration is called "duration at fifty," or "duration at .050 inch." With this duration, the tappet is .050 inch off its zero position. The duration at .050 is always smaller than the advertised duration, but it's much more useful in all-out race cams and engines.

Comp Cams Comparison

As a test, I selected two cams from Comp Cams with the same duration, 268 degrees. Among this company's offerings are two families of hydraulic profiles: High Energy and Xtreme Energy.

As you might expect from the name, the Xtreme Energy gains 6 degrees of duration at .050 inch and gains .023 inch in valve lift. This means that although the Xtreme profiles are pushed harder and may need better valvesprings, they should make more power.

Cam	Duration (degrees)	Duration at .050 inch (degrees)	Valve Lift (inch)
High Energy	268	218	.454
Xtreme Energy	268	224	.477

Camshaft Terms

Camshaft events are closely related to valve events. You must have a working knowledge of the following terms to be successful when making your cam selection.

Lobe Base Circle

This is the lowest part of the cam lobe, or profile. It is also where the tappet spends most of its time. As the cam lobe has more cam lift, the base circle is ground closer to the center of the shaft.

Separation Angle

The manufacturer grinds this specification into the camshaft; it is the angles of the intake and exhaust lobes relative to TDC. A low lobe-center angle (less than 110 degrees) produces better peak horsepower and a wider lobe-center angle (more than 112 degrees) tends to help torque and spread the power over a greater range of RPM.

The installed center can change, but as you move the intake in one direction, the exhaust goes in the other direction.

Lobe Nose

The highest point of the lobe is the nose, and its farthest from the center of the camshaft. The nose is a rounded point; the longer the duration of the cam, the more rounded the point becomes.

The nose is almost always at the same height relative to the center of the cam because the nose must fit through the cam bearings, which remain at the same diameter.

Therefore, more cam lift is always gained by machining the base circle. The exception is if you go to larger-diameter cam bearings, which allows the nose height to increase and the shaft to become thicker and stiffer.

Lobe Profile

Everything between the base circle and the nose on both sides (opening and closing) is considered the lobe's profile. Every manufacturer produces its own equations, which are closely guarded secrets.

These equations determine lift and duration specs.

Lobe Ramps

Every cam lobe profile has an opening ramp and a closing ramp. They may be similar but they are not exactly the same. The ramps' job is to start the tappet moving upward, away from the base circle (opening ramp). On the other side, the closing ramp gently allows the tappet to come to rest on the base circle.

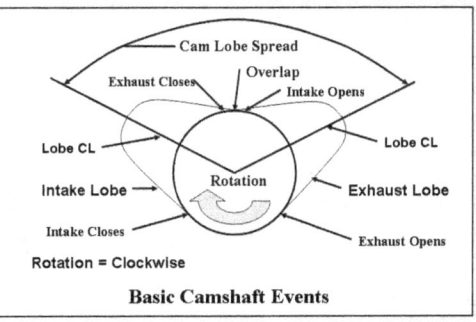

The specifics of the individual cam lobe listed here are only the beginning. To make a cam that will operate the engine properly you also must make an exhaust lobe; now you have the various relationships of the intake lobe to the exhaust lobe. The cam manufacturer provides this information.

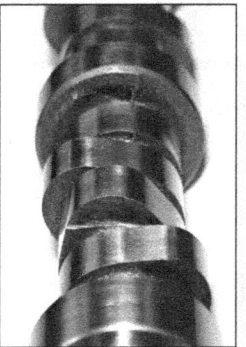

This mild cam is designed for the hydraulic roller tappets. The first lobe (just above the cam journal) and the third lobe up make up a cylinder's worth of cam lobes. The angle between these two lobes is the lobe center for each. The hydraulic roller does not use any taper to the lobe but the standard hydraulic cam does.

Lobe Taper

The lobe is ground at this angle. If you look at a lobe from the side, the lobe's face angles in one direction; a zero-taper lobe has no angle.

A mechanical cam has a very low taper, almost flat, along with an almost-flat tappet face. Hence, the common mechanical cam name "flat tappet."

A typical hydraulic cam uses a higher taper and a more radiused tappet face. The reason for the higher taper is that they are generally considered street cams and you want the tappet to spin (or rotate) in the tappet bore, especially at lower engine speeds. To do this, you have to increase the taper and put more radius in the tappet face to match.

Magnum hydraulic roller tappets and cam lobes are flat.

Valve Lash

Used with mechanical cams only, it is the free lash (gap) between the rocker arm and the valve tip when the tappet is on the base circle. Valve lash numbers are typically between .020 and .035 inch. Ramp design has an impact on the specific valve lash numbers given by the manufacturer. ■

Events

The engine cycle includes four cam events: intake opens, intake closes, exhaust opens, and exhaust closes. These four events are measured in degrees relative to TDC or BDC. The cam's duration can be calculated if you know the event measurements.

Overlap

A cam's overlap is the amount of time that both the intake and exhaust valves are open. It is defined as the sum of the intake opens event (before TDC) and the exhaust closes event (after TDC).

Street cams have low overlaps and race cams have high overlaps.

Centerline

After a manufacturer grinds a cam, there is only one specification that you can change, the installed cam centerline. This is the relationship of the cam to the crankshaft, sometimes called the intake centerline.

The manufacturer grinds the cam centerline (or lobe centers; see sidebar "Camshaft Terms") into the cam, and after it's ground, you can't change it. You can, however, adjust cam advance or retard.

For example, a 340 may be ground on 114-degree centers and installed at 114 degrees intake. By definition, the exhaust is also at 114 degrees. So, if you install this cam 5-degrees advanced, the intake becomes 109 degrees and the exhaust becomes 119 degrees.

Geometry

Valvetrain geometry starts with the camshaft location and the tappet angle (all production small-blocks use a 59-degree tappet angle). This geometry is suitable for many high-performance street applications, but as you get into all-out racing cylinder heads and racing valvetrains, improvements can be made.

Most valvetrain issues become apparent at high RPM, and that's usually more than 7,500 rpm. If your engine generally runs more RPM and makes more horsepower, the first major improvement is changing the tappet angle.

If you draw a straight line from the race rocker arm pivot in the typical race cylinder head to the center of the camshaft, the tappet angle is 48 degrees. It is very difficult and very expensive to change to this angle

Geometry is an overused term in cams and valvetrain discussions. For the rocker arm, it relates to the center of the rocker arm tip being centered over the valvestem. A Magnum valvetrain is shown.

Cam Specs and Installation

When you buy a new cam, you also receive an installation sheet that gives you specifications and tips on how to install it.

The two basic methods are called "event" and "centerline." Both start by lining up the dots, which gets you in the area by plus or minus 10 degrees. To be more precise (at one specific location), you need to use one of these procedures.

For the centerline method, the install sheet lists two numbers: the profile's duration and the installation centerline. For the event method (popular aftermarket approach), you have five numbers on your sheet: the profile's duration and the four events (intake opens, etc.). Use these five numbers to perform the centerline method. I focus on the intake side for this timing procedure. Assume that your new cam has a duration of 284 degrees and the intake opens at 32 degrees before TDC and closes at 72 degrees after BDC. This is typical event method data.

First, add the numbers to determine the duration: 32 + 72 + 180 = 284.

Next, divide the duration by 2, which is 142. Because the intake opens at 32 degrees before TDC, the center must be located 142 degrees later, or at 110 degrees (142 - 32).

To use the centerline method, you only have two numbers: duration and centerline. Assume that the cam has 292 degrees of intake duration and an intake centerline of 114 degrees.

First, you divide the duration by 2, which is 146 (292 ÷ 2).

You know that the intake opens at 32 degrees BTDC (146 - 114) and the intake closes at 80 after BDC (32 + 180 = 212) and (292 - 212 = 80). ■

The pushrod angles to the tappet must be within spec. In this view, the tappet and the pushrod are almost in a straight line. You really want more intake airflow, so you may need to move the pushrod over and use offset rocker arms. The trick is the side view (looking at the pushrod to tappet angle from the front of the engine/head). These are 59-degree tappets and the straight line occurs with 48-degree tappets.

The A-engine front cover is unique (hole in the side). MPI fuel injection can be installed on the A-engine by removing the eccentric and placing a fuel pump block-off plate over the hole in the front cover. The Magnum cover (shown) has no mechanical fuel pump boss. If you want to add the mechanical fuel pump capability to a Magnum engine, you should change both the camshafts (use A-engine style) and the A-engine front cover plus the A-engine water pump. I recommend using the March serpentine front-drive conversion, so you don't end up running the water pump backward.

With the cam installed, the thrust plate bolts to the two bolt holes above the cam and the one bolt below and at the left of the cam.

on an existing block. Knowing this, Mopar Performance added material to its race blocks to allow for a 48-degree tappet. The casting is designed to allow machining of the race blocks with either-style tappet. If you have a race block machined for 48-degree tappets, you must use camshafts that are ground for 48-degree tappets.

Cam Oiling

All cams are oiled from the main bearings. Magnum engines oil the rest of the valvetrain through the pushrods from the tappets.

All A-engines oil the heads and valve gear through the block and head (machined passages). This oiling path starts at the number-2 and -4 cam journals (the cam has five). It is a good idea to be sure that any cam that you use has the number-2 and -4 cam journals drilled through and grooved to help move oil to the cylinder heads and upper valvetrain at all engine speeds.

Cam Gear

Magnum engines use a forged steel cam and special hardened oil pump drive gear that mates to it. These look similar to the standard A-engine gear/drive, but they should not be switched. You cannot use a standard A-engine intermediate shaft and gear on Magnum cams.

If you want to use steel cams (and, until recently, race mechanical rollers) in an A-engine, you have to change the gear to an aluminum-bronze gear. It is gold colored, which is very obvious. This aluminum-bronze gear or shaft assembly is available from Crane or Comp Cams. It also works with Magnum cams.

High-Performance and Race Cams

These are considered to be any cam that is larger than stock or is a service replacement. They are typically made by the aftermarket or Mopar Performance. You should always replace the tappets when you replace the camshaft.

Big Hydraulic

The 340 cam is the largest of the production designs, so these cams start in the .450-inch lift area and go up. Big hydraulic cams may have .480- to .520-inch lift. The advertised durations tend to be in the 280- to 290-degree area.

Hydraulic Roller

The hydraulic roller cam is standard in all 5.2L and 5.9L Magnum engines. The Magnum roller cam is shorter than the typical A-engine cam because the fuel pump eccentric was removed from the front of the Magnum cams.

The tappet location spider and figure-eight (dog bone) hardware does not fit the typical A-engine block. The exception is the 1988 to

CAMSHAFT, LIFTERS AND CAM DRIVE

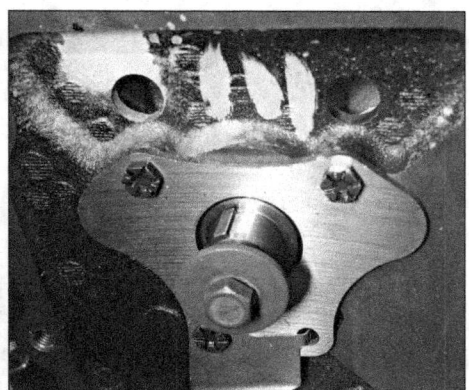

Three bolts hold the plate and the small bracket in place. The small bracket has an index tab that locates it properly; it fits into the fourth hole in the plate.

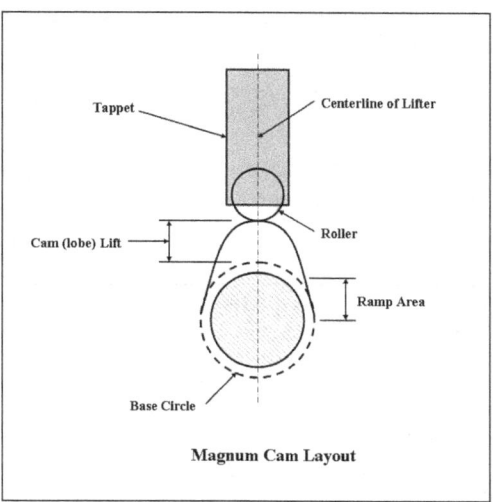

The guide bar must keep the tappet squared to the cam lobe or the cam lobe and tappet will both fail.

Magnum engines already have a hydraulic roller cam and the hardware to allow its use. The A-engine does not have this hardware and swapping the Magnum hardware to the A-engine is not recommended. To install hydraulic roller cams in the A-engine, use a complete conversion kit from a cam manufacturer, such as Comp Cams or Crane. The major difference between the Magnum roller hardware and the aftermarket is how the guide bar systems work on the two tappets.

1991–1992 A-engines, which had hydraulic roller cams also. To convert an A-engine to a hydraulic roller cam, use the Comp Cams or Crane conversion kit, cam, and tappets. To install bigger hydraulic roller cams in the Magnum, install better valvesprings.

The 1986–1991 318 and the 1987–1992 360 cams are at the end of the LA-engine's long production run and they were switched to hydraulic roller cams before the basic engine conversion to the Magnum family. This makes them unique in the LA family. Crane offers cams for these engines. The 1985 and earlier cams do not work in these engines.

Mechanical

Select a mechanical cam when your engine needs a cam that's bigger than the .520-inch-lift hydraulic cam. Mechanical cams with .500-inch-lift area were produced, but lifts of .550 to .600 inch are more common.

In addition, you must install adjustable rocker arms when a mechanical cam is added. The exception is the 340 6-barrel engines, which already have adjustable rockers. Mechanical cams may also require an upgrade in valvesprings, such as a dual spring.

Mechanical Roller

For the past 20 years, Pro racing classes and similar engines have used mechanical roller cams. They allow more lift without breakage than the standard mechanical. For many years, mechanical roller cams peaked at about .700- to .750-inch lift. If the cylinder heads were limited (such as stock castings that were ported or heads limited by their valve size), around .650-inch lift was more likely.

Then, better and bigger cylinder heads were introduced, and mechanical rollers grew even bigger and the valvesprings became stronger. The upper limits are still open, but valvespring loads are more than 750 pounds and valve lifts are approaching 1.00 inch. Part of the technology that allows these very large changes is the big 60-mm roller cam bearings.

Roller Cam Bearings

The 50- and 60-mm roller cam bearings require their bearing bore diameter in the block to be larger; it must be much larger in the 60-mm version. Cam bearing bore cannot be increased on stock production blocks because the bulkhead does not have enough material to bore. Mopar Performance race blocks, called R3s, have material added and allow for this modification.

Cam Selection Process

Selecting the correct cam for an engine combination is dependent on a wide range of factors, so you should take a methodical and detailed approach when determining the specific cam for your engine. Be sure your cam works in conjunction with and complements the entire engine package, including heads, intake, carb, and exhaust.

If you put all that stuff into a chart, it would be so complicated that no one would ever figure it out. Instead, I have included my recommendations in two charts for each cam, the second one shows some of the engine hardware that will work.

CHAPTER 4

Basic Cam Recommendations and Hardware Packages

The following five cam charts divide the cam selection into groups based on type of cam: hydraulic, hydraulic roller, mechanical, street mechanical roller, and race mechanical roller. Each group is divided into three or four levels based on the desired output; more lift equals more horsepower. Each cam chart is followed by a hardware package for heads, intakes, carbs, etc. These work best with the cam listed to make an engine package that works together for best overall performance. The hardware packages are matched to the each specific cam level.

Street Hydraulic Cam

Cam Level	Company	Profile	Lift (inch)	Duration (degrees)	Duration at .050 inch (degrees)	Centerline (degrees)
MP-H1	Comp Cams, P4120249	20-212-2	.454/.454	268/268	218/218	110
	Crane Springs, P4120249	272H10	.454/.454	272/272	216/216	110
MP-H2	Comp Cams, P4120249	20-232-4	.480/.480	280/280	230/230	110
	Crane Springs, P4120249	284H12	.480/.480	284/284	228/228	112
MP-H3	Comp Cams, P5249847	20-243-4	.501/.501	292/292	244/244	110
	Crane Springs, P5249847	H-232/3360	.504/.504	304/304	232/232	106
MP-H4	Comp Cams, P3614542	20-244-4	.525/.525	305/305	253/253	110
	Crane Springs, dual, P3412068	H-312-2	.528/.552	312/322	242/252	108

Hydraulic Cam Levels H1 through H4
MP-H1 Stock 340/360 heads, dual exhaust, stock 4-barrel intake, 650-cfm 4-barrel carb. Electronic ignition, high-performance air cleaner
MP-H2 2.02 intake, street headers, aluminum dual-plane intake, high-performance plug wires
MP-H3 Back-cut valves, 750-cfm 4-barrel carb, 9:1 CR
MP-H4 Better heads (higher flow), single-plane intake
Note: With 318 engines, use a one-step smaller cam; with 400-inch engines, consider a one-step bigger cam. With any given engine package shown above, you can always use a smaller cam but you should not move to a bigger cam without upgrading the engine package to match.

Hydraulic Roller (Magnum) Street Cam

Cam Level	Company	Profile	Lift (inch)	Duration (degrees)	Duration at .050 inch (degrees)	Centerline (degrees)
MP-HR1	Crane	2030	.458/.467	260/264	204/208	114
	Springs, P5249464; Retainers, P4452032					
MP-HR2	Crane	HR-208/292	.467/.482	264/272	208/216	110
	Comp Cams	20-744-9	.480/.480	258/264	206/212	112
	Springs, P5249464; Retainers, P4452032					
MP-HR3	Comp Cams	20-746-9	.506/.506	265/273	216/224	114
	Comp Cams	20-604-9	.512/.512	264/274	210/220	112
	Crane	HR-214/325	.520/.531	276/282	214/220	114
	Springs, P4876062; Retainers, P4452032					

Note: Each cam level has a recommended valvespring along with a retainer listed below the cam; all single springs.

CAMSHAFT, LIFTERS AND CAM DRIVE

Hydraulic Roller Cam Levels HR1 through HR3
MP-HR1   Cat-back exhaust, low-restriction AC
MP-HR2   Computer upgrades, headers
MP-HR3   Single-plane intake

Note: These engine packages assume a Magnum multi-point injection (MPI) engine. The standard 2-barrel throttle body is okay for airflow, but the 4-barrel tends to be overkill. However, the next step is the 4-barrel throttle body, a matching 4-barrel intake along with electronic control module (ECM) re-flash and new injectors. A 400-inch version requires a similar engine package.

Note: The first two levels use a single spring; the last two levels recommend a dual spring, which is based on valve lift.

Mechanical Cam and Street Cam

Cam Level	Company	Profile	Lift (inch)	Duration (degrees)	Duration at .050 inch (degrees)	Centerline (degrees)
MP-M1	Crane	F-238/3200	.480/.500	300/310	238/248	114
	Comp Cams	20-247-4	.495/.495	282/282	236/236	110
	Springs, P4120249					
MP-M2	Crane	F-244/3454	.518/.536	280/288	244/252	106
	Comp Cams	20-248-4	.525/.525	294/294	248/248	110
	Springs, P5249847					
MP-M3	Crane	F-256/383	.575/.585	312/316	256/260	108
	Comp Cams	20-249-4	.555/.555	306/306	260/260	110
	Springs, dual, Crane: 99836; Comp Cams: 995-16					
MP-M4	Crane	F-274/412	.618/.620	306/324	274/288	108
	Springs, dual, Crane: 99838					

Note: The first two levels use a single spring; the last two levels recommend a dual spring, which is based on valve lift. Both MP-M3 and MP-M4 can use Chrysler P3412068 dual spring.

Mechanical Cam Levels M1 through M4
MP-M1 2.02 340/360 heads, street headers, aluminum dual-plane intake, high-performance plug wires
MP-M2 Back-cut valves, 750-cfm 4-barrel carb, 9:1 CR, upgrade ignition
MP-M3 Better head, single-plane intake, more CR, upgrade oiling system
MP-M4 Ported head
Note: A mechanical cam is not needed to use a ported head, but if you use a mechanical cam with this much lift, you need more airflow, such as with a ported head.

CHAPTER 4

Mechanical Roller (Street) Cam						
Cam Level	Company	Profile	Lift (inch)	Duration (degrees)	Duration at .050 inch (degrees)	Centerline (degrees)
MP-MRS1	Crane	SR-238/350	.525/.543	288/296	238/246	112
	Springs, dual, Crane: 99838*; Chrysler: P3412068 optional					
MP-MRS2	Comp Cams	20-701-9	.550/.550	288/288	243/243	110
	Crane	SR-246/362	.543/.561	283/293	246/254	112
	Springs, dual, Crane: 99838; Comp Cams: 995-16*; Chrysler: P3412068 optional.					
MP-MRS3	Comp Cams	20-702-9	.575/.575	308/308	262/262	110
	Springs, dual, Comp Cams: 995-16*; Chrysler: P3412068 optional					

* All levels: Magnum heads require spring set modification for dual springs. Magnums use P4876862.
Note: All valvesprings are dual springs because of the basic valve lift.

Mechanical Roller (Street) Levels MRS1 through MRS3
MP-MRS1   Better head, single-plane, more CR, race headers
MP-MRS2   Ported head
MP-MRS3   400 inches
Note: You do not need a mechanical roller cam to use a ported head or 400 ci.

Mechanical Roller (Drag Race, Competition Only)*						
Cam Level	Company	Profile	Lift (inch)	Duration (degrees)	Duration at .050 inch (degrees)	Centerline (degrees)
MP-MRR1	Comp Cams**	20-719-9	.649/.651	296/303	263/270	106
	Comp Cams**	20-718-9	.654/.655	302/309	269/276	106
	Crane**	R-260/420	.630/.630	292/298	260/266	108
	Springs, dual or triple	N/A	N/A	N/A	N/A	N/A
MP-MRR2	Crane***	R-256/452	.746/.746	285/297	256/268	110
	Crane***	R-274/482	.723/.735	318/334	274/278	108

* High-lift cams (.630 to .750 inch) require special parts, such as long valves with 2.00-inch installed heights. I have listed the easiest solution and generally accepted, least expensive package.
** Use high-lift, dual springs P5249849/Crane #99885/ or Comp Cams 622-16 for lifts over .625 inch and less than .660 inch. Caution: High-lift springs use tall, 2-inch installed height, which requires longer valves.
*** Valve lifts over .660 inch require tall installed heights (2 inches), which require longer valves. Use Crane #96883 installed at 2.050 inch gained with long valves for these cams. Triple springs, such as P4007536 or Crane #961246, or Comp Cams #946 are optional.

Mechanical Roller (Drag Race, Competition Only) Levels MRR1 to MRR2
MP-MRR1 and MRR2 Race engine

These recommendations are for basic street and dual-purpose engines. Typical race engines use large, mechanical roller cams, but they change frequently. The heads keep getting better and the ports' roller cams are getting bigger so they can keep up.

For a dual-purpose car, you can usually use a bigger cam in a larger-displacement engine than you can in a small-displacement engine. For example, if you have a 360, you can use a one-step-bigger cam than you can in a 318. Likewise, you can move up one step with a 400-ci engine instead of a 360.

For cylinder heads, level-3 engines should have a good, high-flow head; level-2 engines could have an upgraded standard head; and the level-1 engines could have a standard high-performance head (non-318).

CAMSHAFT, LIFTERS AND CAM DRIVE

Performance Packages

In an effort to tie all engine hardware together, I created five performance packages. They vary from 250 hp to more than 700 hp and all are intended for street/strip applications. (Remember that the cam affects many of the other selection processes.)

Package Options	No. 1	No. 2	No. 3	No. 4	No. 5	5 (Optional)
Comp Ratio	9.0	9.5	9.5	10.5	11.5	11.5
Cam	HP	H1	H2	H3 or M2	M3	M4 or MRS3
Duration at .050 (degrees)	200/210	215/220	225/230	220/250	255/263	270/290
Carb, 4-barrel (cfm)	650	750	750	750	850	850
Intake manifold	Dual Plane	Mod	Single Plane	Single Plane	Single Plane	Fabricated
Head	2.02 I	bowl	Edelbrock Indy, B1-BA	bowl E, I, B	mild-port E, I, B	full I, B
Intake flow (cfm)	190	220	260	280	310	340
Estimated hp/ci	.63/.70	.85/.91	1.10/1.20	1.32/1.44	1.56/1.68	1.88/1.99

Note: Use this chart as a guideline; it is not a definitive resource for performance packages. For example, you could use a 220-degree cam in the No. 1 package or a bigger carb (cfm) and so forth.

	Cam Level	Best Valvespring
Package Nos. 1, 2	H1, H2, M1	P4120249 Mopar Performance
Package No. 3	H3, M2	P5249847 Mopar Performance
Package No. 4	M3	P3412068 or Crane/Comp Cams dual
Package No. 5	M4, MRS3	P3412068 or Crane/Comp Cams dual

Cam Installation

Properly orienting the cam with the crankshaft requires some detail work so the engine performs well. The factory method of lining up the dots on the crank and cam sprockets is a starting point, but if you bought a new cam, follow the manufacturer's recommendations. Often, an aftermarket cam must be installed in a different location. To find this installation location, you need a degree wheel and a dial indicator.

Using a Degree Wheel

As I recall, high school geometry says that a circle is divided into 360 degrees. Engine builders use a degree wheel to install and centerline camshafts and to check camshaft locations relative to the crank. My recommendation is to use the 0-180-0 version (available from Mopar Performance) because I prefer to think of the relationship of the crank to the camshaft in terms of the cam centerline, which is one number that defines one engine aspect.

The other version (0-90-0-90-0 style) is designed mainly to work with the four-event installation method, which has degrees for the four events: intake opens (IO), intake closes (IC), exhaust opens (EO), and exhaust closes (EC). You also have to consider the locations before or after TDC and BDC.

Adjusting the Centerline

After you have determined the cam's actual centerline, slip the cam sprocket off the nose of the cam and remove the stock key. Install the new offset key and slip the sprocket back into position. It is easier to adjust the centerline using the dial indicator than it is to calculate which direction it goes, offset to the left or offset to the right. If you guess wrong and the offset is installed incorrectly, the dial indicator and degree wheel tell you.

Aligning Timing Marks

Each tooth in the cam sprocket is about 7.5 degrees wide; aligning the dots is only accurate to 7.5 degrees. The installed centerline could be 107 or 123, which is one tooth off in each direction. Therefore, if you want to install the cam at 112 or 118, you can't get there with the lining-up-the-dots method. However, actually doing the lining-up-the-dots as the first step saves you a lot of time in the long run. It also catches a one-tooth-off error.

MOPAR SMALL-BLOCK ENGINES: HOW TO BUILD MAX PERFORMANCE

CHAPTER 4

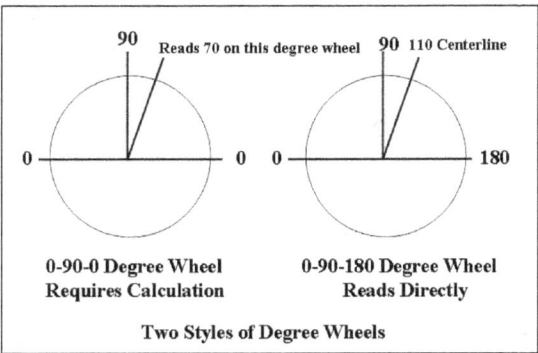

0-90-0 Degree Wheel Requires Calculation

0-90-180 Degree Wheel Reads Directly

Two Styles of Degree Wheels

Most degree wheels read 0-90-0 so that a cam centerline of 115 degrees will actually read as 65 degrees on the degree wheel. You can subtract the actual reading (65) from 180 degrees for the actual cam centerline (115). The 0-180–degree wheel reads 115 degrees directly; no calculations required.

There are two styles of degree wheels: the 0-90-0-90-0 layout and the 0-180-0 layout (shown). I recommend this version because it is much easier to focus on one number, the centerline. You will make fewer mistakes.

Cam Degreeing

Degreeing the cam (centerline installation method) requires a degree wheel. Always remember that the cam needs to have a specific relationship with the number-1 piston. So the zeroing process, which is the first step, is extremely important.

Advancing/Retarding

When degreeing a cam, the cam movement (changing the centerline) is called advancing or retarding the cam. If you start with a 115-degree centerline, and you move the centerline toward 100 degrees, you are advancing the cam. If you move the centerline away from 100 degrees, you are retarding the cam.

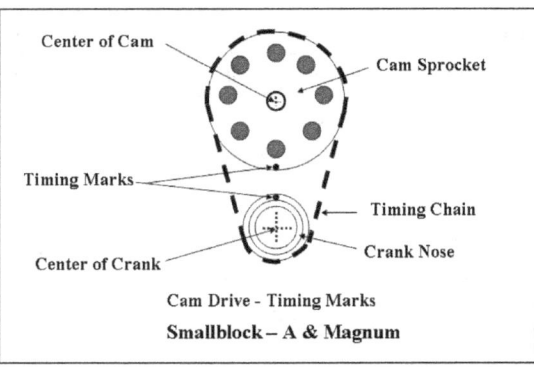

Cam Drive - Timing Marks
Smallblock – A & Magnum

With the cam installed in the block, the next step is to line up the dots on the crank and cam sprockets and install onto the cam and crank. Get the number-1 piston to TDC and line up the dots so they are opposite each other. Then rotate the cam so that the keyway in the sprocket lines up with the key in the cam. Slip the timing chain over the crank sprocket and slide the cam sprocket over the nose of the camshaft. Slip the cam sprocket into place and check to see if the dots line up.

Lining up the dots on the crank and cam sprockets is the first step in installing the cam correctly. It will save time and effort in the long run. You can fine-tune this process by using the steel scale to line up the dots with the centers of the crank and cam sprocket.

Next, the degree wheel is attached to the nose of the crank with the dampener bolt and a large washer (use extra washers as necessary). Use a piece of bent wire as a pointer; select two front cover bolt holes to which you'll attach the pointer. Place the dial indicator on the top of the number-1 piston and rotate the piston to TDC and zero the indicator. Rotate the piston so that the indicator now reads .050 inch and read the pointer, which indicates 20 degrees. Reverse the direction of rotation and bring the piston up to .050 inch below TDC and read pointer again; it should indicate 30 degrees. If the pointer was properly zeroed, it will read the same at both locations. Because there is a 10-degree difference, bend the pointer 5 degrees toward zero. Repeat procedure and both readings should now be 25 degrees.

CAMSHAFT, LIFTERS AND CAM DRIVE

Install the tappets into the tappet bores for the number-1 cylinder. Lube with very thin oil. Reposition the dial indicator to the top of the intake tappet (outside edge, flat surface). Rotate the crank one full revolution and return to TDC with both tappets on the base circle. Carefully rotate the crank in the clockwise direction until the intake tappet reaches max lift; zero the indicator. Rotate the crank clockwise until the tappet reaches the base circle and starts to lift again. Stop at the point .050 inch below max lift point and read the degree wheel; it should be 85 degrees. Continue rotating clockwise through max lift and back to the .050-inch down point and stop to take the second reading. It should be 145 degrees. The centerline is halfway between these two points, at 115 degrees.

If you wanted the cam installed at 115, you are finished. If it measures 107 degrees, then you are a tooth off on the sprockets or the dots are out of line by one tooth. If you want to install the cam at a point between these two numbers, you will have to use offset cam keys or multi-key sprockets.

Tappets

A tappet is about 1 inch in diameter and 2 to 3 inches long. The face of the tappet rides directly on the lobe of the cam. Therefore, the tappets must be the same as the cam design, that is, hydraulic to hydraulic, mechanical to mechanical, etc.

The most common mode of tappet failure is scuffing. Always replace the tappets when you replace the cam and keep the tappets matched to the lobe number-1 intake tappet on the number-1 intake lobe.

Cam Drive

You should always replace all three pieces of the cam drive if it appears to be showing too much wear. You should replace the cam drive on high-mileage engines.

Belt, gear, silent, and roller are the four cam drive types. The belt drive is made by Jesel and should be considered a drag racing part. Several companies make gear drives but I recommend Milodon because it fits under the stock front cover (most gear drives replace the stock front cover). The silent chain is the typical production version and should be replaced for any performance application.

Crane, Comp Cams, Milodon, and Cloyes make roller or double-roller timing chains. Cloyes has several versions of the roller-chain cam drive with three or nine keyways for cam alignment, along with standard and billet gears.

Cloyes offers a hex-adjust option for the Mopar big-block but not the small-block yet, maybe soon. Any of the roller assemblies are fine for the street, but the special tensioner offered by Mopar Performance (Mancini Racing in Detroit) is a nice trick for the street: durability and accuracy over time.

Cloyes makes a multi-keyed sprocket, which is a version of the roller chain. The difference is in the two sprockets because they have more than one keyway for installation. And it doesn't require offset keys to centerline the cam. There are often three keyways but there can be as many as five. Each keyway has a unique dot for alignment.

The valve-to-piston clearance is an important clearance; with bigger cams, valve notches are typically cut into the top of the piston. As a general statement, advancing the cam (moving centerline from 115 to 105 degrees) will hurt valve-to-piston clearance, while retarding the cam tends to help the valve-to-piston clearance. You generally want to measure the piston's valve-to-piston clearance early with the cam properly centerlined (and adjust the valve notch size) to avoid future problems.

MOPAR SMALL-BLOCK ENGINES: HOW TO BUILD MAX PERFORMANCE

This is the most common tappet used in production and also for street/strip. It adjusts automatically for wear and removes any lash that is in the system. Typically, this type of tappet is used with a stamped rocker arm that requires no adjustment. The 1970 340 6-barrel engine used a hydraulic cam with adjustable rocker arms. If you are going to use a hydraulic cam with adjustable rocker arms, adjust the rocker to zero lash as you would for a mechanical cam and then turn the adjusting screw down one more full turn. Note the oil feed hole in the side two-thirds up from the bottom.

The hydraulic tappet is quite complicated inside and it is designed to adjust about .100 inch up and .100 inch down. You do not want to get too close to either end of the adjustment range. The insides of the standard hydraulic tappet and the hydraulic roller tappet are very similar. The primary parts are the main tappet body, the small spring, the plunger, the plunger cap, and the retainer clip.

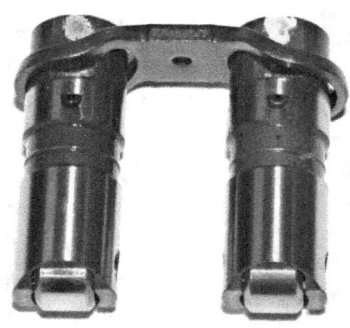

The Magnum hydraulic roller tappet adjusts for wear and lash automatically. The mechanical roller or race setup uses a guide bar to keep the roller square to the cam lobe as the cam rotates, and it usually attaches to the tappet body by a slot, pin, or button. The Magnum's production location system has a yoke that slips over the outside of the tappet body, which is square on the top. The yoke acts like a guide bar and keeps the tappet from turning in the tappet bore. A spider bracket holds the eight yokes (one per cylinder) in place; three bolts attach it to the center of the tappet chamber.

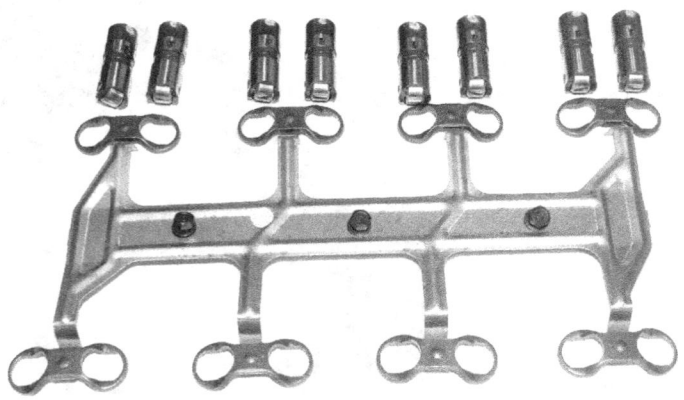

Magnum blocks have three machined bosses in the tappet chamber to accept the spider's attaching bolts. These bosses are not in an A-engine block, so it is difficult to add the spider to the earlier engines. In addition, the top of the tappet bore is not machined to accept the yoke. The aftermarket hydraulic roller cam conversion kits for the A-engine use a hydraulic roller tappet that uses a guide bar to control rotation rather than the yoke. These aftermarket kits allow you to convert the A-engine to the hydraulic roller cams.

The hydraulic roller tappet should be installed with the oil hole in the side of the tappet body pointing toward the center of the engine, away from the tappet wall. In the tappet on the right, the oil hole is just above the top of the tappet base and pointing away from the block.

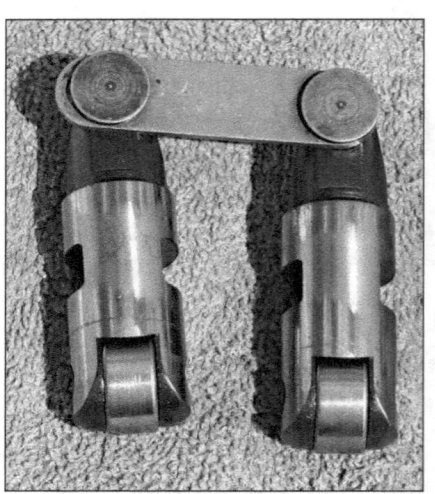

These mechanical roller tappets have been around racing for over 40 years and now, after a slow start, almost all race cams are based on the mechanical roller cam. The mechanical roller uses a guide bar, typically attached to the tappet body, which means that these tappets are installed in sets of two.

CAMSHAFT, LIFTERS AND CAM DRIVE

Timing Sets

Magnum engines use special hardened gear on the intermediate shaft. Production A-engines use a cast-iron gear. With any steel cam (typically a roller), an aluminum-bronze gear (brass/gold in color) must be used.

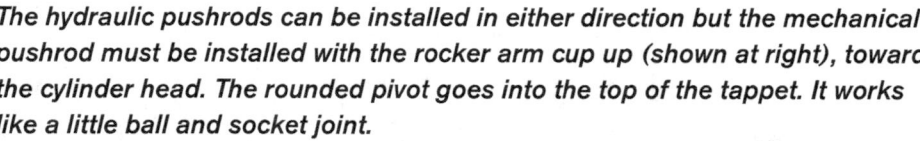

The hydraulic pushrods can be installed in either direction but the mechanical pushrod must be installed with the rocker arm cup up (shown at right), toward the cylinder head. The rounded pivot goes into the top of the tappet. It works like a little ball and socket joint.

Gear drives are used for racing. The most popular style of gear drive has two small gears mounted to a crossbar that holds them in place between the crank and cam sprocket.

The silent chain is the standard cam drive in production, but you always upgrade to a roller chain for performance applications. The silent chain crank sprocket has the wide teeth rather than the sharp, bicycle teeth used on the roller chain.

The roller chain or double-roller chain looks like a bicycle chain with two rows of links rather than a single row. This is the standard performance setup. Note that the crank sprocket has more than one keyway in it.

Oil Pump Drive

Max-performance applications require the use of a hardened oil pump shaft and an upgraded oil pump gear. A high-volume pump places a higher load on the oil pump shaft, so it needs a hardened tip. Mopar performance offers upgraded pump driveshafts and distributor gears.

The camshaft drives the oil pump and the distributor off the gear at the rear of the cam. The gear actually drives an intermediate shaft. For max performance it is a good idea to upgrade this shaft to a race unit. The one tricky part is roller cams. All mechanical roller cams are steel; the Magnum's hydraulic roller cam is a steel alloy.

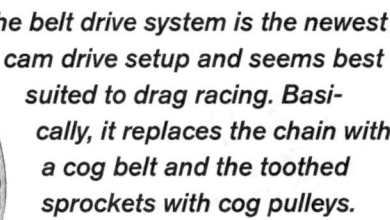

The belt drive system is the newest cam drive setup and seems best suited to drag racing. Basically, it replaces the chain with a cog belt and the toothed sprockets with cog pulleys.

The Magnum engine uses a special hardened gear on the intermediate shaft. The A-engines use the aluminum-bronze gear, which looks like brass with any steel cam

CHAPTER 5

CYLINDER HEADS

Selecting the best cylinder head for your application takes careful consideration and requires weighing many factors so you have the correct casting that matches your engine package. Heads flow air and manage the combustion of the fuel charge and, therefore, are critical for attaining the proper output level. You need to have your application and performance targets clearly defined so you end up with the correct head.

In the following sections, I cover most of the original production and the performance heads, but I focus on currently available heads. In the early 2000s, Chrysler/Mopar offered more than 30 different heads for the Mopar small-block engine, and this number does not include any actual current production heads. The aftermarket offers many more performance heads, which I also cover.

The head must work with all other engine components for the engine to be successful. The short block's displacement, the compression ratio, the intake manifold, throttle body/carb induction system, camshaft, and valvetrain all play important parts for the team that makes the final output of torque/power. If the short block is not up-to-snuff, the best heads can't deliver the desired power. No air flows through the ports in the head unless the valves open (and the cam opens the valves), so the cam is a very important part of the airflow team, even though it doesn't flow air.

Once you define your application and what you expect from the engine, you can select a set of heads to best suit this application. Prepping the heads properly and matching the rest of the engine parts to this head are the key factors to making high torque and power outputs.

Identification

Looking at the casting number is the most reliable method to identify a head. Typically this number is located on the top of the cylinder head but inside the valvecover gasket area, which means that you can't observe it if the valvecover is installed.

So the first tip is that the A-engine uses a 5-bolt attaching pattern and the Magnum engines use a 10-bolt attaching pattern. The next tip is that A-engines use a 7-digit casting number and Magnum engines use an 8-digit casting number.

Some performance (non-production) and aftermarket heads are aluminum or cast iron and have unique casting numbers or other logos to identify them. Notice that the specifications are very similar among production-based heads, but

The A-engine and Magnum cylinder heads are similar but not the same. The Magnum head shown has a 10-bolt valvecover; the A-engine has a 5. The Magnum head uses vertical intake manifold attaching screws and the A-engine intake attaching screws are perpendicular to the manifold face. Other differences are more subtle.

CYLINDER HEADS

Cylinder Head Specs

	273/318	340 (1968–1971)	340 (1972–1973)	360	5.2L/5.9L
Valve centers (inches)*	1.870	1.870	1.870	1.870	1.870
Valve size (inches)	1.75/1.50	2.02/1.60	1.88/1.60	1.88/1.60 1.92/1.625	
Valve angle (degrees)**	18	18	18	18	18
Valveguide (inches)	3/8	3/8	3/8	3/8	8 mm
Spring installed height (inches)	1.68	1.68	1.68	1.68	1.64
Valve length (inches)	4.90I/4.91E	4.90I/4.91E	4.90I/4.91E	4.90I/4.91E	4.90I/4.91E
Weight (pounds)***	45	45	45	45	45

* W7/W8/W9 aluminum racing heads use 1.936-inch valve centers
** W7/W8/W9 racing heads use 15-degree valve angles
*** Production heads with air pump provisions are approximately 4 to 5 pounds heavier

Cylinder Head Casting Numbers

As you can see in the chart below, there is a large variation in combustion chamber size (volume); plus, at a typical rebuild, the head is milled, which makes the volumes smaller than the numbers listed. The only reliable way to identify a cylinder head is by the casting number. Most of the production cylinder heads are listed below, but it is not a complete listing of all casting number possibilities.

Year	Engine	Casting Numbers	Combustion Chamber Volume (cc)
1964–1966	273	2465315, 2536178	57.0–64.5
1967–1971	273, 318	2658920, 2843675	57.0–64.5
1973–1976	318	2843675, 3769973	61.0–67.5, 63.0–69.0
1977–1983	318	4027163, 4027593	64.5–71.5
1981–1983	318 HP	4027596, 4071051	66.0–72.5
1984–1991	318	4323302	56.0–65.0
1984–1987	318 4-barrel	4323475	69.0–77.0
1968–1971	340	2531894	63.0–73.5
1970	340 6-barrel	3418915	65.0–73.0
1972–1973	340	3418915, 3671587	65.0–73.0
1971–1974	360	3418915, 3671587	65.0–73.0
1975–1976	360	3671587, 3769974	65.0–73.0
1977–1979	360	4027596, 4071051	66.0–72.5
1980–1985	360	4027596, 4027593, 4071051, 4027163	66.0–72.5
1986–1989	360	4343923, 4323345, 4343475	66.0–72.5
1990–1992	360	4323308	68.0–74.5
1992–2002	5.2L	53006671, 53030466	57.2–62.8
1993–2003	5.9L	53006671, 53030466	57.2–62.8

Note: Although A-engine casting numbers have seven digits, Magnum 5.2L/5.9L engines use eight digits.

CHAPTER 5

the best spec is the intake valve head diameter, which is 1.92 for the Magnum and 1.75, 1.88, or 2.02 for various A-engines.

It is very easy to install large valves if the cylinder head is rebuilt, so using the actual valve's head diameter to determine which version of a head that you have is flawed.

Production Cylinder Heads

Most production LA-engines are more than 40 years old, so the key is having one set of heads in good shape to use in a performance engine.

When building a max-performance small-block of 500 hp or more, one of the latest aftermarket cylinder heads produces much more performance than many of the cast-iron OEM heads. Cast-iron or aluminum Indy heads are an excellent choice. Although production heads can be ported and modified to accept modern valvetrains, you're going to save time and money by starting with a current aluminum aftermarket model.

340

The 340 head provided exceptional performance and was highly desired and sought after for the A-engine. These heads are referred to as "915" heads because the last three digits of the casting number are 915. But they are also called "X" and "J" heads based on the cast letter on the head in addition to the casting number (versions of the 894 head).

These were good heads in 1968, but there are better castings in the production head lineup. The 308 head is regarded as the best A-engine casting, and it was in production from about 1988 through 1992, but it was not an exclusive casting.

Another aspect of these production heads is that the 1981–1987 318 4-barrel engines used 360 heads as part of the E48 high-performance 4-barrel or police option. After 1971, all high-performance production 340/360 heads had a 1.88 intake valve, which can easily be upgraded to a 2.02-inch intake valve for max-performance applications.

308/576

The 308 head is the best production cylinder head, and it uses a copy of the W2 exhaust port (perhaps the best-flowing exhaust port in *any* small-block head). It just flows more air. The roof of the intake is raised. With matching valve size, it makes more power.

Introduced in the late 1980s the 308 was one of three 360 castings that were installed on trucks from 1988 to 1992, so it is difficult to find in the typical junkyard. Mopar Performance began selling these 308 heads around 1990 as a service for Mopar Stock and Super Stock racers.

Although A-engine production stopped in 1992, dealers often were lucky to get them when ordering service heads. Then Mopar Performance sold the 308 castings machined as 360 production heads with 1.88-inch intake valves, and eventually a 340 version with 2.02 valves was offered.

Later, the casting number changed to "576" (the last three digits). It had the same ports as the 308 and they flowed the same; only the casting number changed. Both heads had the same open combustion chamber as the other 340/360 heads and the same 1.88/1.60 valve sizes. Mopar Performance created an offset pushrod version to duplicate the 340 T/A heads, but it wasn't very popular. The 308/576 cast-iron head was quite popular for about 10 years when production stopped.

W Head

The "W" series of small-block heads are high-performance heads. The W2 was introduced in the early 1970s. It was probably the best cast-iron small-block head for 40 years. The W2 has a casting number of 3870810, and the large, oval intake ports easily identify it. The W2 was offered as an economy version with cast pedestals; the race version had offset rocker shaft stands.

The second-generation W2 was introduced in 1989–1990.

The third-generation W2 was unveiled in 1998 and is visually dif-

Chrysler made many different versions of the cast-iron W2 head. It uses the A-engine five-bolt valvecover pattern. The five rocker pedestals are machined flat but not taken completely off. This W2 race head uses aluminum rocker stands bolted to the flat pedestals. Note the second pedestal from the left has an almost double bolt hole compared to the other four.

CYLINDER HEADS

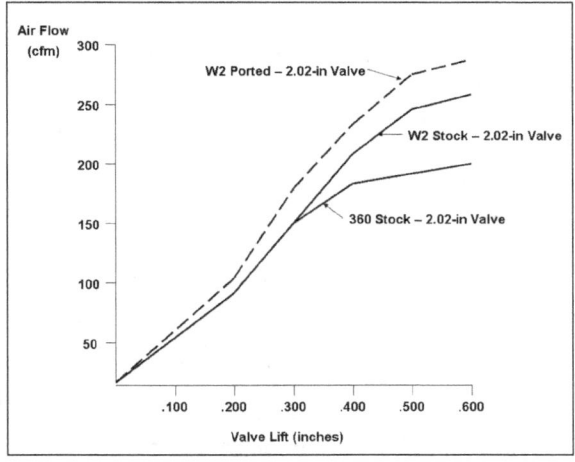

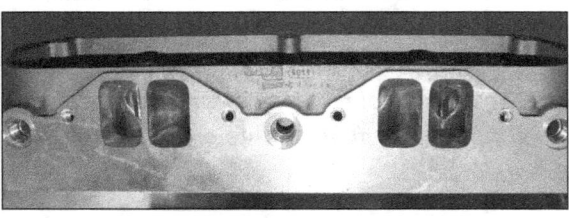

Stock heads provide a good baseline for comparing intake flow numbers. The W2 head flows much better than the stock head using the same intake valve size. The ported W2 flows even better. This is a hand-ported W2, not CNC-ported. The W2 was designed to flow as cast, out of the box. Many aluminum heads are designed to be CNC-ported and do not flow well as cast.

The W9 aluminum head flows well out of the box (as-cast) and in a full CNC-port (shown). Note the height of the intake port above the bottom of the head. These W9 heads require the intake manifolds that are made for the W9 heads. Also note the unique water exits: three, one on each end and one in the middle.

The fully CNC-ported W9 aluminum head also has raised exhaust ports but not as much as the intake side. The unique exhaust bolt pattern was used on all the W8 and W9 heads. These are suitable for engine packages of 500 hp or more.

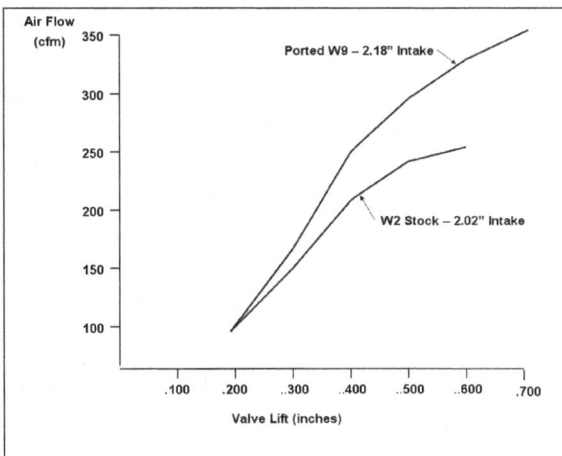

The stock W2 intake port is a good baseline for any high-performance head comparison. The fully ported CNC-intake port uses a larger intake valve (2.18 inches), which is allowed by the wider valve spacing used on the W8 and W9 heads. This flow curve is a few years old, and I am sure that the CNC-porting services today can exceed these numbers.

ferent from the first two versions. Two large external ribs were added to each end of the head on the exhaust side and smaller ribs were added on each side of the short head bolts (exhaust side).

A closed-chamber version was added at this time, along with the capability to be used with the new 48-degree tappet blocks. This last version is a machining change and not a unique casting. By the early 2000s, Mopar Performance offered 10 different W2 heads.

Introduced in 1988, the W5 is an aluminum head that weighs about 25 pounds, but it is no longer available.

The aluminum W7 was introduced a couple of years later. It had large ports and flowed a lot of air but was the last head designed before CNC-porting became readily available.

The aluminum W8 was introduced in 1998 and was only used in the NASCAR Craftsman Truck series and the NHRA Pro Stock Truck series. It weighs 35 pounds and was designed for CNC-porting. It also uses 15-degree valve angles rather than the standard 18 degrees.

The W9 head was introduced in 1999. It weighs about 22 pounds, or 20 if it is ported. It was also designed for CNC-porting but some versions were designed for use without porting; it flowed 290 cfm out of the box.

Magnum

Released in 1992 on the 5.2L engine, Magnum heads use a "bathtub-shape" closed-style chamber rather than an open chamber. The Magnum chamber is smaller in volume than the A-engine chamber (60 versus 70 cc). It also uses a 1.92-inch intake valve and a 1.625-inch exhaust

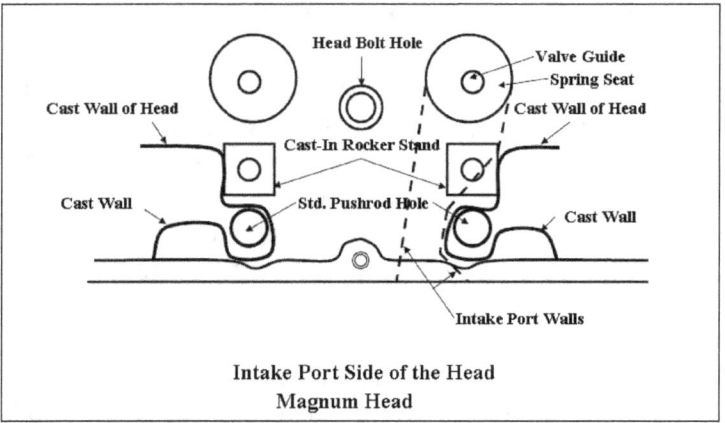

The 1992–2003 Magnum engines had a similar problem fitting the intake ports around the intake pushrods, and the tall hydraulic roller tappets made the pushrods shorter. Shorter pushrods change angles more going through the same valve lift. This added pushrod movement required larger pushrod holes in the head. This larger hole was cast into the head. This means that the pushrod bump in the intake ports is even bigger on the Magnum engines than it is on the A-engine. (This illustration shows the view from the top.)

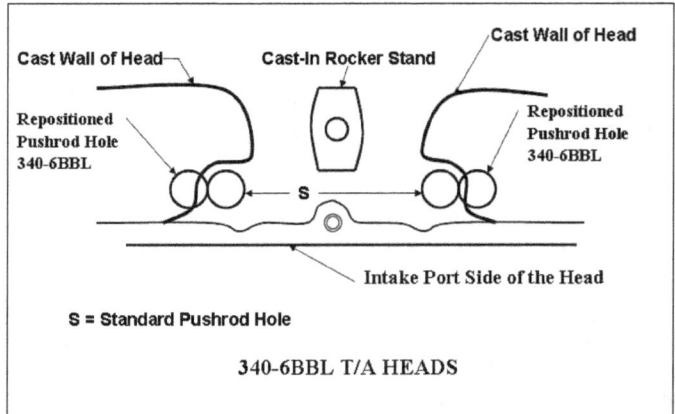

The 1970 340 6-barrel Trans-Am engine used the 340/360 cast-iron heads but they moved the standard intake pushrod holes away from the intake ports. The actual T/A pushrod holes were partially outside of the casting; the hole broke out. This allowed offset intake rocker arms (right and left offsets) to provide clearance for bigger intake ports.

valve, which is larger than the production 360 but smaller than the 1968–1971 340. The stock Magnum's intake port flows slightly better than the 360 A-engine's intake port (190 versus 170 cfm), which may be due to the larger valve.

Another unique feature of Magnum heads is that there is no heat crossover in the center of the intake face. Because it is fuel injected, it does not need the heat in the intake manifold for driveability advantages.

Magnum heads have 10 valve-cover attaching screws and 8 rocker stands, one for each valve.

R/T

The cast-iron high-performance R/T head was designed for the Magnum engine as a direct replacement, and it's essentially a Magnum engine W2 head. It flows more air than the standard head (229 versus 190 cfm) and has larger intake ports (180- versus 153-cc intake) using the same valve size. It has the "R/T" logo and the "Mopar" logo cast into the exhaust face between the short head bolts.

T/A

The 340 Trans-Am engine was produced with special cast-iron cylinder heads based on the "915" casting (3418915 casting number). The 915 was going to be the 360 production head in 1971 and the 1972–1973 340 head, and was specially machined for the T/A program.

The main differences were the use of the larger intake valve (2.02 inches), and the intake pushrod hole (machined) was moved away from the intake port. The actual as-cast ports were the same as the standard 915 heads. The moved pushrod required offset rocker arms (mechanical or adjustable) on all the intake valves.

Commando

The aluminum Commando head for A-engines was introduced in 2001. It was designed to be a "street" aluminum head, so it was interchangeable with the standard 340 heads. The intake ports were larger than stock cast-iron heads at 177 cc, and flowed better than stock cast-iron heads, at 222 cfm. These heads could be used with the standard stamped rocker arms. There was also a large-port, Super Commando aluminum-head version that required offset intake rockers.

Aluminum Magnum

Designed for "street" use, the aluminum Magnum head was introduced in 2000. It was interchangeable with stock cast-iron Magnum heads. The intake ports were larger than the stock cast-iron heads (at 177 cc) and they flowed more air (at 222 cfm).

With any of the 360 and 1972–1973 340 cast-iron heads, you should always upgrade the 1.88-inch intake valve to the 2.02-inch valve.

CYLINDER HEADS

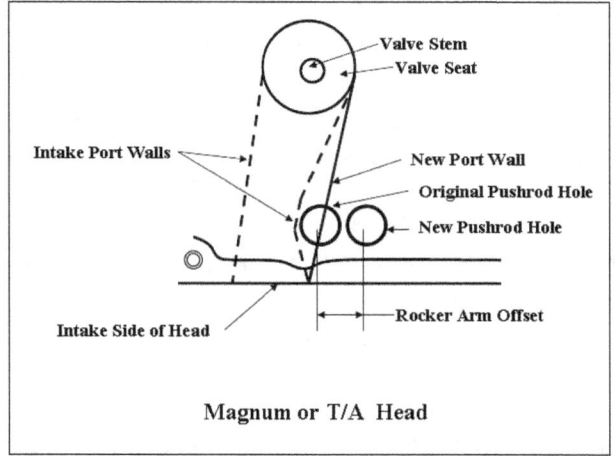

Magnum or T/A Head

The A-engine head's original pushrod hole is severely compromised by the intake port. Manufacturers moved the pushrod hole away from the intake port for the W2, all other W heads, and many aftermarket heads. This straightened out the intake port so that it flowed more air.

Head Spec Comparison

Many specifications relate to a cylinder head, and they can be used to compare one head to another. Many people focus on flow numbers, and most often the peak flow on the intake port, while exhaust is rarely considered.

A flow bench generates a curve of port flow according to valve lift, and the peak flow is at the peak valve lift. Valve lift is often disregarded, but it's important. When comparing different heads, make sure the valve lift is the same and then look at the flow numbers so the comparison is valid.

For example, let's assume that you are building a street/strip engine and have selected a .500-inch-lift cam. One head flows 280 cfm at .500-inch lift and another flows 300 cfm at .700-inch valve lift. The key is to look at the flow at .500 lift. The 300 cfm head may be 250 or 260 cfm at .500 lift, and therefore the 280 cfm head becomes the better choice. Another thing that makes comparisons difficult is valve size. The 280-cfm head might have a 2.020-inch intake valve and the 300-cfm head might have a 2.100-inch.

Bigger ports are not always better and, in fact, ports need to be correctly sized to the engine package. Ports are usually sized by volume (in cubic centimeters). The typical 360 port is 166 cc and the ported W9 aluminum head was in the range of 260 to 270 cc. The W9 tends to be flowed at high lifts, such as .700 to .800 inch, and the 360 is flowed at lower lifts such as .500 to .600 inch.

With differences such as these, the first measurement needs to be taken at your cam's max valve lift. In our example, it's .500 inch. If that is close, determine flow at half lift, which is .250 inch in the example. Usually the flow curve shows the flow at .200 and .300 inch, so pick one and check the flow at that point.

Predicting Horsepower

The technicians at SuperFlow have developed an equation for calculating an engine's potential horsepower output based on the cylinder head's airflow numbers. The equation assumes that gasoline is the fuel:

$$HPC = CP \times TF$$

Where:
HPC = horsepower potential per cylinder
CP = coefficient of power (for 28-inch test pressure, it is .26, per SuperFlow)
TF = total flow per cylinder (in cfm)

For example, if the test head is a ported W9 aluminum head that flows 356 cfm at 28 inches of water, using the equation, HPC is 92.56 (.26 x 356) per cylinder, or 740 for an 8-cylinder engine (92.56 x 8).

SuperFlow also developed an equation for predicting peak power RPM based on airflow numbers. This equation is:

$$RPMPP = CPRPM \div (D \div 8) \times CFM$$

Where:
RPMPP = RPM at peak power
CPRPM = mathematical constant of 1,196 for 28-inch test pressure
D = engine displacement (in ci)
CFM = cubic feet per minute airflow

Let's assume a 340-ci engine and its ported W2 head flows 280 cfm, and the RPMPP is 7,879 (1,196 ÷ 42.5 x 280)

Keeping the same head, if you install a 4.00-inch crank for a 400-ci displacement, the RPMPP is 6,697 (1,196 ÷ 50 x 280).

Note that the long-stroke crank costs you about 1,000 rpm in peaking speed. ■

Flow Bench

Airflow for most cylinder heads is rated as cubic feet per minute (CFM). This rating is measured at a specific pressure drop given in inches of water, and the most common pressure drop is 28 inches of water.

SuperFlow learned that testing a port's airflow at 10 inches of water and converting it to 28 inches of water produces the same data as testing the port at 28 inches. Here is the industry formula for converting CFM from one pressure to another:

$$CFM28 = CFM10 \times (28 \div 10) \times .5$$

Where:
CFM28 = CFM10 × (28 ÷ 10) × .5
CFM28 = CFM at 28 inches of water
CFM10 = CFM at 10 inches of water
28/10 = the pressure ratio of 28 inches divided by 10 inches
.5 = the square-root of the pressure ratio

For example, if a W2 head flow number of 165 cfm was measured at 10 inches, the cfm for this head at 28 inches is 276 [165 × (2.8).5 - 165 × 1.673].

The flow bench is an excellent developmental tool and can be very useful in comparing cylinder heads. However, you must remember that the bench results can vary depending on how the cylinder head is tested. Is the inlet opening radiused? Does the exhaust have a short pipe? Is the bore size adjusted for specific engine cylinders? The key is to keep all the test hardware the same when comparing heads. ■

The higher flow at the .200/.300-inch point is the better head for your application if they were tied at .500 lift.

The valve and the valve job also affect the airflow capability. It's also important where the valve sits in the chamber (don't sink the valve) and how the air enters the chamber at low lifts (chamber reliefs). The valve job angle and the shape of the underside of the valve head are also important to the airflow numbers.

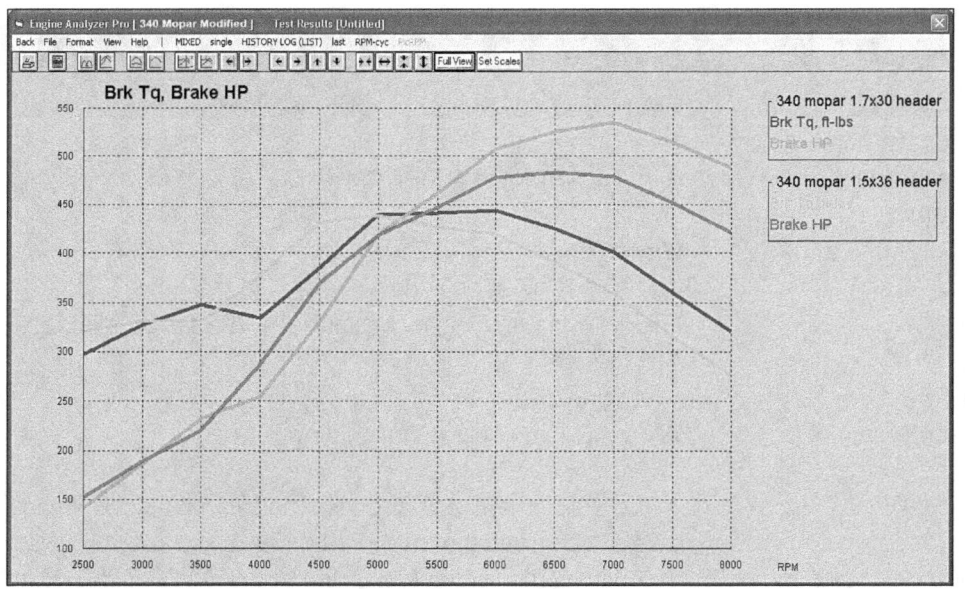

This Performance Trends program shows an exhaust header comparison between 1½- and 1¾-inch headers. It shows torque and horsepower just like a regular dyno test. As you might expect, the 1¾-inch headers make more power. The trick is to note that the peak power is at 7,000 rpm and it runs to 8,000 rpm.

Combustion Chamber Shapes

Combustion chambers are available in two basic shapes: open and closed. Open chambers are round and extend almost to the edge of the cylinder bore. Closed chambers are smaller and only cover a small part of the bore. They generally are not round.

The original 273 chamber was somewhat oval. The Magnum closed chamber is considered a bathtub (rounded rectangle) shape. One 318 head has a heart-shaped chamber, which is popular for some aftermarket heads. Most race/max-performance heads have a modified heart-shaped chamber crossed with the bathtub.

The key is to relieve the chamber around the valves, which helps the valves flow more air. This makes the chamber slightly larger but the net gain is positive.

CYLINDER HEADS

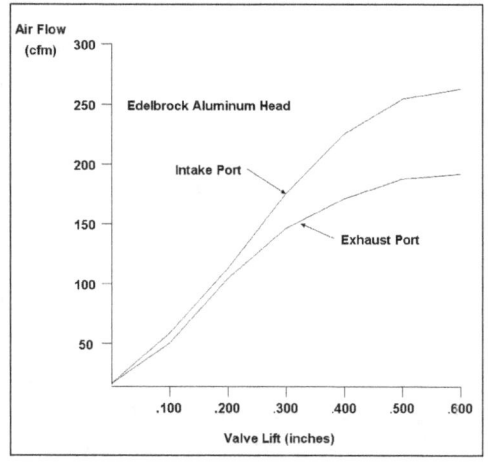

When comparing cylinder heads, always examine both the intake and the exhaust flow. Most customers do not bother with the exhaust flow and just want to discuss the intake flow. In most cases, the exhaust flow should be about 75 percent of the intake flow. Big intake valves and big intake ports help the intake side but this ideal is not always met in high-performance heads. A 260-cfm intake should have about 195-cfm exhaust, which is a little bit short.

The Edelbrock aluminum head machining takes a cut around the intake and exhaust port opening as shown (this is the exhaust). It is not fully ported. The machining only goes in a short amount, maybe 1/4 to 1/2 inch and tapers away. It makes the head look nice for the customer.

The A-engine small-block Edelbrock aluminum heads have good airflow numbers. The closed combustion chambers are shaped sort of like a bathtub. The lower row of pushrod holes at the bottom across from the valveguides or valve centers doesn't require the offset rockers of the W2/W5 etc. group.

Aluminum Heads

Most aluminum heads use larger port volumes than the similar cast-iron heads. During the cast-iron head drought, the aluminum heads were the only choice. Aluminum castings lend themselves to low-volume production, so these may be made in batch runs of 100, 500, and 1,000. This makes them popular with the aftermarket for racing applications, which spills over into many other performance uses.

The aftermarket built the first aluminum cylinder heads for the Mopar A and Magnum small-blocks. Chrysler made the only cast-iron service heads for the A-engine small-blocks and they were kept in stock for 10 years or so. Mopar Performance had provided heads for most engines. Between 2000 and 2010, all this changed and most Mopar heads were no longer available. In the past couple of years, this has changed again; there are now several versions of aluminum heads.

The three aluminum heads from Edelbrock, Indy Heads, and B1-BA all flow about 260 cfm in stock configuration. That means that economics should decide your selection. These heads are also offered in ported form where the Indy Heads version (339) and the Brodix B1-BA version (340) are equal, so economics can again be used to select between these two heads. The latest data indictes that the newest B1-BA CNC-ported head by Koffel's Place makes more than 360 cfm, which makes it the best-ported small-block head to date!

Edelbrock Aluminum Heads

Edelbrock offers several aluminum heads for A-engines (five valvecover screws). The 1968–1971 340 "A" head features a larger, open combustion chamber. It provides clearance for the piston because it sits above the deck at TDC. With all other A-engines (including 318s, 1972–1973 340, and all 360s), the pistons sit below the top of the block, so this special feature is not required.

The aluminum A-engine head has chamber volumes of 63 and 65 cc, intake port volume of 171 cc, and valve diameters of 2.02-inch intake and 1.60-inch exhaust. These dimensions are the same as for the 1968–1971 340.

Edelbrock carries aluminum heads for Magnum engines. These heads have chamber volumes of 58 cc, intake port volume of 176 cc, and valve diameters of 2.02-inch intake and 1.60-inch exhaust. Although these dimensions are the same as the 1968–1971 340, the heads are different from the production Magnum.

Edelbrock also offers aluminum heads for use with hydraulic cams

CHAPTER 5

The Edelbrock's aluminum Magnum heads have the 10-bolt valvecover and the vertical intake attaching screws. Also note the Magnum-style valve gear (no rocker shaft pedestals) and the tall bosses for the upper row of head bolts. Flow numbers for the Magnum are similar to the A-engine version, using equal valve sizes. Several options are available.

Indy Heads offers the only new cast-iron head currently available for the A-engine. Note that five pedestals are machined in this head. Both the A-engine and Magnum configurations were designed and cast with machining in mind. Next to each valvespring is an unmachined square boss that is used to attach the rockers in the Magnum machined version; these are not machined in the A-engine version. Also note that only 5 valve bolts are used in the machined head, but the bosses are there for the Magnum 10-bolt version. My six-step chart of packages would put it in the 520- to 610-hp range, but I think you could push it.

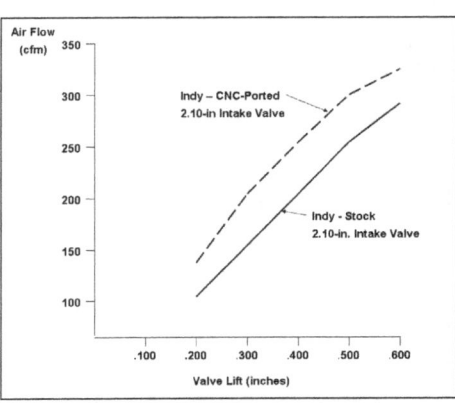

Indy Heads offers many different valve size and port configurations for A-engines. The best comparison seemed to be with the 2.10-inch intake valves, which is much larger than the 2.02-inch that was standard in the heads and the W2. It doesn't require the wide-spaced centers as with the W9. The CNC-ported versions were the last two packages; these two are in the 600-hp-and-higher range. In race configuration, it might make more than 800 hp.

and hydraulic roller cams. Similar to the A-engine, heavier valvesprings are used for a hydraulic roller that has higher-load springs. These heads also use 11/32-inch valvestem diameters and manganese-bronze valveguides. They use 14-mm x 3/4-inch–reach spark plugs (recommended Champion RC12YC or equivalent). The valvespring installed height is 1.800 inches.

ARP lists the same head bolts for the Edelbrock Magnum heads as for the production version, which means five extra-long head bolts. Caution: The specs indicate that these heads use 3/8-inch rocker studs, which may mean that you need larger bolts or must change the valve gear.

Both Edelbrock aluminum heads (A-Engine and Magnum) flow the same 260-cfm intake at .600-inch lift and 251 cfm at .500-inch lift. Both are very good numbers.

Edelbrock aluminum heads flow excellent out-of-the-box, and lead the affordability list at most shops. It is a great bolt-on head. At this time, Edelbrock does not list ported upgrades.

Caution: ARP lists the same head bolts for Edelbrock heads as for the W2, which means two extra-long head bolts (a typical 340 or 360 has five long and no extra-long).

Edelbrock also has an aluminum head for race only, which features a 58-cc chamber and a larger 225-cc intake port. The ports are fully CNC-ported and use 16-degree valve angles. Flow numbers were not published.

Aluminum Indy Heads

The Indy Heads 360-1 and 360-2 are two versions of the company's aluminum Mopar small-block heads. The 360-1 is the rectangular-port version and the 360-2 is the oval-port version (similar to the W2). The 360-1 has a 210-cc intake port, 2.100-inch intake and 1.65-inch exhaust valves, and a 63-cc heart-shape combustion chamber. It also uses .800-inch offset intake rockers.

Indy Heads used many logos and numbers on its casting but the easiest way to identify an Indy head (cast iron in this case) is by the "Indy" logo and the big "X" cast into the head between two spark plugs (number-1 and -3 cylinders on the driver's side). Caution: Check with the manufacturer on the spark plug machining; several sizes are optional.

Many options are offered, such as rocker shafts or Jesel rockers, 10-bolt or 18-bolt head bolt patterns, and several porting options. The stock intake port flows 280 cfm at .700 inch; bowl-port and intake match yields 290 cfm. Super-modified porting yields 309 cfm, and the full porting and polish yields 339 cfm, both at .700-inch lift.

The 360-2 oval-port Indy aluminum head uses a 180-cc intake port and flows 252 cfm at .700-inch lift. The chamber is 63 cc, the intake valve is 2.100 inches, and the exhaust valve is 1.65 inches. In its full CNC-ported configuration, the port size increases to 230 cc and the flow goes up to 322 cfm at .700-inch lift.

B1-BA Aluminum Heads

Koffel's Place designs and Brodix casts the B1-BA Mopar small-block aluminum head. It features 18-degree valves with 2.08-inch intake and 1.60-inch exhaust valves. The exhaust pattern accepts standard headers. Production A-engine intake manifolds and stock, five-bolt valvecovers can both be used. The stock intake port is about 195 cc and the stock combustion chamber is 65 cc. The standard setup uses shaft-mounted rockers.

Many options are offered, including CNC-porting. Recent CNC-ported intake ports have flowed more than 370 cfm.

Cast-Iron Heads

All the cast-iron heads pretty much disappeared in the early 2000s. Cast iron is difficult to pour in limited quantities, and many cast iron foundries have gone out of business. So until about 2014, cast-iron heads were not easy to find. Indy Heads introduced a cast-iron version of its aluminum head and produced it in an A-engine version (with rocker shafts) and in a Magnum version (8 rocker pedestals). Both are machined from the same casting.

Cast-Iron Indy Heads

Indy Heads offers cast-iron 360 LA-X heads for the A-engine, which feature five valvecover bolts and the dual-exhaust bolt pattern. The cast-iron A-engine head has chamber volumes of 62 cc, intake port volume of 179 cc, and valve diameters of 1.92-inch intake and 1.625-inch exhaust (with 2.02- and 2.055-inch options).

The company also offers heads for use with .525-inch lift (hydraulic cams) and .600-inch lift (mechanical cams). The .525-lift version is for hydraulic cams but can be used with

The aluminum B1-BA head cast by Brodix and designed by Koffel's Place is designed with CNC-porting in mind. The wide, flat exhaust face seems to be unique to the B1-BA heads, and many options depend upon your performance needs. At 370 cfm, it has some of the highest intake flow numbers for CNC-ported heads. In stock or mildly ported form, it would fit in the first four performance packages, and in fully ported form it fits in the last two.

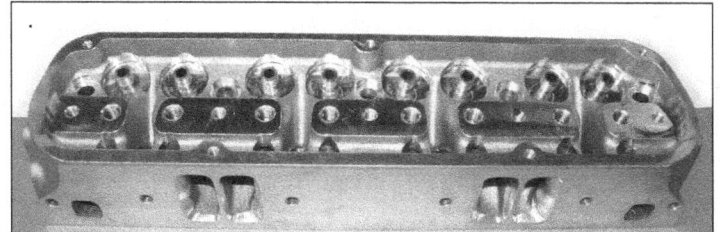

The B1-BA aluminum head is designed to accept the race-style valve gear. The five flat pads running left to right, three wide and two smaller, are for bolting on the race rocker arm systems. It is based on the five-bolt A-engine valvecover.

CNC-Porting

Originally, knowledgeable and skilled engine builders used a rotary tool to port heads by hand, but now CNC machines port heads with unparalleled consistency and accuracy. Typically the CNC machine machines the valveseat at the same time as the port. In most cases, a head should be designed for CNC-porting.

Most race heads, such as the W8 and W9, were designed for CNC-porting. If you have a standard head, such as any cast-iron head, it is not designed for CNC-porting and the porting service must take this into account.

The best CNC-ported head airflow number in the past few years is 350 cfm for the Darren Shumway (Advance Motion CNC)/Mike Chapman version of the W9 aluminum head. The next best are two aluminum heads: B1-BA (Brodix version listed at 340) and the Indy Heads aluminum (listed at 339).

Both manufacturers (and their CNC-porting services) offer an intermediate step: less airflow, less time involved, and therefore less cost. Indy Heads shows two intermediate steps: a 290-cfm version and a 309-cfm version. Brodix B1-BA also offers an intermediate step, 303 cfm.

CHAPTER 5

The cast-iron Indy A-engine cylinder head uses both exhaust manifold-attaching patterns that are machined in. The stock pattern is close to the ports and the wide pattern was used on the W2 original heads. As a precaution, I recommend plugging the holes that you do not use with small Allen screws. This is an ideal head for street and street/strip applications.

low-lift mechanical cams if desired; there just aren't many mechanical cams that lift only .525 inch. The .600-inch-lift version, a mechanical cam, is most often used because very few hydraulic cams have lifts in the .525- to .600-inch range. The valvespring is the change and valve lift is the key. These heads also use 5/16-inch valvestem diameters and stainless valves.

Caution: These heads use five extra-long head bolts similar to the Magnum, plus they may not use standard 340/360 spark plugs.

Indy Heads also makes a cast-iron head for Magnum engines called the 360 MA-X. Its specifications are similar to the above A-engine head with valve size and spring options.

The Indy Heads cast-iron head is the best available today. Both A-engine and Magnum versions are available. Both of these iron heads feature a 62-cc chamber.

Bare Heads

Several aftermarket manufacturers offer bare (rough) heads. Chrysler referred to these as partially machined heads; Edelbrock called them raw or semi-finished. Essentially, the head has been machined with the exception of the valveseats, combustion chamber, and ports, which are as-cast. In most cases, the valveguide hole is machined, but guides may or may not be installed.

These heads provide engine builders the latitude to machine the heads to specific requirements, and therefore can be CNC-ported. Most manufacturers offer this option, but only Edelbrock puts details in its catalog and on its website.

Cylinder Head Selection and Prep

When selecting the head for your build, focus on three features: material (cast iron or aluminum), valve size (intake and exhaust), and peak intake flow. Although there's more to a cylinder head than these specifications, they are very important.

With so many head models, designs, port sizes, and combustion chamber shapes available, you need to select the head for your build very carefully. There should be no reason to hunt through junkyards and hope you find the specific head for your performance use.

Several considerations must be addressed first, such as aluminum versus cast iron and repair versus new versus used. Cast-iron (Indy) and aluminum heads (Edelbrock, B1-BA, Indy) are available today that do a good job for the Mopar/Chrysler small-block. Originally, cast-iron heads were less expensive but today cost close to the same as aluminum heads. Aluminum heads offered more flow, but that may not be the case today, short of the W9 head and CNC-ported heads in general.

Overall, I do not recommend going the used route, but there are exceptions. So the choice comes down to buying new or doing repairs.

The Indy Heads, Edelbrock, and B1-BA/Brodix are excellent choices for max-performance street use. The best small-block head is the W9, either as-cast or ported. Availability is the factor.

The W8 head was a good head but is no longer available. To recommend it, the head must be cost-effective and readily available, so the Edelbrock aluminum head is my first choice.

Currently Available Hardware

	Estimated hp/ci	Best Head
Package No. 1	.85/.91	Bracket valve job (back-cut valves) with 2.02-inch intake valve
Package No. 2	1.10/1.20	Edelbrock aluminum, Indy, or B1-BA
Package No. 3	1.32/1.44	No. 3 with bowl work
Package No. 4	1.56/1.68	No. 3 with intermediate CNC-porting
Package No. 5	1.88/1.99	Indy Heads or B1-BA fully CNC-ported

CNC-porting obviously increases performance, such as going from 260 to 340 cfm. CNC-porting outside of the manufacturers is done at companies such as CFE, which developed the best W8 port, and Advance Motion CNC (with Darren Shumway), which did the W9.

CYLINDER HEADS

Cost is the deciding factor between the Indy head and the B1-BA. Brodix provides more technical information on the B1-BA in its catalog and the company offers both the standard 18-degree valve angles and the 15-degree angle that were common in the W8 and W9 heads.

All three manufacturers offer CNC-ported versions and there seems to be more information on the Brodix and Indy Heads versions. Based on flow numbers, the CNC-ported Indy head makes 339 cfm with a 2.100-inch intake valve, and the CNC-ported Brodix B1-BA makes 347 cfm with a 2.14-inch intake valve. Brodix shows the stock or as-cast B1-BA flowing 269 cfm, which is also very good. CNC-porting makes more horsepower but a full porting job is probably not needed for the street/strip application.

Remember that other specifications must be kept in mind too. They include: compatibility, port volume, bolt patterns, and combustion chamber type.

Compatibility

All parts of an engine must function as a complementary system. One cylinder head is not best for all applications. So you need to carefully select the proper specifications for your goals and build. The valves must work with the port, as finished, and the port-valve combination must work with the cam selected. You do not want to use a .700-inch lift port with a .500-inch lift cam, or a .500-inch lift port with a .700-inch lift cam, which are common pitfalls to avoid.

However, the exhaust and intake manifolds, throttle body/carburetor, and cubic inches all play into the same equation. For example, in NHRA Stock and Super Stock classes, which allow only limited modifications, the 340 and 360 engines (using the same head and induction system) do not work well with the same cam, converter, gear, etc. Simply put, the 340 sets up like a short-stroke engine and the 360 sets up like a long-stroke engine.

For an interesting comparison of how heads and cams, valve lift, and compression ratio work together to change the engine's operating band (engine RPM), torque, and horsepower outputs based on horsepower

Cylinder Head Port Volume and Intake Valve Comparison

The port volumes and intake valve sizes listed below vary greatly. The big valve on the W9 is allowed by the increased valve centerline used on the W9 head. Most of the aftermarket heads shown offer valve options and porting, so the numbers listed are only a beginning reference.

The 273/318 port volume is an estimate because it is not used for performance applications.

The W5 is no longer available and only listed for reference.

The W8 was designed for CNC-porting.

The as-cast port was small and almost any valve size could be added by changing the CNC program within valve-center limits.

The Mopar Commando and aluminum Magnum heads are no longer available but the aluminum Edelbrock heads are close in specification.

The only ported head listed is the W9, which is shown as 60 to 70 cc bigger than as-cast. A ported cast-iron head might only increase 20 to 30 cc in port volume. Most of the aftermarket manufacturers offer ported versions of their heads that increase the port volume and increase the airflow by similar numbers. Today, a ported W9 may be even larger than shown and flow much more air. ■

Cylinder Head	Port Volume (cc)	Intake Valve Size (inches)
273/318	130/140	1.75
340/360	166	1.88/2.02
Magnum	153	1.92
R/T	180	1.92/2.02
W2	185	2.02
W5	205	2.02
Commando	177	2.02
Aluminum Magnum	177	1.92
Edelbrock Aluminum A	171	1.88/2.02
Edelbrock Aluminum Magnum	176	1.92/2.02
B1-BA	195	2.08
Indy 360 LA-X	179	2.02/2.055
Indy 360-2	180	2.100
Indy 360-1	210	2.100
W9, as-cast	200	2.15
W8	NA	NA
W9, ported	261/270	2.15/2.18

CHAPTER 5

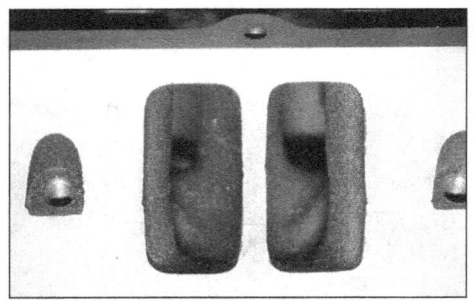

The Magnum intake port has a big bump in it (to the left and right of each port opening) to get around the pushrod. Machining the pushrod hole, as is done by Edelbrock and Indy Heads, allows this bump to get smaller but still limits the big flow numbers.

The A-engine intake port bump is almost as big as the Magnum's. Actually, the stock Magnum intake port flows better than the 360's intake port, at 1.88 inches stock. The 340's bigger intake valve (2.02 inches) helps the A-engine but it also helps the Magnum, at 1.92 inches stock.

Before you send your head out to the machinist, check the depth of the combustion chamber with a dial indicator. The trick is to find a flat spot in the chamber. Each style of casting has different flat spots (a Magnum cast-iron is shown). This allows you to check the amount that is machined off the deck when the head is returned.

per cubic inch, you can review Edelbrock's five basic packages. They include upgrades from 250 to 325, to 400, to 470, to 610, and to 720 hp based on Edelbrock heads and hardware. Information is available on the company's website under "Power Packages."

Port Volume

Many aspects of a cylinder head affect actual port volume. Although valve size stays the same, a slight tweak (grind) on the valveseat sinks the valve slightly and changes the port volume. Changing the valve from a tulip valve to a nailhead valve changes the port volume.

Milling the intake manifold face to make the intake manifold fit after milling the deck surface changes the port volume as well. Any porting that is performed also changes the port volume. That is why port volume is not used as a control specification but as a general guideline.

Intake and Exhaust Bolt Patterns

The Mopar A-engine intake bolt pattern is perpendicular to the manifold face; the Magnum pattern of the attaching bolts is vertical. The 1964–1965 273 heads also used vertical intake attaching screws. Also, the W-series heads, such as the W2, used a wider-spaced attaching bolt pattern for the bolts on either side of the actual intake ports.

The end bolts stay in the same location because the bigger intake ports are best for the higher-flowing ports in performance applications. End bolts stay in the same location (only the ones next to the ports move away from the ports) to gain wrench clearance for the ones on the inside of the turn.

The intake manifold must match the cylinder head ports, so the larger runners crowd the inside-turn manifold bolts (the two closest to the center of the engine) to the extent that you cannot put a wrench on the bolt head. Widening the spacing solves this problem very easily.

The A-engine and the Magnum use the same exhaust bolt pattern. The original W2 cast-iron head spreads the exhaust bolt attaching pattern away from the ports. In the second generation of W2 heads, either the standard pattern or the wider W2 pattern was machined into the head.

You should plug the holes in the dual-exhaust pattern that are not

The original W2 heads used a wide-spaced exhaust manifold attaching pattern because the stock pattern was very close to the larger, raised exhaust ports used in the W2 heads. Later versions of the W2 head machined both patterns into the head and let customers choose which to use. The W2 head was raced frequently. If the head is ported for high flow on the exhaust side, you want to use larger tubes in the headers.

78 MOPAR SMALL-BLOCK ENGINES: HOW TO BUILD MAX PERFORMANCE

CYLINDER HEADS

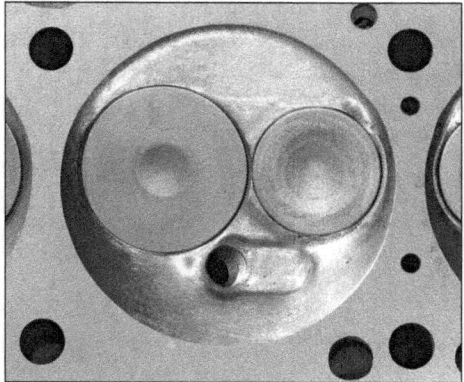

This is a typical A-engine open combustion chamber used in the stock cast-iron heads. If the head is milled extensively, then the section at the top of the circle goes away and what's left of the chamber is somewhat heart-shaped with the point at the bottom.

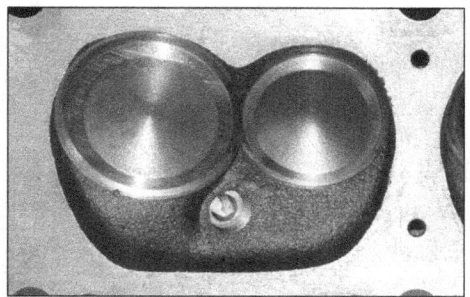

The stock cast-iron Magnum chamber is somewhat heart-shaped and flattened on the bottom. It is often called a bathtub-shape chamber.

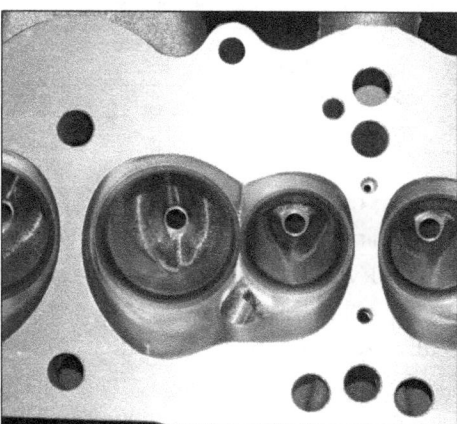

The chamber of the B1-BA is very similar to the W9 and the Magnum, but it could almost be considered a figure-eight shape. Note that the spark plug hole points at the exhaust valve guide and how close it is to the exhaust seat ring; it is very similar to the W9. Then compare this to the stock A-engine chamber, which has the spark plug pointing at the exhaust valve but is much farther away from the seat.

The W9 CNC-ported chamber is shaped similar to the Magnum but has a lot more relief at the bottom of the intake valve. Note how close the valve's seat rings are to the edge of the chamber and the area where the head gasket seal ring is located. This is caused partly by the wide valve centers used on the W9 head. Also note how close the intake and exhaust seat rings are to each other in the center of the chamber.

used to attach the exhaust manifold/header; use small Allen screws and seal the threads. Indy uses this dual-pattern approach. The the Magnum exhaust side uses spark plug shields inserted into the head.

Combustion Chamber Type

Many aftermarket performance heads use a machined chamber, so it is easy to revise. The typical A-engine head uses an open chamber; the Magnum engine uses a closed (bathub) chamber.

The third-generation W2 offered a closed-chamber head as an option with volumes in the 47- to 55-cc range (standard open-chamber volume was 70 cc).

Many aftermarket heads use a heart-shaped chamber. Most chambers are really a modified heart shape, which is pretty close to the bathtub shape. Relieving the chamber around the valves for increasing the port's airflow enlarges the chamber slightly and tends to make the heart into more of a bathtub shape.

High-Performance Valve Job

The two parts of a valve job are half to the valve and half to the cylinder head. Aluminum heads use a valveseat insert into the head; cast-iron heads typically grind the valveseat directly into the casting, but seat inserts can be used for repair purposes. One of the secrets to a valve job with any valve insert is to create a smooth transition from the port to the valve job and into the chamber. This is one of the advantages of CNC-porting, if the CNC machine does the port and the valveseat.

Valve Centers

Almost all A-engine and Magnum heads use the same 1.87-inch size for valve centers. The W9 uses 1.936-inch valve centers for large valves. Aftermarket heads can be modified to add a 1.936-inch valve, but most are built with a 1.87-inch valve.

Air Pump Holes

Most newer A-engine production heads have emission air pump holes in the exhaust flange just below the exhaust port on each cylinder. If the heads are going to be used for racing or other performance purposes,

Head Milling

Milling your heads may be necessary because the deck is not flat, chambers are too large for your desired specifications, or many other reasons. When you mill the deck surface of either the head or the block, also mill the intake manifold face of the head and the front and rear china walls of the block.

To help determine the final compression ratio, you need to define the total amount that the head and block will be milled. If the head is milled .020 inch and the block is milled .030 inch, the actual amount of milling is .050 inch.

Once you determine the total amount to mill off the deck surfaces, you can use the chart below to learn how much should be milled off the intake manifold face. For example, with .050-inch total off the decks .0475 inch should be milled off the intake manifold face.

Although you mill this amount off the intake manifold, I recommend machining the intake face on the cylinder head. If you milled it off the manifold, each manifold you might install would need to be milled this amount or it would not fit the engine. If it is milled off the head, any standard manifold would fit without modification.

The china walls (the third surface in the sealing surface equation) cross the block at the front and rear, and the intake manifold seals against them. As the intake manifold lines up with the ports in the head, the china walls can stop it and cause the ports to not line up, as well as not seal. So the front and rear china walls have to be milled to allow the ports to line up and for the manifold to seal. As an example, the chart shows that .050-inch total deck mill causes the china wall to be milled .072 inch for proper alignment.

By milling all three surfaces the engine geometry is correct and the gaskets can seal the tappet chamber.

The other aspect of milling the deck surfaces is that changing the head's combustion chamber size changes the volume. The chamber volume change affects the engine's compression ratio. The milling operation only makes the chamber smaller, which increases the compression ratio.

Small changes in compression ratio can be accomplished by milling, but large changes should be made by changing the pistons and adjusting the compression height.

A common question can be asked in two ways: I want to drop the chamber volume by "Y" cc, how much should I mill? or, I milled the deck "X" amount, how much volume did I lose?

To answer the first question, assume that you want to lose 7 cc. With an open chamber (column one in the chart below), you mill a total of .0336 inch off the deck surfaces. With a closed chamber (column two in the chart below), you mill .0476 inch.

To answer the second question (using our previous example of .050-inch total mill), you lose 10.42 cc with the open chamber or 7.36 cc with the closed chamber (according to the chart below).

Indy Heads ships its 360-1 and 360-2 heads with a 63-cc combustion chamber and states that it can be milled to 53 cc. This small chamber can help achieve high compression ratios (see package No. 5, 11.5:1) without using domed pistons, at least with displacements of more than 360 cc. ■

Milling Specifications

Total Amount Milled from Head/Block Deck Surfaces (inch)	Amount to Remove from Intake Manifold Face (inch)	Amount to Remove from Front and Rear China Walls (inch)
.010	.0095	.0144
.020	.0190	.0288
.030	.0285	.0432
.040	.0380	.0576
.050	.0475	.0720
.060	.0570	.0864

Combustion Chamber Volume Adjustments

Amount to be Milled (inch)	A-Engine Open Chamber Volume (cc)**	Magnum Closed Chamber Volume (cc)***
Mill Cut*	.0048-inch	.0068-inch
.010	2.08	1.45
.020	4.17	2.94
.030	6.25	4.41
.040	8.33	5.88
.050	10.42	7.36
.060	12.50	8.82

* This figure can be used to calculate volume for any amount of milling.

** Most production A-engines and the original W2 used an open chamber.

*** All Magnums have a closed chamber along with early 1964–1965 273 and new W2.

CYLINDER HEADS

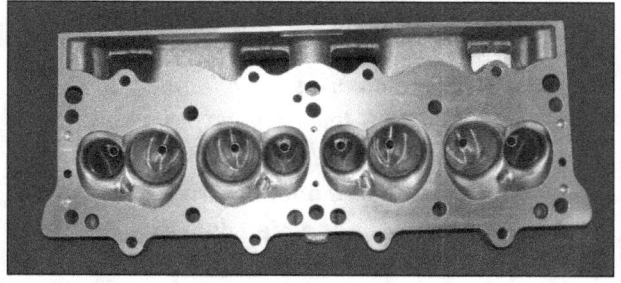

The W8 and W9 aluminum heads were designed for the six-bolt cylinder head attaching pattern. The two extra bolts around each chamber are smaller than the standard head bolts. The four added bolts across the bottom of the head are easy to see. The other four bolts are directly opposite just inside the intake manifold flange. If you want to use this head on a standard four-bolt block, the top and bottom bolts are not used. And, you will have to use the four-bolt head gasket.

The A-engine valvetrain has an oil hole drilled in the block up from the cam journal. The large hole just above the two intake valves is the head-bolt hole. The small hole above the head-bolt hole is the drilled hole that mates up to the hole in the block that allows oil into the valve gear.

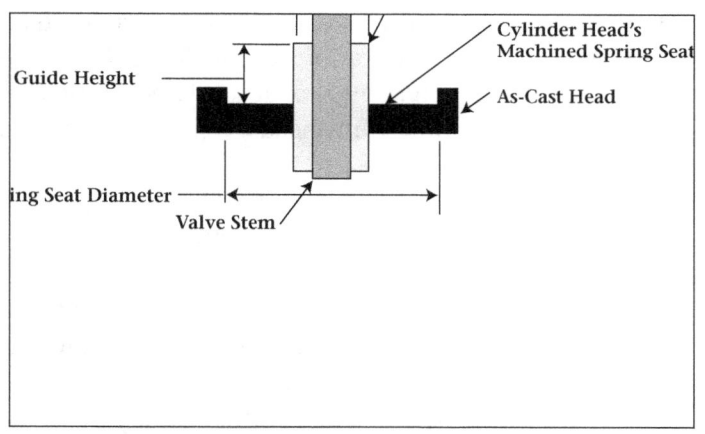

The production heads have the valveguide machined into the casting. The height of the guide above the spring seat is set by the factory and is designed for the stock lift of the cam. With the standard valves and stock installed heights, the keeper-to-guide clearance can be below minimum limits with the high-lift cams common today. To solve this problem, you can shorten the guides to give the required clearance. The longer guide gives better valveguide durability so you don't want to do this if you don't have to. Note that the spring seat is generally machined into the head casting and doesn't always have the lip all the way around the seat (as shown).

plug the threaded hole with an Allen screw. If the air pump holes are left open, they leak exhaust gas when headers are installed.

These holes are not machined on the 360 high-performance (E58 option) or the 340 cast-iron heads.

Rocker Stands

Rocker stands fit between the rocker shaft and the cylinder head; basically, they replace the cast-iron rocker pedestal. To use rocker stands the machine shop machines off the pedestals. The most common use of rocker stands was for race W2 heads.

The rocker stands allowed the rocker shaft to be raised, which allowed a longer valve and taller valvesprings, and offset away from the valves, which allowed the rocker arms to be stronger (no increased relief on the underside).

The econo-W2 head used as-cast pedestals.

Special Head Considerations

Many cylinder head and overlap features are important to the engine's operation and performance. Compression ratio and airflow are key players in the performance equation and are affected by the cylinder head.

Compression Ratio Measurement

The first step in measuring your engine's compression ratio is to cc the combustion chamber in the cylinder head. Initially, you only need to measure one chamber. I recommend one of the two center chambers.

To cc the combustion chamber in the head, you need the following: a 100-cc burette; a flat, clear, 1/4-inch thick Plexiglas plate; a cc-ing fluid, such as parts cleaning solvent or rubbing alcohol with food coloring added; and a light grease such as petroleum jelly.

Compression Ratio Calculation

The formula for calculating the engine's compression ratio is detailed in Chapter 3. Basically, it is the VBDC divided by the VTDC. The biggest part of the VTDC is the chamber volume, which must be cc'd.

You want to know your basic compression ratio as soon as possible so you can order pistons, mill decks, mill piston tops or to have the

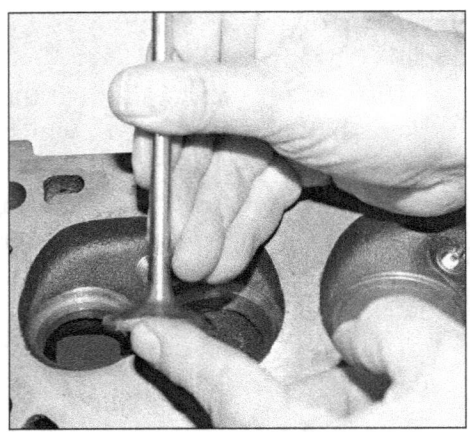

Place the deck surface up and support the head above the workbench. It should be almost horizontal, but slightly higher on one end or on one side. Install a clean spark plug. Next, select a clean intake and exhaust valve and place a thin bead of the light grease around the valve head on the 45-degree seat of each valve. Slip each valve into the proper guide in the selected center chamber. Push down firmly to seat and wipe off any excess grease.

Now run a thin bead of light grease around the outside of the edge of the combustion chamber. The 1/4-inch-thick plastic plate should have a small hole in one corner or toward one edge; add a 3/8-inch hole if one is not already present. Place the plate over the chamber with the small hole on the high side. Push the plate down firmly to seal against the light grease. The chamber should be completely covered.

Fill the burette with colored cc-ing fluid. The color helps you read the burette more accurately and see the fluid in the chamber as it fills. Do not fill the hole in the plate, just up to it. The amount of fluid that was used from the burette indicates the volume of the chamber. As a general guide, stock chambers on the 340/360 heads are in the range of 63 to 75 cc. The 318 heads are about 3 to 5 cc smaller. Magnum heads are in the 60- to 65-cc range.

compression ratio where you want it for your application and fuel use.

If you are shooting for a compression of 9:1 and you find that it is 10:1, you must lower the ratio by one point. If you are building the engine, a new set of pistons is the best solution. If it is already built, try a thick-head gasket or shim.

If the ratio is 8.5:1, you could probably mill the block and heads to gain the 1/2-point of ratio. However, if it is 8:1, new pistons are best because it would require too much milling, which causes other problems.

Displacement Calculation

The first part of the compression ratio equation, or VBDC, is basically the displacement of one cylinder plus the VTDC. This makes it important to calculate your exact cylinder displacement.

For example, if your engine has a 3.94-inch bore and a 4.00-inch stroke, the displacement is 390.15 ci (8 x .7854 x 3.94 x 3.94 x 4.00).

For use in your compression ratio calculation, you only want one cylinder's displacement (sometimes called swept volume), so you divide the displacement by the number of cylinders. In this case, it's 48.77 ci (390.15 ÷ 8).

To use the number in the compression ratio formula, you need to convert this volume to cubic centimeters, which is 799.17 (48.77 x 16.387).

Shrouding

The combustion chamber allows the valves to open into an area on one side, next to a valve. For about 90 degrees, where the valve is next to the chamber wall, the valve is shrouded as it lifts off the valveseat.

On production cast-iron heads, a valveseat cutter generally relieves this area for each valve. Enlarging this basic relief helps airflow. However, you must not get carried away because the seal ring on the head gasket must seal to the head surface in this area so any increased relief must stay inside of the gasket's seal ring. This is commonly performed on aluminum heads, especially the ones that are CNC'd.

Valves

A-engine and Magnum engine valves open on-center. Simply put, this orientation means that the head diameter runs across the widest part of the

---

Displacement Formula

To calculate displacement, use the following equation:

$$D = N \times .7854 \times B \times B \times S$$

Where:

D = displacement
N = number of cylinders
$.7854$ = mathematical constant
B = bore
S = stroke

bore. As a result, big-valve 340 heads can be used on small-bore 318 blocks. It also means that if the valves are the same size, such as 2.02 or 1.60 inches, the valves are less shrouded as they approach max lift.

Magnum engines and A-engines do not use the same valves. Because the diameters are slightly different, the Magnum uses a slightly shorter valve by about .060 inch. It also uses a thinner valvestem. They are not interchangeable.

Length

The Magnum intake valve has a length of 4.91 inches and the exhaust length is 4.92 inches. A-engine intake valves are 4.98 inches long and the exhaust valve lengths are 4.97 inches.

Race versions of the W2 and W5 A-engine heads use .300-inch-longer valves, 5.28-inch intake and 5.29-inch exhaust. This increases the valvespring installed height from 1.70 to 2.00 inches. More installed height allows the use of bigger springs, which allows more valve lift, which works with the big ports that flow more air at high lifts.

Some aftermarket heads use longer valves with the increased installed height/max valve lift.

Stem Diameter

A-engines, both the 273/318 group and the 340/360 group, use 3/8-inch valvestems. All Magnums use 8-mm valvestems, which is very close to 5/16 inch. In the aftermarket, 11/32-inch valvestems are popular. Some aftermarket heads use 11/32 x 5/16 stems.

The aluminum roller-tip rocker arms on this aluminum head (A-engine) are basically straight across from the adjusting screw.

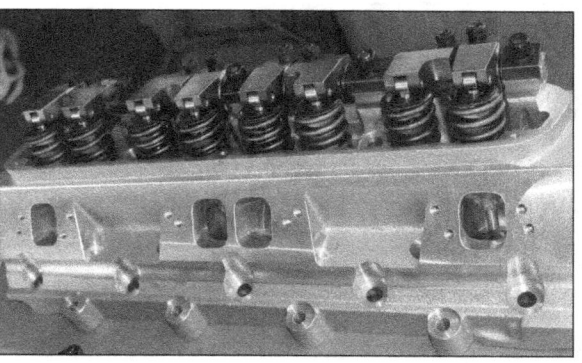

The aluminum roller-tip rocker arms on this aluminum head have straight rockers on the exhaust (first and fourth measuring from the right side) and offset rockers on the second and third valves. This offset allows the intake ports to be much larger.

Head Diameter

The 340 valves' head diameters are the most popular at 2.02 and 1.60 inches for the A-engine. The 1.88-inch intake (360) is also popular. Oversize valves, such as 1.65-inch exhaust and 2.08-inch intake, are also common. If a 2.15-inch intake valve is to be used, wide valve centers must be used. The Magnum uses a 1.92-inch intake valve and a 1.625-inch exhaust valve, with oversize intakes of 1.97 and 2.02 inches also available.

Material

Both intake and exhaust valves are made from steel. In general, the intake and exhaust are not made from the same steel alloy. The exhaust valve sees more heat so it uses a special alloy. Most aftermarket performance valves are made of stainless steel. Stainless steel is also harder and stronger than standard valve material and this hardness helps the engine if unleaded gas is used. Stainless offers an option to hardened valveseats.

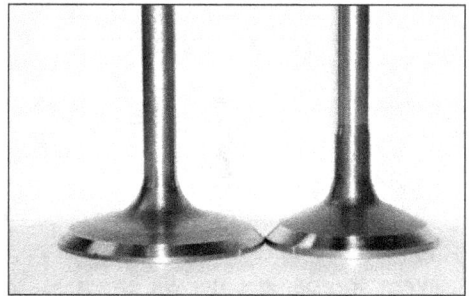

The valve on the left is an intake and the one on the right is an exhaust. Note that the underhead angle of the intake valve is much less than the underhead angle on the exhaust valve. The intake valve is considered a nailhead valve and the exhaust valve is considered a tulip valve or a semi-tulip valve. Notice that these valves do not have the "ski jump" just above the valveseat.

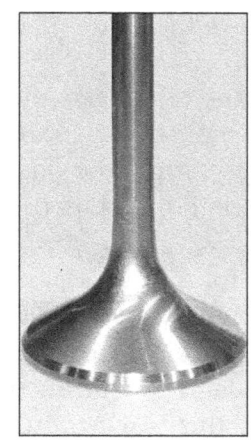

This is more of a true tulip-shaped underhead-angle valve. It is also a pyramid with a stem attached to the top. Tulip valves are often used in the exhaust ports of wedge cylinder heads.

CHAPTER 5

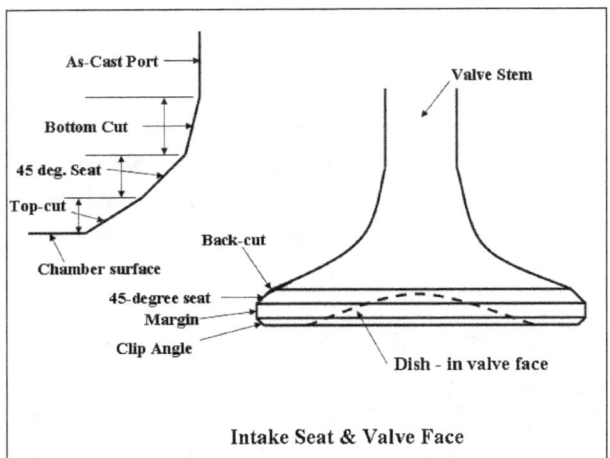

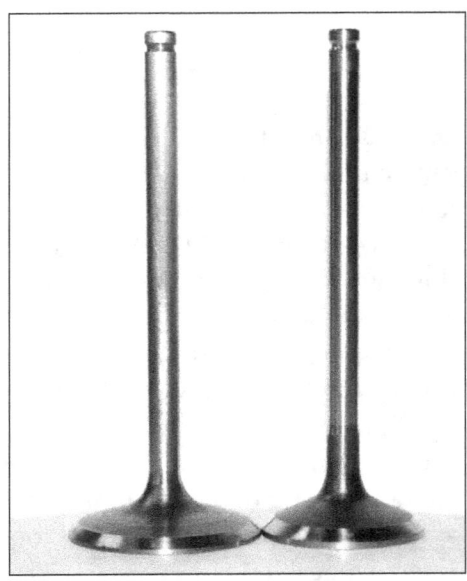

After you get into the racing side of performance, the valve work gets more complicated and there are more angles to grind. The bottom must be cut to blend the valveseat into the port and a top should be cut to help the air enter the combustion chamber, especially at low lifts. The back-cut is only used on valves that have a ski jump. The clip angle is also optional. The size of the dish in the face of the valve varies but is larger and more commonly used in exhaust valves or tulip valves.

Production valves, such as these Magnums, generally have a small flat area on the underside of the valve head. I call this a "ski-jump" because the air coming down the backside of the valve head hits this flat area and it jumps off the valve head. The valveseat is cut at a 45-degree angle, so if you select an angle less than 45 but greater than the underhead angle and back-cut the valve, then this ski-jump disappears and the air has a smooth transition from the underhead angle to the valveseat angle and better flow results. This is a very inexpensive performance tip.

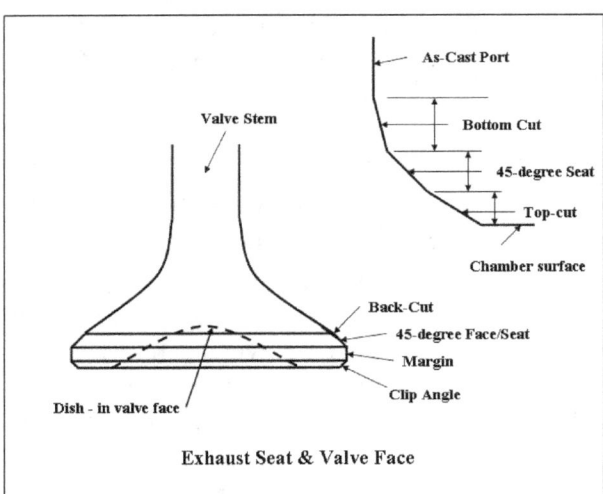

The exhaust valve is smaller in diameter than the intake and the dish in the face tends to be larger because the exhaust valve usually has a higher underhead angle, which means it is more tulip-shaped. The dish takes weight out of the valve head. Only professionals did this type of valve job because it took so many cutters. Today, however, if the head is CNC-ported, the machine can cut the seats at the same time it cuts the port. Moreover, multi-angles are easy for the CNC-machine.

The production A-engine valves have several keeper-groove alignments of one groove (right), two grooves (middle), or three grooves (left). The two-groove alignment is not common. The three-groove alignment is generally used on the exhaust valve. Most of the intake valves use a single square groove. All the Magnum valves are single round grooves. All aftermarket max-performance valves are single groove (square) designs unless they are made for the Magnum engines.

For max-performance applications, the aftermarket offers titanium valves, which are considered race-only parts. They are lighter than stainless valves and are also strong, but they are quite expensive. As valve heads become larger and valves become longer, they are heavier. Titanium is one way of making the valve lighter without giving up diameter or length.

Valve Seals

High-performance valve seals are made of high-temperature Viton. The standard A-engine valve seal has an umbrella seal that slips over the valvestem; the Magnum valve has cup-style seals that fit over the valveguide and must have the guide sized to accept it.

Seals must be inserted inside the valvespring. The umbrella seals fit inside of the single spring; the dual spring does not. High-lift cams use dual springs.

One option is to use a PC seal in place of the umbrella seal. The PC seal fits over the guide and requires the top of the guide to be machined to accept it. Also, this seal requires

.100-inch clearance, so you lose the thickness of the seal off the valve lift.

If you plan on running on the street, you want to use a production seal (umbrella or Magnum-style), which means using a single spring with dampener (optional). There are good single springs that allow .500-inch valve lift, up to .535-inch valve lift.

Head Gaskets

Today most of A-engine and Magnum head gaskets are about .040-inch thick. Most use MLS construction.

Four- and Six-Bolts

The production small-block gasket uses four bolts around each chamber (10 bolts per head). For very high compression ratios and racing applications, Mopar/Chrysler introduced blocks and heads that featured six bolts around each chamber (18 bolts per head). Cometic, Fel-Pro, and others offer special six-bolt head gaskets for this application. The W8 and W9 heads were designed for the six-bolt pattern.

The six-bolt pattern is designed so that if you have a six-bolt head or block but do not want to use this feature, you can use a standard four-bolt gasket. For example, if you have an R3 bolt with the six bolts machined, but you have an Indy four-bolt head, you can use the four-bolt gasket and leave the extra bolt holes empty.

Street Supercharger

Several aftermarket companies offer street supercharger kits for Magnum engines, and most kits are set up for the Dakota, Ram trucks, or Jeeps because the engine compartments are large. Magnum engines in these vehicles were built with a compression ratio over 9:1, but a supercharged engine on pump gas (92 octane) should have an 8:1 compression ratio. If the ratio isn't changed, the engine detonates and breaks parts, blows head gaskets, scuffs pistons, etc.

Changing the pistons to reduce the ratio one full point is expensive and time-consuming. Cometic offers an MLS gasket that is .120-inch thick, which drops the engine's compression ratio about one full point and solves the problem.

Copper Head Gasket

Copper head gaskets are suitable for supercharged race engines because they support high compression. Typically they are used with O-rings. They come in thicknesses of .042, .051, .062, and .081 inch. Manufacturers also offer special bore sizes.

If the copper gasket is not damaged, it can be re-used.

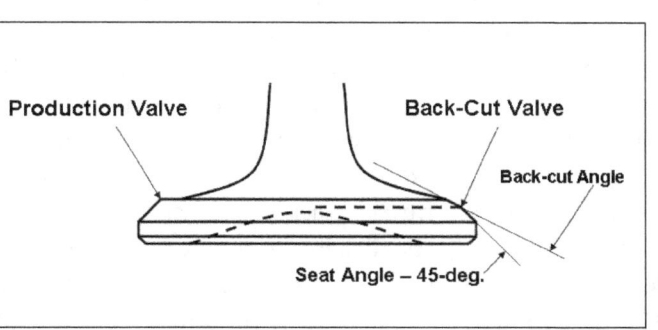

The Magnum valvespring installed height is 1.64 inches; the A-engine installed height is 1.68 to 1.70 inches. The long-valve W2 and W5 heads use a 2-inch installed height. The basic installed height defines the valvesprings that can be used. Even though the specs are close, the Magnum uses different valvesprings than the A-engine (see Chapter 7).

Production valves generally have a small flat area on the underside of the valve head that I call a ski jump. Air comes down the backside of the valve head, it hits this flat area, and then it jumps up off the valve head. The valveseat is cut at a 45-degree angle. If you select an angle less than 45 degrees but greater than the underhead angle and back-cut the valve, this ski jump will disappear. The air will have a smooth transition from the underhead angle to the valveseat angle and better flow results. This is a very inexpensive performance tip.

CHAPTER 6

VALVETRAIN

You need aftermarket roller rockers, pushrods, and valves. When building a 500-hp (or greater) engine, I recommend upgrading from the stock stamped steel to heavy-duty aluminum roller rockers. The roller rockers provide much more strength, they tend to maintain geometry better, and roller design is more efficient.

High-performance engines run greater valve lift and, as a consequence, they use heavier springs. Thus, the aluminum rockers are more suited to these engine setups. In fact, with the higher spring loads the pushrods tend to pierce the stamped rocker arm. The basic upgrade from the stamped rocker is the ductile iron rocker. These rockers are available from Crane and Isky; Crane also offers a 1.6-ratio version.

The ductile iron rocker is the standard street/strip setup. The next upgrade is to aluminum roller rockers, and these include Crane's 450-, 600-, and 700/900-pound valvesprings, which is the open load rating for the springs. None of the hydraulic or mechanical cams require this much spring load so any of these rockers should work for a street/strip application. These high loads are used with mechanical roller cams, which I don't recommend for the street.

T&D, Jesel, and Comp Cams offer mini-shaft kits, and some heads, such as the W8 and W9, require this kind of valvetrain. However, these are commonly relegated to a race engine. Valves are discussed in Chapter 5 and lifters are covered with the camshaft in Chapter 4. Pushrods, rocker arms, rocker shafts, pivots, rocker stands, valvesprings, retainers, and keepers are part of the system.

You need to select the compatible valvetrain for the hydraulic or mechanical cam for the A- or Magnum engine. Remember, you can use a mechanical valvetrain on a hydraulic cam, but you cannot use a hydraulic valvetrain on a mechanical cam. The one crossover example is the 1970 340 6-barrel, which used adjustable rockers on a hydraulic camshaft.

Oiling system health is important. Getting oil to the valvetrain is one of the biggest challenges for the oiling system. The valve tip is at the end of the oil path. Any problem with oil pressure or delivery and the rocker arm, rocker tip, valve tip, valvestem, or pushrod ends will scuff and/or fail. For this reason, do not restrict the oil to the heads on the A-engines because it causes engine and valvetrain failures.

Magnum pushrods are much shorter than A-engine pushrods by

The A-engine and Magnum are fitted with either hydraulic or mechanical rockers. The production A-engine and the Magnum valvetrains look similar because they are both hydraulic and center on stamped steel rocker arms. This A-engine with adjustable mechanical rockers has aluminum roller-tip rockers.

VALVETRAIN

Valvetrain Specs

	318/340/360	340 T/A	5.2L/5.9L
Rocker Shaft Outside Diameter (inch)	.872–.873	n/a	n/a
Tappet Diameter (inch)	.9040–.9045	.9040–.9045	.9040–.9045
Pushrod Hydraulic Outside Diameter (inch)	.309–.315	mech	.309–.315
Pushrod Length (inches)	7.495–7.525	7.23	6.915–6.935

The A-engine hydraulic rocker arms are stamped steel and look similar, but there is actually a right and a left. The pushrod bump at the top of the rocker is slightly offset to the left in the left rocker arm and offset to the right in the right rocker. Note that there is no spacer between the two rockers.

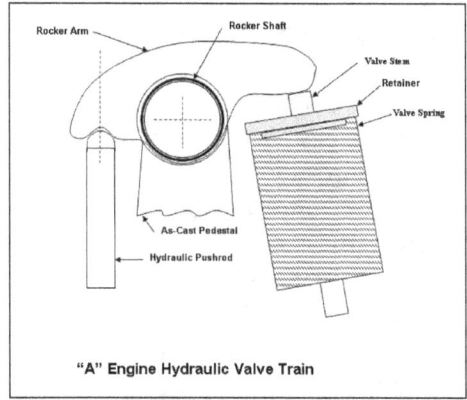

The A-engine uses one large rocker shaft per head and has cast-in pedestals (five per head). The valvespring is smaller than big-block springs and uses a shorter installed spring height. The race W2 system machined the as-cast pedestal off slightly below the bottom of the saddle and replaced it with a rocker stand (not shown).

almost 1/2 inch because Magnums use tall hydraulic roller tappets. Also, the only mechanical valvetrain is the 1970 340 T/A and its pushrod is shorter than the hydraulic pushrod. Note these differences when swapping parts. The early 273 engines also used mechanical valve gears, but this hardware is not up to the heavy-duty requirements of max-performance engines today. Use 340 T/A or W2 hardware for these applications.

Oiling System

The Magnum and A-engine use different valvetrain oiling.

The A-engine oils up through the block and heads; the Magnum oils the valvetrain through the pushrods. The A-engine valvetrain gets oil from a drilled passage in the block from the number-2 and number-4 cam journals. See Chapter 4 on cross-drilling and grooving those journals. In the head, the oil passage intersects the second or fourth rocker shaft pedestal attaching bolt hole.

The rocker shaft hole for the attaching bolt is slightly larger to allow oil into the hollow shaft. The bottom of the rocker shaft has small holes for each rocker that allow oil into the rocker. From there it drips on the valve tip and a hole in the rocker's pushrod cup oils the pushrod end.

The mechanical valvetrain for the A-engine is somewhat unique. The oil gets to the rocker shaft the same way, but the mechanical rocker arm has a hole in its underside to spray oil on the valve tip. It also has a small hole drilled through the adjuster threads that allows oil to drip into the pushrod cup or an optional hole on the underside of the arm to spray oil on the pushrod cup.

The Magnum oils the valvetrain through the pushrods, so it starts with the small hole in the side of the tappet. Passages inside the tappet and a hole in the pushrod cups (one in the lifter and one in the pushrod) allow oil into the hollow pushrod. A small hole in the upper ball pivot and a matching hole in the rocker arm cup allow the pushrod oil to pass into the rocker arm, lubricating the pushrod end along the way. The oil in the rocker arm collects in the lower area and lubricates the rocker arm pivot. As the rocker arm moves through its normal motion, the oil that has collected in the center of the rocker spills over the end of the arm onto the valve tip and retainer area and lubricates the valve tip and the valvestem.

A-Engine

The A-engine is fitted with either hydraulic or mechanical valvetrains. The hydraulic system uses a stamped steel rocker arm while the mechanical uses a cast rocker arm with an adjuster on the pushrod end. The adjuster is required to set valve lash on each valve. In the mechanical valvetrain group, the straight on the standard engine and offset on the W2 and W5 engines are the two designs.

Changing the pushrods and rocker arms can convert from the standard hydraulic valvetrain to a mechanical valvetrain. For this swap, you use 16 straight exhaust rockers

CHAPTER 6

from either a W2 package or a 340 T/A package. The W2 valvetrain package of rocker arms uses eight straight exhaust rockers and four right- and four left-offset intake rockers. Roller rockers can be used with either hydraulic or mechanical cams, and they are available in straight or offset styles. In addition, roller-tip rockers and double roller versions with roller tips and roller pivots are available.

The rocker arm offset allowed by the rocker shaft is one of the big advantages of rocker shaft systems because it allows the pushrod to move away from the intake port wall, which allows the intake ports to be larger and flow more air.

Magnum Engine

The basic Magnum valvetrain oils the rockers through the pushrods. This means that the lifter or tappet must have "oil through the pushrod" capability. If you want to use a mechanical cam in a Magnum engine, buy a 360 Jeep (AMC) V-8 mechanical tappet readily available from Crane, Comp Cams, and others. In addition, the rockers have to

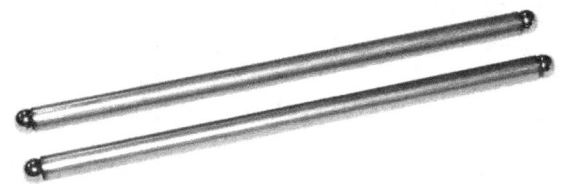

The typical pushrod is long and straight. Hydraulic pushrods have a round ball on each end and can be installed in either direction. A Magnum's pushrod is shown.

be switched to ones with an adjuster such as the Harlen Sharp aluminum roller rockers for the Magnum engines.

Pushrods

Stock pushrods are not suited for max-performance engine builds of more than 500 hp. For more than 500-hp builds, use a mechanical pushrod. If the valvespring is upgraded, the rocker should also be upgraded and the ductile iron adjustable rocker requires new mechanical pushrods (cup on the upper end rather than a ball). You could buy (or make) rockers with a cup on the end of the adjusting screws, but they are not readily available and might cost

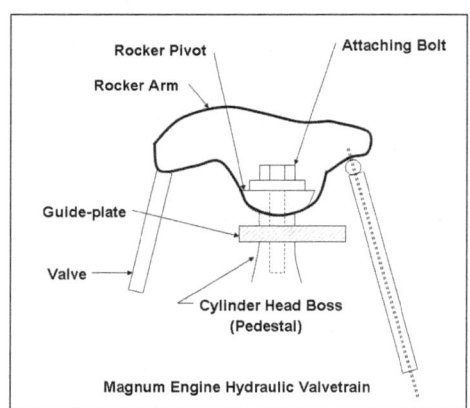

The Magnum's valvetrain includes the T-shaped pivot at the bottom of the rocker and the individual attaching bolt. The guideplate (one per cylinder) fits between the pivot and the cylinder head boss on the short pedestal. If a mechanical cam is used in the Magnum engine, adjustable rockers must be installed.

a lot more. However, you might consider upgrading to a 3/8-inch pushrod in the area of 600 hp or when you install an actual mechanical cam with .550-inch lift or more.

The mechanical pushrod has a ball-end on the lower end (the one in the lifter) and a cup on the upper end (at the rocker arm). Be sure you install them correctly. The 1970 340 TA-engines used mechanical pushrods. They can also be used with other mechanical cams as long as adjustable rockers are used: T/A-style, W2-style, or aluminum/aftermarket roller rockers. Magnum engines use hollow pushrods but also have a small hole in each ball-end to allow oil to pass through. If mechanical cams are used on the Magnum engines, the mechanical pushrod must also have small holes in the ball-end and cup-end to allow oil to pass through.

Cam companies, along with specialists Trend Performance and Smith Bros., make pushrods. They both make pushrods of any length, hydraulic or mechanical. The common sizes are 5/16 (stock), 3/8 (most common upgrade), and 7/16 inch. Smith Bros. only offers a .116-inch wall in the 5/16 pushrod but offers .083, .120, and .145 inch in 3/8-inch pushrods and similar sizes in 7/16-inch rods. Trend offers two wall thicknesses in the 7/16-inch and two in the 3/8-inch. When ordering pushrods, pay very close attention to how the company you are dealing with wants the pushrod to be measured. I recommend in general the

The Magnum engine's valvetrain uses a stamped steel rocker with the small flap (or tab) over the pushrod oil hole to help deflect the oil. The bolt in the center holds the T-shaped pivot and rocker to the cylinder head.

VALVETRAIN

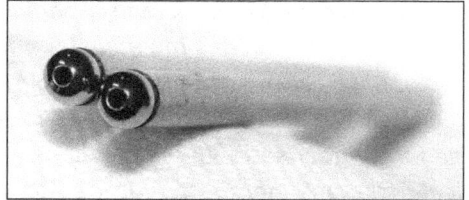

The pushrod tube is hollow, and the small round hole in the center of each ball is how the oil gets from the tappet into the pushrod and then up to the valvetrain.

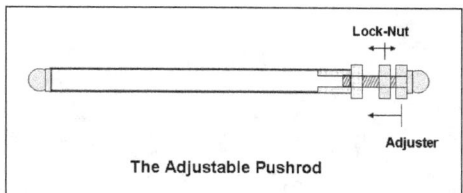

The adjustable hydraulic pushrod (shown) can solve many problems. After it is adjusted to the desired length by threading the adjuster in or out, the lock nut is turned down against the insert and locked in place. The adjuster is generally placed at the top.

Rocker Arms

Both Magnum and A-engine rockers are stamped steel. They are not interchangeable. The A-engine uses a driver-side and passenger-side rocker, with a slight offset to the pushrod hole. The Magnum uses all the same rockers. The 1970 340 TA-engine used cast rocker arms. The T/A and the W2 both use left- and right-offset cast-iron rockers on the intake side. The early 273 engines also used mechanical cast rockers (all straight), but they are not up to the spring loads and aggressive cams used in today's high-performance applications.

Stamped versus Cast

The vast majority of Mopar small-block rocker arms are stamped steel. Only the 273 and the 1970 340 T/A used cast rocker arms. The W2 systems are all cast rockers.

If you use too much valvespring load, you may pierce the stamped rocker arm with the pushrod end. High valvespring loads lead to cast rocker arms because they don't pierce. The 273 cast rockers do not like high valvespring loads either.

3/8-inch thin wall tubing for street/strip engines.

The hydraulic lifter has about .150 inch of adjustment and is designed to operate in the middle of this adjustment range, .075 inch in either direction. In most cases, the tappet adjusts for a head mill of .030 inch. However, if you start milling a total of .075 to .100 inch off the head and block, you should consider changing the pushrod length.

On the mechanical pushrod side, you may think that the adjusting screw fixes everything. Caution: If too many threads are showing on the adjusting screw below the rocker arm's lower surface, you may have trouble. One full turn below the arm or less is desired. If you have two threads showing below the arm, the oil that is supposed to travel down the threads to lubricate the pushrod cup is shaken off and the no-lubrication situation smokes the pushrod ends.

"The Problem Solver"

An A-engine may have more than 200,000 miles and may have been rebuilt several times since new. At each rebuild, the head and mating surfaces were machined. After three or so rebuilds, the valvetrain is not working. Tappets didn't bleed down or there was a "tick" coming from the valvetrain.

The Smith Bros. adjustable pushrod is the problem solver. It's suitable for a hydraulic valvetrain fix because the mechanical system has adjustment in the rocker arm. Although the adjustable hydraulic pushrod has a ball-end on both ends, it has a threaded adjustment on one end, which goes into a threaded insert pressed into the end of the tube, as well as a lock-nut between the tube-insert and the ball-end, which is used to lock the adjustment setting once determined.

So many problems with a multi-rebuilt engine's valvetrain, end up with the stock pushrod being too long or too short. An adjustable pushrod solves all of these assembly problems, even though the pushrod itself was not the cause of the problem.

These hydraulic pushrods can be adjusted during installation in the engine. I recommend that the length of the adjustable pushrod be determined and test fit. Then make all 16 pushrods to this length on the bench prior to installation into the engine.

Smith Bros. makes Magnum adjustable pushrods, too, but the Magnum engines don't seem to have these problems yet. I think this is because they aren't as old.

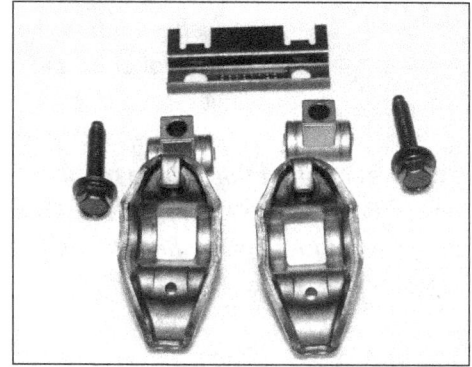

The Magnum engine valvetrain uses the stamped steel rocker, a T-shaped pivot (shown just above the top of the rocker arm), and a steel guideplate with one attaching bolt per rocker.

The A-engine mechanical valvetrain starts with the adjustable rocker arm, which is generally cast iron. These rockers are actually aftermarket parts, but look very similar to the straight T/A and W2 exhaust rockers. Note the spacer between the two center rockers.

The W2 rockers (both mechanical and adjustable) are offset on the intake side (left) and straight on the exhaust (right).

The mechanical Mopar/Crane A-engine rocker arm system has the adjuster on top of each rocker arm along with the lock nut. The hydraulic rocker shaft is generally not used with the mechanical rockers. Either the T/A or the W2 shaft can be used; aftermarket manufacturers of the rocker arm systems also supply their own shaft. The T/A and W2 shafts were ground "round" and the hydraulic production shafts are not. Mechanical rockers need a round shaft. Note the spacer between rockers.

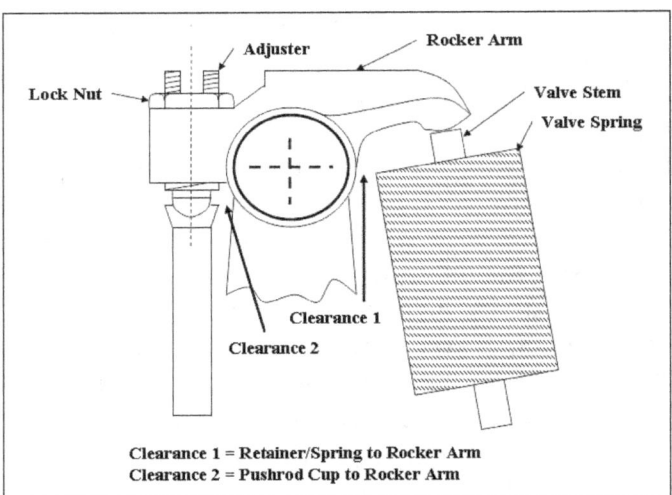

The rocker arm in mechanical valvetrain systems often has clearance issues with the valvespring and retainer and also with the pushrod cup. Most mechanical rocker arms have a relief under the arm near the valve tip for retainer clearance and a relief on the underside of the pushrod arm to clear the cup-end. As the cam lifts get higher, the outside diameter of the valvesprings increases. These issues must be addressed.

The aluminum roller-tip rocker arm is adjustable (the screw hole is visible but the screw is missing). It has the small roller on the valve-tip end but the center slides on the rocker shaft in the same manner as on the other A-engine rockers. The cut or relief just above the roller is for retainer clearance.

T/A and W2 cast rockers have a clearance relief under the valve-tip arm. This is required to clear the valvespring and retainer. If this clearance relief is enlarged, the rocker is weakened and may fail.

For any cast rockers (T/A, W2, or ductile iron) any failure is at higher horsepower than is common in street engines but very high spring loads are the cause, not the actual horsepower. I estimate that these loads would be greater than 450 to 500 pounds; with loads that high, you need valve lifts over .650 inch, which is in race territory. With high loads and high lifts in racing, geometry and friction issues come with a pad-style rocker rather than a roller.

Aluminum

Almost all early aftermarket rocker arms were made of aluminum. They also had a roller on the valve-tip end. These rockers also have a relief under the valve-tip end, but the arm is thicker or wider and therefore stronger. Because of these early beginnings there have been many more aluminum rockers and rocker systems produced. Although most are aluminum, they now feature double-rollers (valve tip and center pivot) and several offsets and ratios. The actual valvetrain geometry (A-engine) is somewhat improved with the addition of aluminum roller rockers (at the same ratio, 1.5:1).

Investment Castings

After aluminum rockers set the standard for performance rocker arms, several companies introduced investment cast rockers. These rockers make a very good performance system. Generally, they are stronger

VALVETRAIN

My Performance Packages

In an effort to tie all engine hardware together, I created five performance packages. They vary from 250 to more than 700 hp and all are intended for street/strip applications.

	Basic Cam	Best Rocker Arm
Package No. 1	HP Hydraulic	Stock, stamped
Package No. 2	Big Hydraulic	Ductile or Aluminum
Package No. 3	Mechanical	Ductile or Aluminum
Package No. 4	Mechanical	Ductile or Aluminum
Package No. 5	Mechanical or Roller	Aluminum or Race

Note: Package No. 1 and No. 2 could use ductile or aluminum rockers. Any of the five packages could use a race-style rocker system.

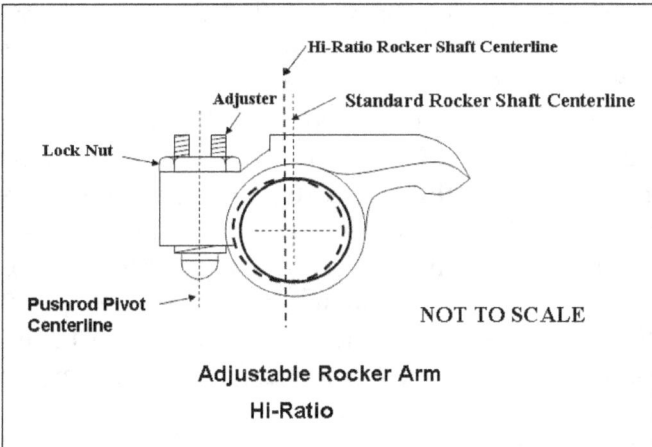

You can move the pivot (shown) or move the adjuster's centerline (not shown) to change the rocker arm ratio on a given engine. The manufacturer can do either depending upon the ratio desired and the casting or forging being modified. Once machined, offsetting the center pivot is the only reasonable method. Remember, a little (such as going to a 1.7 ratio) is okay but a lot will cause failure.

These are offset Crane mechanical rockers. The first and last rockers are somewhat straight for the exhaust valves, while the second and third rocker arms are offset about 3/4 inch for the intake valves. An offset is to the left and also to the right. They are always installed this way. The pushrods for those valves move away from each other so the intake ports below the offsets can get much larger. The Mancini Racing flat bracket holds the rocker shaft in place and spreads out the bolt's clamping loads around the shaft. That helps keep the shaft round, which is desired for mechanical rockers.

than the standard cast rocker but may not be as available.

Rocker Ratio

The typical stock rocker ratio for the A-engines is 1.5; for the Magnum engines, 1.6. Aluminum roller rockers from the aftermarket come in the stock 1.5 ratio and the optional 1.6 ratio for the A-engine and 1.6 and 1.7 ratios for the Magnum (Harlen Sharp, Crane, Comp Cams, Indy Heads, Isky).

Most companies have only one aluminum roller rocker, but Crane has three grades of roller rockers. For street/strip use, cost is the best guide (depending on desired ratio); a 1.6 rocker is unique (Crane has one). Some versions use a double roller: one on the valve tip and one at the rocker shaft. The race systems from T&D and Jesel also offer ratio options.

There are not as many rocker arm options for the Magnum, which has a standard 1.6 ratio, but Harlen Sharp offers a 1.7 ratio. It requires extra pushrod clearancing, which is okay at initial buildup but not a quick swap at the track.

In general, for street/strip engines, switching from a 1.5 (stock)-ratio rocker system on the A-engine to a 1.6-ratio rocker arm gains about .030-inch valve lift with the typical hydraulic cams. This change should yield gains similar to installing the next bigger camshaft except that the durations stay about the same, as does the overlap.

With standard cams (in the .500- to .600-inch area), going from 1.5 to 1.6 ratio or from 1.6 to 1.7, the same cam picks up about .030- to .040-inch valve lift, which makes more power without affecting torque because it increases the lift and has little effect on the duration. Caution: 1.7 rockers

CHAPTER 6

These special alloy cast rocker arms are stronger than the standard cast-iron rocker. They are generally adjustable rockers and have a roller on the valve tip. These are the almost-straight versions but offset versions are available for the W2.

Race rocker arm systems are offered in several styles. These have a roller valve tip and a roller at the center pivot. The rocker shafts are shorter and smaller in diameter. Note that there is a bolt on each side of each rocker. In general, the bolts that you can see actually bolt into a bracket, and the bracket bolts to the head.

Rocker Tip Alignment

The typical rocker pad on the rocker arm is larger (wider) than the valve tip. Therefore, having the rocker centered over the valvestem isn't really for contact. The loads in the rocker arms with hydraulic cams aren't that high but can become very high with mechanical and mechanical roller cams and dual and triple springs. Rocker tip alignment isn't critical in the stock A-engine or Magnum hardware. For tip alignment you try to have the rocker-tip pad centered over the valvestem. Because the pad is larger, you have some leeway in positioning relative to valve movement. If the pad is not centered, however, it edge-loads the valvestem and this tends to wear out the guide very quickly.

To improve alignment, the rocker must move because the valve has to stay in its location. In general, this alignment is only done with mechanical valve gear. If the rocker is next to a pedestal and needs to move away from the pedestal to improve its tip alignment, add a rocker shaft shim between the rocker arm and the pedestal. If the rocker needs to move toward the pedestal, the shoulder of the rocker on the pedestal side has to be milled, by machine shop. Then that rocker must stay in that location at final assembly.

cause the pushrods to hit the head on the Magnum engines and clearance must be added. Similarly, 1.6-ratio rockers on the A-engine can cause the pushrods to move closer to the block/head. Be sure to check this at installation; go through the full range of travel to check all clearances.

Rocker Offset

T/A and W2 rockers are both known as offset types, but in reality, only the intake rockers are offset. The rockers have left and right offsets, which depends on the cylinder they are designed to fit. The offset rocker allows the pushrod to move away from the wall of the intake port, which allows the intake port to be larger. With the W2 ports, the rockers were larger (wider) as-cast. With the T/A ports, the offset allowed for more porting, which yielded larger, higher-flowing ports. Most newer performance heads (W7, W8, W9, Indy, Edelbrock, and B1-BA) have a combination of these two features, with CNC-porting.

Race Rockers

With the introduction of W7, W8, and W9 race cylinder heads, race-only rocker systems became common. T&D and Jesel offer these systems. When the race W2 head was introduced in the early 1970s, Chrysler machined off the five cast-in pedestals and threaded the flat pad to accept a rocker stand and attaching bolt. This five-rocker stand system allowed Chrysler to move the rocker shaft away from the valvespring and retainer. By using taller rocker stands, the shaft could be moved upward to match up properly with longer valves used in the race W2 package. This change also accommodates the new high-lift

VALVETRAIN

High-Ratio Rocker Clearance

Knowing the valve lift from the cam and rocker arm ratio, and the engine RPM expected by the engine's hardware (heads, carb, manifold), the valvesprings are basically dictated. Going to long valves and large-diameter valvesprings can cause problems with rocker arm clearances. The mechanical rocker arm is already too close to the spring and there are reliefs on the underside of the arms. Long valves and the 2-inch valvespring package work great but it is much more expensive than just a set of springs. Plus there are rocker arm clearance concerns.

You may want to use the A-engine springs at the A-engine installed height. Or, you can use dual spring P3614542 (up to .610-inch valve lift) or P3412068 (up to .620-inch valve lift) installed at the A-engine installed height of 1.68 to 1.70 inches and keep the stock-length valves. They are only 1.45 and 1.46 inches in diameter. The taller springs are around 1.60 inches in diameter or more.

On the Magnum, you can use P4876062 for valve lifts up to .580/.600 inch. (Most of the cams discussed in Chapter 4 have lifts less than .600 inch.)

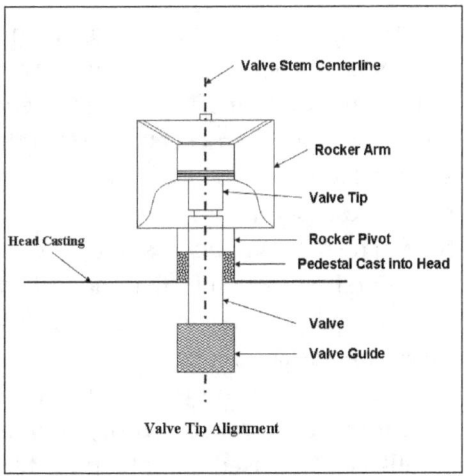

The cams are more aggressive on mechanical rockers and spring loads are higher so alignment is more important. Obviously, you want the rocker-tip pad centerline to line up with the valvestem centerline. What if it doesn't? Assume that a pedestal is to the left and another rocker arm is to the right. To move the rocker to the right, away from the pedestal, you use rocker shaft shims. These are thin, round washers with .030- and .060-inch thicknesses. If the rocker must move to the left, the bracket on top of the shaft, which is held on with the attaching bolt, has to be shaved or the left side of the rocker has to be shaved.

In some cases, the race valvetrain adapts to the existing head and in other cases it works with the race valve gear. Indy Heads and Edelbrock heads are designed for the standard setup but accept race setups. The B1-BA was designed for the race setup but can also be used with a shaft system. This B1-BA head is set up for the race-style valve gear with bolt holes by every valve. Typically, a bracket bolts into these holes; the mini-shafts and rockers then bolt to the bracket.

cams, and allows the use of bigger and longer valvesprings.

The original W2 system moved the shaft away from the spring by about .180 inch, but it does not allow for more clearance. When moving the shaft farther out, the attaching bolts break through the wall of the shaft and cause the shaft to break. To remedy this situation, aftermarket race valvetrain suppliers made a plate that bolts to the head where the pedestals were located in most cases. The steel plate runs the full length of the head, and it's machined to accept a mini rocker shaft; one for each valve, or one plate for two valves in some cases. Two screws secure it to each shaft and to the plate. The double-roller aluminum rocker then pivots on each small shaft and can have the required offset.

T&D offers a T/A offset of .450 inch; a W7, W8 offset of .550 inch; a W2, W5, B1-BA offset of .700 inch; and an Indy 360-1 and 360-2 and Edelbrock Performer RPM offset of .800 inch. The supplier part numbers for the individual heads are all unique, but they share the same amount of offset. The W9 uses several of these offsets.

A-Engine Rocker Shaft

The rocker shaft is used in the A-engines only, and it features a long, thick-wall tube with holes drilled in it. The typical stamped rocker hydraulic valve gear isn't very fussy about the rocker shaft, but the mechanical rockers are. For use with mechanical rockers, the shaft should be straight and round. To get it round, the shaft generally has to be ground.

CHAPTER 6

The special T/A rocker shaft is the best one, if you can find one (it was ground and had banana grooves to help oil the mechanical rockers). The shaft is attached to the head by five screws into the pedestals that were cast into the head. The race W2 rocker shaft package machined the pedestals flat and drilled and tapped the pad to receive rocker stands and attaching bolts.

Although other makes used stud-mounted rocker stands, Mopar small-blocks used shaft-mounted stands, and these are suitable for max-performance engine builds. Comp Cams, Crane, Harland Sharp, and others offer upgraded aluminum shaft-mounted rockers that provide exceptional performance.

Crane, Comp Cams, and Indy Heads all offer ground rocker shafts. The ground rocker shaft can be used with either stamped rockers or mechanical rockers. The production shaft can only be used with stamped rockers. The Comp Cams shaft features hard-chrome on the surface, which might be an advantage for some rocker arm systems.

Alignment

The rocker arm pad should be aligned over the valvestem, but you must also align the rocker shaft. First, small holes drilled for each rocker arm in the bottom of the shaft must face down. Second, on the bottom of the shaft, the centerline of the attaching bolts should be straight up or centered. The small holes are located to one side of center, and this offset should go toward the valves when installed. Finally, a notch in one end of the shaft goes to the front on the driver-side head and to the rear on the passenger-side head. The notch should always be at the bottom.

Offset Rocker Shaft

The race W2 valvetrain used rocker stands instead of pedestals, which allowed the rocker shaft to be offset. The rocker stand allowed the rocker shaft's attaching bolt to be offset from the center of the shaft. This required the actual rocker shaft to have its attaching hole offset, not on center as with the typical attaching hole. This offset attaching hole is very easy to spot because one side of the shaft is very thin next to the hole; the opposite side is very thick.

Rocker stands and special shafts were used to move the shaft up and away from the valvesprings. This allowed for taller valves, which allowed for taller springs, which allowed for more valve lift.

Rocker Stands

Aluminum rocker stands basically do the job of cast-in pedestals, and they have two wide and three narrow stands. The narrow stands are for the first, third, and fifth positions. The two wide stands are for the second and fourth positions, and these also have the oiling hole drilled next to the attaching bolt hole.

The W2 race package has the most common rocker stands, which were also used on the T/A race engines. Each rocker stand system is unique and has a large hole in it at a specific height above the flat bottom. The shaft passes through this hole. A much smaller hole is for the attaching bolt to be threaded into the hole in the head.

Rocker stands are not used on Magnum engines.

Rocker Pivots for Magnum Engines

Rocker pivots are used on Magnum engines only. The pivot fits inside the saddle in the stamped rocker arm and the bottom of the T-shaped pivot fits against the flat top of the pedestal. On these engines, the bottom of the pivot is square, and it fits into the guideplate that sits next to the cylinder head. The attaching bolt passes through a hole down the center of the pivot and connects the rocker arm to the head. It is lubricated by oil passing into the rocker arm from the pushrod. There is one pivot per rocker arm and one guideplate per cylinder.

Valvesprings

Straight single springs or beehive springs are commonly selected for max-performance engines of 500 hp or more. For performance applications, you want a single spring with dampener. The dampener is a thin piece of flat steel wound like a spring in the opposite direction of the main spring and inserted inside the main spring. Generally a valvespring is designed to work at a certain installed height and has specific outside and inside diameters.

Specific valvespring recommendations are made with the camshaft

The single spring with dampener (just inside the outer spring at the top) is the standard performance spring for street use. The dampener is wound in the opposite direction from the main outer spring. The trick to any valvespring is to select the spring to work with your camshaft and the desired valve lift. Springs also must be selected to work in your engine's intended installed height.

VALVETRAIN

Beehive springs are used on the Magnum engines. With a beehive spring, the top diameter is smaller than the bottom diameter and they do not usually have a dampener.

The dual spring consists of an outer spring and an inner spring plus a dampener that fits between them. They must be selected to work in the A-engine's installed height. Dual springs are typically used with mechanical cams but they are sometimes recommended for high-lift hydraulics.

recommendations in the cam charts in Chapter 4. I recommend the springs by part number but allow the specific cam manufacturer to suggest the spring that works with the chosen profile.

Beehive

The basic Magnum engine has beehive springs. At the time, production beehive springs could not handle a high-performance cam and there were no aftermarket beehive springs to meet this need, so Mopar Performance designed special valvesprings (straight or non-beehive) and a retainer. Today, Comp Cams seems to have the best beehive spring for the Magnum engines, with a 1.415-inch outside diameter, 137 pounds at 1.70-inch closed, and 305 pounds at 1.10-inch (or .600-inch lift capacity). Check with Comp Cams to see if a steel production retainer can be used.

Dual Spring

Dual springs have an outer spring, an inner spring, and a dampener installed between the two springs to help with dynamics. The typical A-engine dual spring has about the same outside diameter as the single spring and it uses the same installed height. The second spring increases the seat load and the open load, so that it works better with more aggressive performance cams.

As a general guideline, dual springs should be used with mechanical cams. The A-engine's 1.68/1.70-inch installed height is a challenge for valvesprings so consider springs such as P3614542 (up to .610-inch lift) and P3412068 (up to .620-inch lift) or the recommended Comp Cams or Crane springs for their A-engine cams.

Most dual springs that are at stock height when installed also have the same outside diameter as the high-performance single spring. Street engines need an actual valve seal, and the typical one doesn't fit inside of the second spring. One solution to this problem is to use a PC seal, which is small and attaches to the guide. Some guide machining is required to allow this installation. Some seals similar to the Magnums fit on the guide, so guide machining may not be required.

You don't want just any single spring; you want the specific high-performance single spring (no dampener? don't use it) such as P4120249 (up to .500-inch lift) or P5249847 (up to .535-inch lift) for the A-engine.

Magnum valves and keeper position the retainer very close to the end of the valve tip. Double-check that the keepers are installed at the same height in the retainer.

MOPAR SMALL-BLOCK ENGINES: HOW TO BUILD MAX PERFORMANCE

Installed Spring Height

The valvespring must work with the cylinder head, valves, cam, and rocker arms, and to do so, it must be installed at the correct spring height. It is one of the most important measurements that you take during the engine building process. It is defined as the distance between the spring seat in the head and the valvespring retainer with the valve closed or on the seat. It is measured without the spring by pulling the retainer and valve against the seat and holding it while the height is measured. It is typically measured with a snap gauge and a micrometer.

Everything about the head, valve, retainer, keepers, rocker arms, and cam enter into this number. However, the key is that the valve lift has to match the valvespring lift capacity. Several common Mopar installed heights are: 1.64 inches for the Magnum, 1.68/1.70 for the A-engine, 1.86 for big-blocks, and 2.00 inches for long-valve and racing applications.

A single spring and dampener has one installed height. However, the dampener height must be less than the spring height. A dual spring has two installed heights, one for each spring. The dual-spring dampener length has to be less than either spring length. The inner spring is usually shorter than the outer one. The inner spring seat in the head, common on production heads, is machined flat to the outer seat. Performance heads come with the inner seat flat to the outer seat. Therefore, the difference in installed spring heights is controlled by the retainer, which has an inner seat and an outer seat.

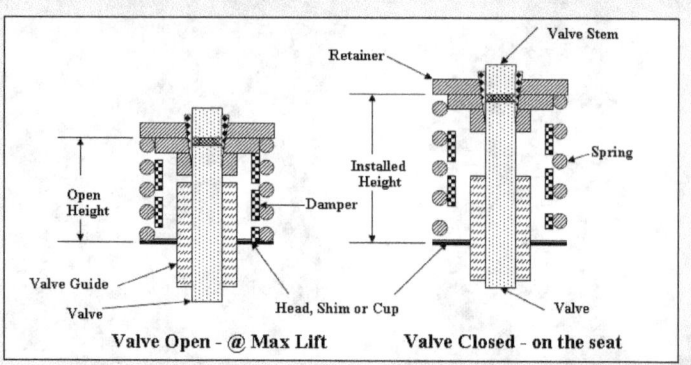

The A-engine's installed height is 1.68 to 1.70 inches; the Magnum's is 1.64 inches. This isn't an issue, but the smaller outside diameter of the Magnum spring means that the spring seat cut into the head was smaller, which prevents use of the A-engine springs in the Magnum. The guide height, guide diameter, and valve seal clearance are all closely related to the installed spring height.

To double-check your selected spring, measure the spring's solid height (coil bind). The solid height can be checked in a spring tester or vise. Use a steel scale or a dial vernier to take the measurements. Next, you need the cam's valve lift (not cam lift). It is best to use actual measured numbers; you can use those from the cam manufacturer. Add .100 inch to the solid height and then add the valve lift (from the spec sheet). This calculated number is considered the minimum installed height. If the actual installed height is larger, it's a plus for the valvespring. ■

The Magnum engine uses both the straight single spring (early) and a beehive (newer), but the A-engine springs listed above do not fit the Magnum head's machined spring seat. Removing the heads to machine the spring seats is expensive. The Magnum HP single springs are P5249464 (up to .525-inch lift) and P4876062 (up to .600-inch lift), and

Valve Lift

The cam and the rocker arm ratio dictate the valve lift, and the valve lift dictates the valvespring. Performance springs are designed for valve lifts in the .450- to .500-inch area, which could also be called street use. Engines planned for street/strip use typically have valve lifts in the .500- to .600-inch range. Lifts over .600 inch are considered race. Remember, if you have a given cam lift and rocker ratio and you switch to a higher-ratio rocker, the selected valvespring must be able to work with the higher lift.

For example, a hydraulic cam and 1.5 rocker that yield .500-inch valve lift picks up .033 inch of valve lift if the rockers are switched to 1.6 ratio. That means that the valvespring has to be able to accept .533-inch lift, not just .500 inch.

Spring Load

You need to understand closed (or seated) and open spring pressure. For the A-engine, the closed load should be measured at 1.68 to 1.70 inches; for the Magnum it is at 1.64 inches. Generally you want to measure the open load at the installed height minus the max valve lift.

For example, if your cam has .500-inch lift, measure the open loads at 1.20 inches (1.70 – .50 = 1.2).

If the max valve lift changes, so should the open load height. Loads are best used to identify weak springs. For this selection process, open loads are better than closed loads.

Valvetrain Parts

Performance heads (aluminum) use a large, flat spring seat, but cast-iron heads machine the seat into the cast iron with the outside diameter of the seat cutter, which leaves a recess in the head that the bottom of the spring must fit into. Magnum heads use a 1.42-inch seat diameter and A-engines use 1.50 inches, which is why A-engine performance springs do not fit Magnum heads. Production heads with an inner spring seat are typically milled flat for performance applications if the heads are off the engine.

If you bought a finished head from any popular manufacturer, all of the hardware has been installed, so you just need to verify that the hardware is suitable for the RPM range and horsepower targets. Comp, Crane, Isky, Edelbrock, and others sell the hardware that is suitable for a cam setup, and for simplicity, you should use that hardware. If you are going to use another manufacturer's hardware, communicate with the company. Tell them the head, cam, and other relevant information so you're sure the hardware is suitable.

The valveguide's outside diameter and height above the spring seat are important, especially with dual valvesprings. The guide height must allow the valve lift dictated by the cam, rocker arm, and installed height. You should use a steel spring cup for aluminum heads, so the steel valvespring tips don't dig into the aluminum spring seat in the head.

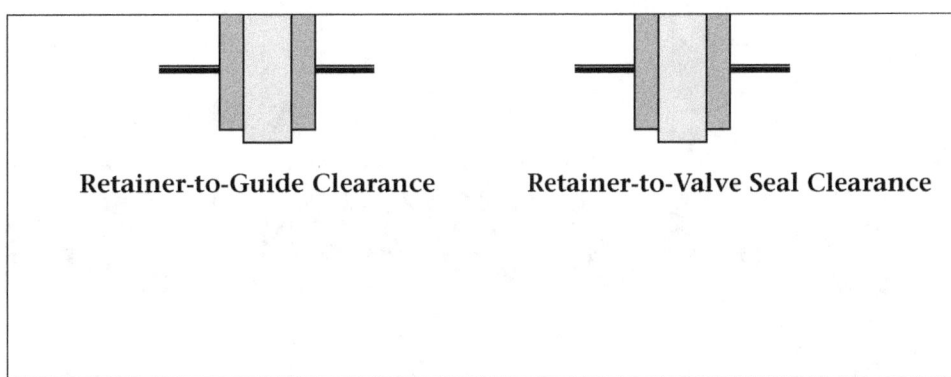

The clearance between the bottom of the retainer and the top of the valveguide in the head (distance A) is important to the proper function of the valvetrain. For street use, the distance between the bottom of the retainer and the top of the valve seal (distance B) is even more important. You want to have at least .050-inch clearance to the seal at max valve lift.

Retainers and Keepers

Valvestem grooves and diameter require certain locks (or keepers). The retainer is determined by the valvespring (outside diameter, inner diameter, inner spring seat). They join at the angle of the keeper, 7 or 10 degrees. The retainer must match the keeper's angle. Production keepers are 7-degree designs; race-only keepers are 10-degree designs. With very aggressive high-lift race cams, the high-load springs required with these cams, try to pull the 7-degree keepers through the retainer. The 10-degree keeper/retainer package solves this problem. I wouldn't consider this until you have mechanical roller-cam designs and lifts over .650 inch.

Retainers are made from several materials: steel (chrome-moly), aluminum, and titanium. Race engine builders prefer titanium retainers. In many cases, the street engine builder wants to use steel retainers because they accept much abuse.

A suitable retainer attaches the valvespring to the valvestem and must match the valvespring type: single, dual, or triple. It also must match the keepers (7- or 10-degree) and valvestem diameter (3/8, 11/32, and 5/16 inch, plus 8 mm). If you have a dual spring, 3/8-inch valvestem, and 7-degree keepers, there is a retainer to match those specs (available from Mopar Performance, Crane, or Comp Cams).

Keepers must fit into the valvestem grooves and match the common 3/8- and 5/16-inch, or 8-mm stem size. The 11/32-inch valvestem is used in some performance applications. Although one-, two-, and three-groove keepers are available, the one-groove is the most popular in performance engines. The A-engine uses 3/8-inch-stem valves; the single groove is square and located in the middle of the keeper. The Magnum engine uses 8-mm valvestems and the single groove is round and at the top of the keeper.

Rotators

Occasionally you may run into an A-engine truck head that has exhaust-valve rotators. These are basically very thick retainers. For any performance engine, rotators should be removed and replaced with the standard hardware discussed above.

CHAPTER 7

INTAKE MANIFOLDS

The A-engine and Magnum intake manifolds are not interchangeable without modification. The aftermarket offers intake manifolds that are machined with a dual attaching bolt pattern. However, almost all factory and aftermarket manifolds are machined specifically for the Magnum engine with vertical attaching screws or A-engine with perpendicular-to-head-face attaching screws. One unique aspect of the two related engines is that all Magnum production engines are fuel injected (multi-point injection or MPI) and most of the A-engine manifolds are carbureted. A few A-engine versions were sold in the mid- to late 1980s and early 1990s with 318 and 360 engines that used throttle body injection. These throttle bodies were small 2-barrel units and did not lend themselves to performance applications.

Production Intakes

The A-engine family has had a very wide range of intake manifolds, from small 2-barrel units, to 4-barrel units (both AFB and AVS) and large spread-bore 4-barrels (mainly the Carter Thermo-Quad), and the 6-barrel. In addition, the aftermarket has offered tunnel-rams (2- and 4-barrels), cross-rams (2- and 4-barrels), and many other options.

All A-engine production intake manifolds are made of cast iron except for the 1970 6-barrel, which was cast in aluminum. All Magnum manifolds are made of aluminum. The 340 and 360 4-barrel manifolds are good manifolds for torque and power. The 318 4-barrel manifolds (1978–1989) are basically unchanged 360 versions.

The first couple years of 273 production used vertical attaching screws, so they are unique. All other A-engine intake manifolds are interchangeable. To identify an intake manifold, say the 2-barrel versus the 4-barrel, the vertical attaching screws are easy enough to spot, If you want to tell a 1972 340 4-barrel intake from a 1974 360 4-barrel intake, I strongly recommend using the casting numbers, which are on the top of the intake and easy to see, even with the manifold installed. Both of those intakes used spread-bore carburetors (ThermoQuads), which are easy to differentiate from the 1968 340 4-barrel, which is not a spread-bore design (it has huge secondaries).

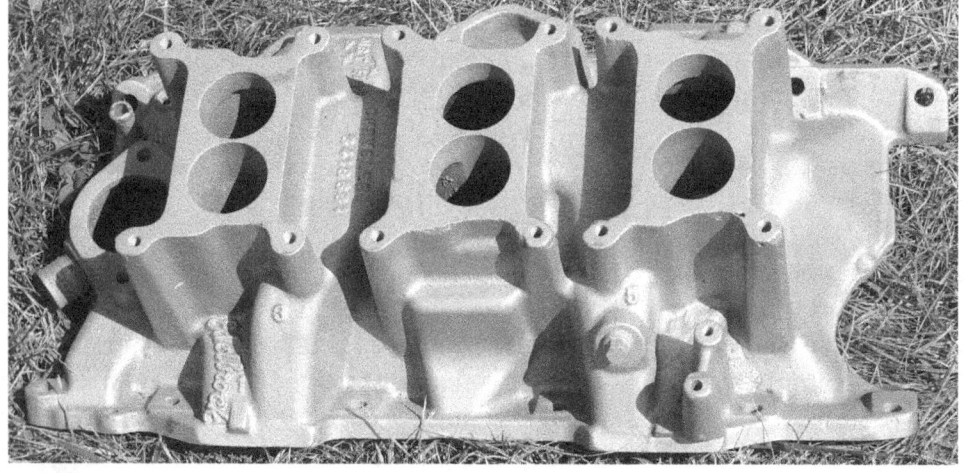
The 340 6-barrel is the most unique production intake manifold. This dual-plane manifold is aluminum and holds three inline Holley 2-barrel carburetors. The casting number, 3418681, is between the first and second carb pads on the left.

INTAKE MANIFOLDS

The high-performance 340 4-barrel intake manifold fits the Carter/Edelbrock AFB and AVS carburetors. It is cast iron and has the casting number 2531915 on the rearmost runner.

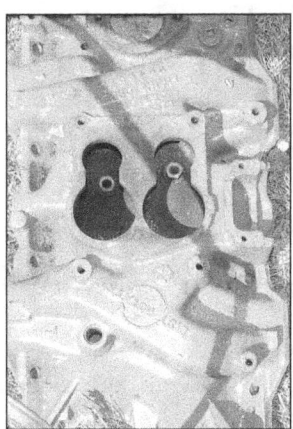

The 1972–1973 340 4-barrel engine used the Carter ThermoQuad carburetor, which had very large secondaries. Many manifolds had to be redesigned to accept these large secondaries. The cast-iron dual-plane intake has the casting number 3671918 on the front runner (shown at top).

Intake Manifold Casting Numbers

Year	Engine	Casting Number(s)	Material
1964–1965	273 2-barrel	2463252	Cast Iron
1965	273 4-barrel	2465726	Cast Iron
1966–1969	273 2-barrel	2536559	Cast Iron
1966–1967	273 4-barrel	2536563	Cast Iron
1967–1974	318 2-barrel	2468960, 2951185, 3698431	Cast Iron
1975–1979	318 2-barrel	3830941, 4100331	Cast Iron
1978–1979	318 4-barrel	3830945, 4100340	Cast Iron
1980–1989	318 2-barrel	4100331, 4201120, 4104506	Cast Iron
1980–1989	318 4-barrel	4100340, 4173915, 4323352	Cast Iron
1981–1991	318 TB	4210397, 4343969, 53006607, 53005764	Cast Iron
1968–1970	340 4-barrel	2531915, 3462848	Cast Iron
1970	340 6-barrel	3418681	Aluminum
1971–1973	340 4-barrel	3512100, 3671918	Cast Iron
1971–1978	360 2-barrel	3418435, 3698437, 3830943	Cast Iron
1974–1978	360 4-barrel	3698434, 3830945	Cast Iron
1979–1984	360 2-barrel	4100334, 4201120	Cast Iron
1979–1991	360 4-barrel	4100340, 4173915, 4323352	Cast Iron
1989–1992	360 TB	4344000	Cast Iron
1992–2003	5.2L/5.9L	53006614	Aluminum

Note: The 318-TB and 360-TB are fuel-injected engines based on throttle body injection. They are not multi-point injection systems. The 5.2L/5.9L engines are multi-point injection systems.

All production manifolds have easily visible casting numbers. Aftermarket manifolds tend to use logos, such as "Edelbrock" or "Indy." Manifolds designed by Mopar Performance typically have the "Pentastar" and/or the "Mopar" logo.

Although the Carter AFB and AVS were the most popular production 4-barrel carburetors, most of the popular aftermarket aluminum 4-barrel manifolds have both the Carter and Holley attaching bolt patterns. Edelbrock offers an adapter so the AFB/AVS/Holley carbs can be mounted on spread-bore manifolds, such as ThermoQuad versions. It also works in the opposite direction, to adapt Thermo-Quad or spread-bore Holley carbs to the AFB/AVS/Holley-style manifolds.

Unlike many production engines, the 340 and 360 cast-iron dual-plane OEM intake manifold is a very good piece, and for a long time, the aluminum dual-plane was only slightly better. The Mopar Performance aluminum dual-plane was the first step forward. Edelbrock's high-rise dual-plane is the best one today. In addition, Weiand offered an aluminum dual-plane intake for the W2 heads, which was a good option for street/strip use but availability is an issue.

Many aluminum single-plane intake manifolds have been produced and the Offy Port-O-Sonic was the original best, especially for manual transmission use, and the Holley intake was as good for the automatic and more user-friendly. The only real advance on this situation is the Mopar Performance intake, which is now the best single-plane. That statement only applies to stock cast-iron heads.

Dual-Planes

The aftermarket aluminum dual-plane intake is much better at

CHAPTER 7

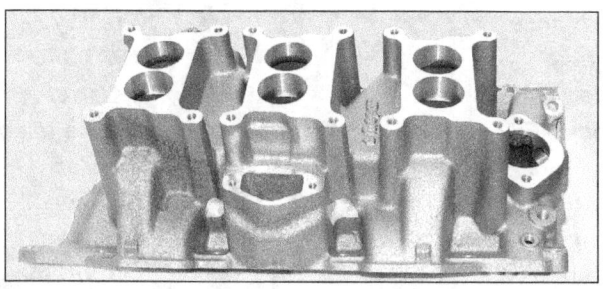

Mopar Performance and Edelbrock both produced this six-pack manifold. These are an effective upgrade from a stock cast-iron manifold, but a lot of performance can be gained through porting.

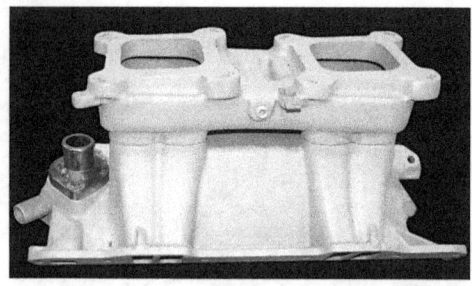

In early days, the tunnel ram intake was the top dog in the horsepower race. They sit very tall and typically required large, tall hood scoops.

making power than the production versions, but this advantage is not true of the typical Chrysler intake. With the A-engine, the cast-iron production manifold makes about the same amount of power, but the aftermarket aluminum version is easier to work with and is lighter.

The 1970 6-barrel aluminum intake manifold is also a dual-plane design and uses three Holley 2-barrel carbs. With 318-style small intake port heads, you are still better off to use the 340/360 large runner intakes even though the ports do not line up. Use 340/360 intake gaskets in this situation.

The original W2 intake was a single-plane design, but several W2 dual-plane intakes were produced in the 1990s and early 2000s. There were no dual-plane manifolds built for the race heads such as the W7, W8, and W9.

Single-Planes

For many decades, the single-plane intake has been the race manifold and the horsepower winner. But a lot of research and development has taken place to create single-plane high-performance street manifolds. The original 273 manifolds were single-planes, but they were a long way short of the 340 and 360 manifolds.

The first of the single-plane horsepower winners was an Offenhauser Port-O-Sonic, but it needed a lot (at least four) of fuel distribution dams in the plenum. Next was the Holley 4-barrel intake manifold, which was the best for automatic transmission cars. The original W2 single-plane made good power with W2 heads. The next step up was the introduction of the Mopar 340 single-plane, which was the best 4-barrel intake at the time. Next came the influx of big-port high-flow cylinder heads, so Mopar introduced a race version of the 340 single-plane. It had bigger and taller ports to work with the bigger port in the heads, such as the W5 and the W7. This was the horsepower champion but without the big ports. The original Mopar single-plane is a better choice.

The W9 equipped with the best manifolds was designed as a CNC-ported head, but there is one version that may have the best as-cast port ever produced. The intakes designed for the W9 heads were designed to work with this head (or the bigger CNC-ported versions) and were leading-edge technology at the time.

Mopar Performance made all of these intake manifolds. Also, with the race intakes, such as the W9, watch for the two deck heights used in the race blocks: standard tall, 9.56/9.60-inch, and short 9.0/9.2-inch manifold width changes.

Throttle Body Injection

The intake manifold used a throttle body injection system from 1981 through 1991 on the 318 engine and from 1989 through 1992 in the 360. This type of system works more like

Intake Port Size and Shape

The most obvious port size change is between the small-port (intake) 273-318 and the large-port 340-360. Both are basically rectangular.

The most obvious shape change is the oval-port W2, which is much wider than the 340 rectangular port (requires offset intake rocker arms). The W5 was basically a raised W2 that was rectangular.

Intake manifolds are designed to match these basic designs. When the intake port is raised, the intake manifold has to be wider. Adapter plates can also be used between the standard intake and the raised-port head. Customers have never seemed to like adapter plates so they are used in the early development process and then the manifold is made to the proper width.

With the advent of the racing W7, W8, W9 cylinder heads and availability of CNC-porting, fabricated intake manifolds became more common, and often fabricated parts are used where an adapter plate is used.

a carburetor than the newer MPI system used on the Magnum. For any performance application, remove this system and install a 4-barrel carburetor (and manifold) or the Magnum MPI system.

Magnums

All the Magnum engines (1992–2002) use the same aluminum intake manifold, and there is no big port/small port model. The standard manifold is large and shaped like a beer barrel. These manifolds also have a bolt-on breastplate on the bottom of the intake casting designed to keep hot oil off the runners.

The key issue with Magnum intake manifolds is that all Magnum engines were MPI fuel injected. Also, Magnum heads use vertical intake manifold attaching screws, while A-engines use attaching screws that are perpendicular to the cylinder head's intake face.

Intake manifolds are not interchangeable between Magnum engines and A-engines. The A-engine manifolds could be adapted by welding, but it is expensive and new manifolds are readily available.

The stock beer-barrel Magnum intake manifold is fine for stock applications, but it should be replaced for any performance project (except NHRA Stock class racing where the stock casting is required). The Mopar Performance 2-barrel single-plane intake P5007398 is a suitable replacement. It makes more mid-range and high-end performance, allows use of factory accessories, and is the same height as the stock manifold. Use installation kit P5007638 to help make the swap more user-friendly.

The stock 2-barrel throttle body flows a lot of air because it doesn't have to meter any fuel but performance customers lean toward 4-barrels. This swap requires a 4-barrel intake manifold. Do not install a 4-barrel throttle body onto any of the 2-barrel intakes. The 4-barrel aluminum single-plane intake for the Magnum heads is P5249816 for the right-hand linkage used on trucks or P4876615 for the driver-side linkage used on passenger cars. These manifolds come with a 2/4-barrel adapter so that either the production 2-barrel throttle body or an aftermarket 4-barrel throttle body can be used.

The intake runners on these two intakes are slightly larger than on the replacement 2-barrel intake discussed above and, therefore, make a small increase in power over the 2-barrel intake using the 2-barrel throttle body.

All muscle car engines used a driver-side throttle linkage. The Ram trucks that received Magnum engines use a passenger-side throttle linkage.

To convert an MPI Magnum to carburetor usage, the intake manifold has to be changed along with replacing the throttle body with a carburetor. In the mid-1990s through the early 2000s this swap was popular because Mopar Performance was selling Magnum crate engines converted to carburetor usage.

To convert a stock Magnum engine, you need a 4-barrel intake manifold (P5249501, single-plane) designed for use with a carburetor. It has the Magnum's vertical attaching screws, and the 4-barrel carburetor pad that fits the dual pattern for Holley or Carter/Edelbrock. When converting to a carburetor, you must have either a mechanical fuel pump or a fuel pressure regulator in the system for the carburetor to function properly.

Aftermarket Intakes

All aftermarket intake manifolds are made of aluminum, but that is about the only feature that they share. There are dual-planes, single-planes, race single-planes, 6-barrels, 8-barrels, and even supercharged versions. There are standard, W2, and Magnum port versions. Availability is constantly changing, so double-check any part with

The Magnum intake manifold is fuel injected; it has one injector boss at the end of each runner, just above the manifold face. They are all 2-barrel throttle body designs. The runners go up from the head face and bend over into a big half-circle. The manifold looks like a big barrel, hence its nickname, the beer-barrel.

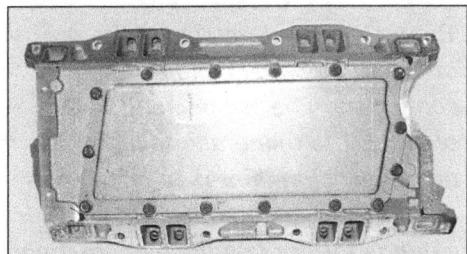

The Magnum intake manifold uses a breastplate on the bottom of the intake manifold to keep oil from hitting the bottom of the runners directly. Keeping hot oil off the bottom of the runners allows them to run cooler. This approach was used on the 426 Hemi intakes.

CHAPTER 7

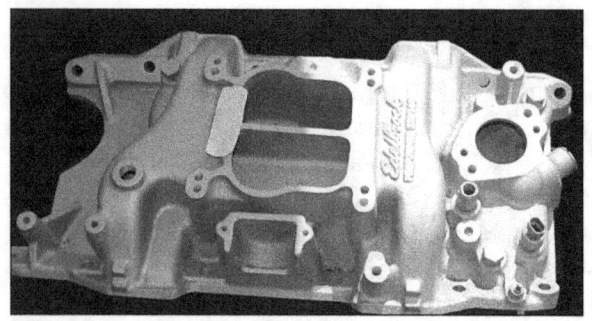

The original high-performance 340 intake manifold was the dual-plane Edelbrock LD340; it looks like this newer version for the A-engine. The LD-340 was designed for the standard Holley/AFB flange and updated to the spread-bore (shown) in the 1980s. The 340/360 4-barrel engines used ThermoQuads; this aftermarket part also has the Holley carb pattern. This would be in either package No. 1 or No. 2. However, the Edelbrock Air-Gap replaced it as the best dual-plane.

The Air-Gap is Edelbrock's high-rise dual-plane. The runners are raised up and a plate is cast across the bottom, which creates a gap for air to pass through. In addition, the plates keep hot oil off the bottom of the runners.

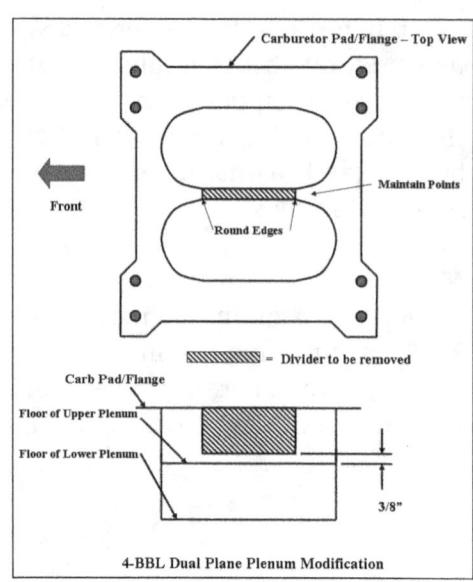

Originally, the old LD-340 aluminum Edelbrock produced the best horsepower and torque numbers. Cutting the divider down between the two plenums delivered more power. You should leave a 3/8-inch-high wall at the bottom, and leave points on either end. This mod is effective for any dual-plane.

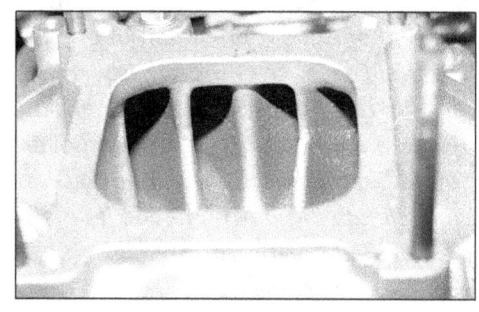

The typical single-plane intake manifold plenum has four runners coming together on one end of the plenum. The runners tend to be tall and somewhat thin. They often enter at an angle; the bottom of the runner extends farther into the plenum than does the top of the runner.

the latest information on what is in stock, what's new, and what has dropped from sight.

Dual-Planes

Edelbrock made the original dual-plane, aluminum intake manifold for the 1968 340, called the LD-340. It's now called the Performer 340/360 (revised and updated). This is a good manifold and was the standard performance part for many years. The trick with aluminum dual-plane intakes to make more power for performance projects is to mill down the divider between the driver's and passenger's sides. This trick works with any dual-plane.

The Edelbrock Performance RPM 340/360 makes more power than the standard Performer because it has somewhat larger runners (1.01 x 2.17 versus .97 x 1.95 inches) and is taller or has a higher rise (raised by about .75 to .72 inch actually).

The RPM Air-Gap 340/360 is the next intake on the performance ladder. It has about the same height and uses similar runner size as the Performer RPM, but it has a plate cast across the bottom of the manifold that keeps the hot oil off the bottom of the intake runners. Thus, it creates an air gap between the bottom of the manifold and the bottom of the intake runners. Edelbrock makes the RPM Air-Gap Magnum, and at this time, it's the only known aftermarket dual-plane for Magnum engines. It is designed for use with carburetors.

Single-Planes

Single-plane manifolds used to be considered a race-only component; low-RPM throttle response was quite poor because engines typically load up on fuel. Improved designs have now made the notion no longer valid. Edelbrock offers the Torker II and the Victor for standard 340/360 rectangular-port heads and a Victor W2 for oval-port heads. It also offers a Super Victor, which is an air-gap design and is about 1.3 inches taller than the Victor. Indy Heads offers large-port (and tall) single-planes

INTAKE MANIFOLDS

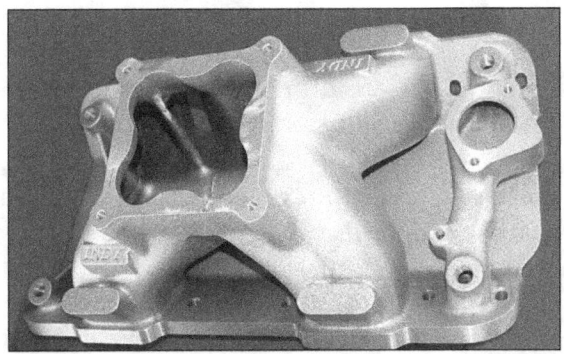

Indy Heads also offers a 4-barrel intake for the giant 4500 Holley carburetor, which is rated at 1,000 cfm, 1,300 cfm, and higher (for one carb). In the past few years, Holley and Quick Fuel have made smaller versions of this big carb. The spacing is still the same, but the airflow drops; this manifold has many more options with these new carbs.

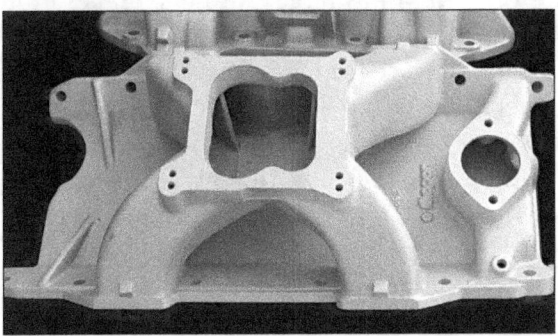

When it was introduced, this was the top performing single-plane intake manifold for the stock 340/360 heads. It was used with the most common 318/340/360 carburetor: the ThermoQuad. It has the dual-carb pattern so other carbs can be used.

When it was introduced, this big-port single-plane intake made the most horsepower; it was designed with bigger ports for use with the big-port heads. Fuel injection bosses were added in preparation for what was coming: the Magnum engines.

Racing builders fabricate intake manifolds for many of the special applications such as big-port heads, raised-port heads, very big carbs (a Holley 4500 is shown), or multiple carbs. This version is considered a 4-barrel tunnel ram because the runners go straight up from the head. (Photo Courtesy L. Lawson)

This manifold was the horsepower champ because it was designed for the W9 heads. Note that the water crossover at the front of the typical small-block intake is not there. Race engine builders created a water manifold, actually a fancy pipe, which attached directly to the heads. In addition, the ports are raised so far that a plate was designed to fit below this manifold to seal the tappet chamber and keep hot oil off the runners.

for standard rectangular-port heads, along with 6- and 8-barrel two-piece single-plane manifolds in several versions.

Multi-Carbs

Several manufacturers offer multi-carb intakes for Mopar big-blocks, but only Indy Heads currently offers a two-piece, aluminum single-plane intake manifold for use with the 6-barrel (three 2-barrels) and the 8-barrel (two 4-barrels).

Tunnel Ram and 4500

The typical tunnel ram intake is designed for using two 4-barrel carburetors in-line; the 4500 is the largest single carburetor offered by Holley and Quick-Fuel. The 4500 does not fit the standard Holley 4-barrel carb pad attaching pattern. These manifolds have been made as castings in the past but are probably fabricated today. Indy Heads offers a 4500 cast manifold.

Fuel Distribution

With any carburetor system, fuel distribution issues are common with the intake manifold, whether cast or fabricated. These problems can be identified by using a dynamometer. The solution is always to put dams (wooden popsicle sticks) in the floor of the plenum. It is an issue with single-plane intakes but is not an issue with dual-plane intakes. Chrysler/Mopar used to provide this information (where to put the sticks), but hasn't done so for the past few years.

Fuel distribution is the basic problem. When you run an intake and carburetor on an engine, all eight cylinders do not receive the same amount of fuel and air; some are rich and some are lean. In general, the overall fuel level is adjusted upward until some cylinders are on longer lean, but that leaves the few rich cylinders. If these cylinders can be brought down to the proper fuel/air ratio, the engine makes more power. This is one aspect of dyno testing that can be a real bonus with any single-plane intake manifold.

Manifold Selection

Because of the many possible choices this is almost as difficult as selecting cylinder heads and camshafts. Popular manifolds are kept in circulation while unpopular manifolds are dropped from production; availability is constantly changing. The same is true for cylinder heads. In addition to all that, fabricated manifolds can be expensive.

The dual-plane is the best street manifold and the Mopar Performance dual-plane has been the best of them. The Edelbrock Performer RPM has larger runners, makes more power, and is definitely the best choice for larger displacements, such as 390 to 400 inches.

Magnum

The best MPI intake for the Magnum is the Mopar Performance design. The traditional aftermarket doesn't offer many MPI manifolds so most of these options are based on the Mopar Performance line. Also, many MP manifolds have fuel-injected bosses (not machined),

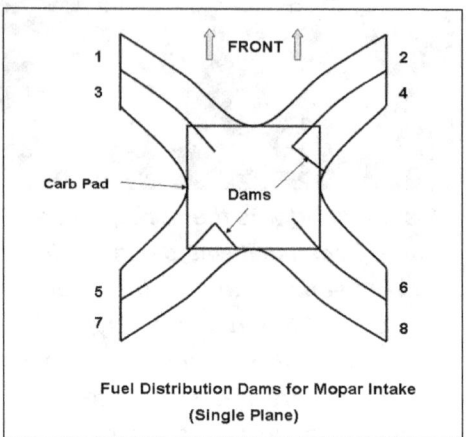

Fuel distribution must be measured on a dyno. Once you have it, the dams are unique to that specific manifold. This fuel distribution setup is designed for a Mopar single-plane intake (PN P4552891). It has two dams, each 3/8-inch high. I suggest that you make them out of wood and epoxy them into place. They are called popsicle sticks because that is what you start with.

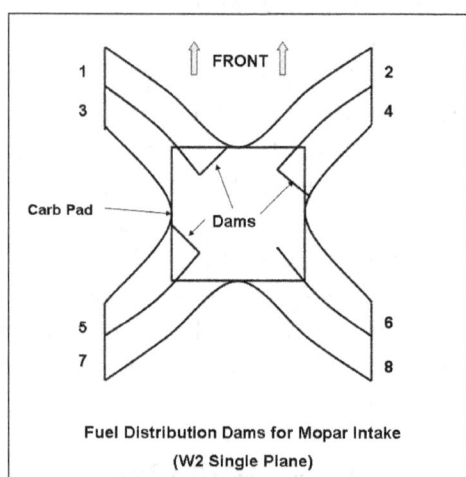

This is the fuel distribution setup for the W2 single-plane (PN P4529408). It requires three dams (or popsicle sticks), each 3/8-inch high. Use epoxy to hold them in place.

My Performance Packages

In an effort to tie all of the engine hardware together, I created five packages, which vary from 250 to more than 700 hp, and all are intended for street/strip applications.

	Best Head	Best Carb (cfm)	Best Intake
Package No. 1	Bracket valve job (backcut valves) with 2.02 intake valve	750	Mod DP
Package No. 2	Edelbrock aluminum or Indy or B1-BA	750	SP or Hi-Rise DP (Edelbrock)
Package No. 3	Edelbrock aluminum or Indy or B1-BA with bowl work	750	SP
Package No. 4	Edelbrock aluminum or Indy or B1-BA with intermediate CNC-porting	850	SP
Package No. 5	Indy or B1-BA fully CNC-ported	850	Fab SP

Note: Any one of these packages could use a 6-barrel system or a 950/1,050-cfm carb.

which can be machined for fuel injectors. Edelbrock and Mopar both offer carburetor versions; a tie.

Single-Plane Intake for Carter AFB/AVS and Holley 4-Barrel

The single-plane is basically a race or horsepower manifold with the possible exception of 390- to 400-ci engines. The two styles of standard 4-barrel carburetors (the Holley and the Carter) work well on the single-plane. The Mopar single-plane is overall best, but the race version is best for ported-head engines and larger displacements. If this manifold isn't available, the Edelbrock Super Victor (air gap) is best.

6-Barrel: Only the standard manifold is available from Mopar. For larger displacements and/or ported-head engines, the Indy Heads two-piece would be interesting.

8-Barrel: Today's choices are limited, but the Indy Heads 2 x 4–barrel intake looks interesting for larger displacement engines.

Manifold Prep

Chapters 1 and 5 discuss various milling ratios: deck, intake face, and china wall. If this milling specification is calculated properly, the intake should drop into place and everything fits and lines up. The first clue that something might be wrong is if the screws do not fit into the screw holes easily. Installing the intake gaskets loosely against the head and carefully placing the manifold on top is the usual way to verify this. For the second part of this checkout procedure, see "Port Matching" below.

Porting Matching

Any time that you port the cylinder head or install a new, high-flow cylinder head (which has bigger intake ports), you should consider matching the ports in the intake manifold with the ports in the head. In most cases, the ports in the head are larger. Also in most cases, port matching is only done on the last inch or two of the manifold's intake runner. Caution: With some of the big-port high-flow heads now available, not all intake runners can be ported to match. For example, you can't port standard 340/360 intakes to match oval-port W2 heads. The manifold must be welded up to allow this porting to occur.

A-engine cylinder heads use a heat-crossover in the center of the intake manifold. The Magnum engine and the W2 heads do not have a heat crossover passage. On A-engines, it was common to block the heat crossover passage at the manifold face to make more power. However, driveability suffers, so if you plan on true street driving or cruising, you want to keep the heat crossover working.

Carburetors

I cover only 4-barrel carburetors for max performance. Although there are several manufacturers, Holley, Quick-Fuel, and the Carter/Edelbrock families provide the best performance and tuning options. Chrysler/Mopar mostly used Carter production 4-barrel carburetors with a few Holleys sprinkled in over the years. A few Rochester carbs were installed on trucks in the 1980s, but they do not seem to be very popular today.

With the introduction of fuel injection across the V-8 production engines, Carter Carburetor went bankrupt. A few years later, Edelbrock bought all the tooling and rights to the AFB and AVS carburetors and they are now readily available along with all the service and tuning parts that you might need.

Before you order a carb, determine which one is best for your engine package. Your carb size must match the amount of air that the engine can flow. If the carb is too big,

---

Carb Math

You can use the following formula to predict your best carb size (based on airflow):

$$CCFM = D \times MRPM \div 3{,}456$$

Where:
CCFM = carburetor flow in CFM
D = displacement of the engine in cubic inches
MRPM = maximum RPM of engine
3,456 = mathematical constant

For example, if your engine is a 340 V-8 and you use a hydraulic cam (maybe 6,000 rpm on the street), your carb CFM should be 590 (340 x 6,000 ÷ 3,456). The small AFB and AVS 4-barrel production carbs were probably about 600–650 cfm.

If your engine is a stroker with 400 ci and a mechanical or roller cam (maybe 8,000 rpm), your carb CFM should be 926 (400 x 8,000 ÷ 3,456).

CHAPTER 7

the engine stumbles and floods at lower RPM. If the carb is too small, the engine does not provide enough fuel at high RPM. When selecting a carb for a street engine, bigger isn't always better so don't make the classic mistake of buying a carb that's too large for your engine package.

Carb Selection

Carburetor selection should be based mainly on the engine's cubic inches, but usage (street) and other hardware (heads and cams) can also impact the selection. The primary factor in recommending a carburetor is availability, along with service parts. One of the problems is that many of the special sizes of carburetors are no longer available.

273: The 273 uses the smallest 4-barrel carburetor possible. Because the AVS is a very good street carburetor, I recommend the 500-cfm Edelbrock AVS.

318: I wanted to recommend a 600-cfm carb for this size engine but Edelbrock doesn't make one, so I recommend the 650-cfm Edelbrock AVS. The best 4-barrel choice might be the small ThermoQuad (1⅜-inch primaries) but they aren't readily available (perhaps from Summit).

340 and 360: I recommend the vacuum secondary 750-cfm Holley (or Quick Fuel) or the 800-cfm Edelbrock AVS. You only need about 650 to 700 cfm for the 340/360 ci, but they are not available from Holley or Quick Fuel with vacuum secondaries. Therefore, the closest vacuum secondary carb is the 750 (as with any street/strip cam or head).

If you have a cam with less valve lift than .475 inch and stock-type cast-iron heads (intake flow less than 200 cfm), you should consider the 650-cfm AVS or a 650-cfm vacuum secondary Holley/Quick Fuel. The ThermoQuad provides exceptional street performance, and you can find remanufactured units at Summit Racing.

The Carter ThermoQuad is a great street carb but new ones are difficult to find and tuning parts are even more difficult to find. You can adapt these big secondary carbs to a standard intake manifold by using the Edelbrock adapter plate and flipping it over.

Most current performance intake manifolds are straight and do not feature wide or spread secondaries. From 1971 on, production carburetors had very large secondaries, which required the manifolds to reflect this size change. Most Chrysler production carbs of this era were called ThermoQuads (made by Carter). The Holley version was called the SpreadBore. The GM version was called the QuadraJet (made by Rochester). These are great street carbs but are difficult to find today.

The readily available carbs today, Holley 4-barrel and the Carter/Edelbrock AFB and AVS, do not have giant secondaries. Why? Production had to meet emissions requirements in the 1970s and didn't want customers complaining that their 4-barrel ran like a 2-barrel. The small primaries in these carbs allowed them to meet emissions standards and have reasonable driveability. The giant secondaries increased airflow and kept

The Carter and Edelbrock (shown) 4-barrel AFB and AVS carbs are readily available. They have lots of parts for tuning and adjusting the carb to your specific engine package. I prefer the AVS versions for street applications.

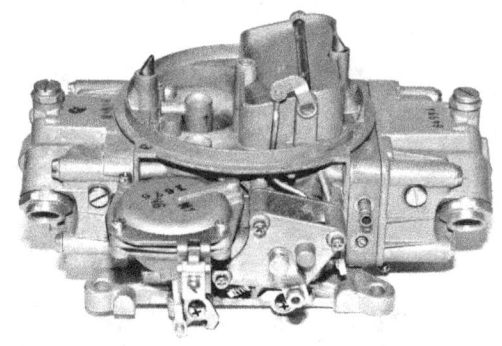

Holley and Quick Fuel (shown) carbs are the standard racing carburetor in classes for which you do not have to use a stock or production carburetor. For street use and any automatic transmission use, I recommend the vacuum secondary versions. This one is a 750-cfm and is a good choice for 340/360-and-larger engines.

INTAKE MANIFOLDS

The Holley (shown) or Quick Fuel double-pumper carburetor has been the standard racing carburetor for many years. It has mechanical secondaries and works very well with manual transmissions.

The Holley three-deuce (three 2-barrels) or 6-barrel setup is one of the best street induction systems based on a carburetor. The two end carburetors are basically the same and have the vacuum pot from the 4-barrel carbs. The vacuum source is the black hose that runs from the center carb to each end carb; it connects just to the right of the vacuum pot. The second black hose leading from the center carb is the ignition's vacuum advance hose.

Carburetion for Magnums

All Magnum engines come with MPI (fuel injection) but some enthusiasts may want to convert these engines to use a carburetor. Manifold availability seems limited with the MPI system, but there are several options for the engines based on carburetor usage. There is no mechanical pump on the Magnum so you have to solve that problem first (convert back to the longer cam and A-engine front cover or install a fuel regulator to reduce the pressure to 5–7 psi). At that point, the carburetor could be selected based on engine size.

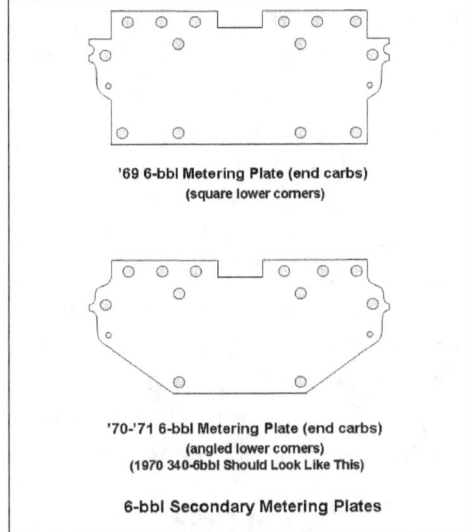

The 6-barrel carb system for the 340 has different metering plates inside the end carbs. The 1969 model has square corners (top); the 1970 and 1971 models (bottom) are the same for both the 340 and 440. The 340 has a unique setup in that the front carb has a fuel distribution tab on the nozzle. You might consider using 440 carbs for a large-displacement small-block. Regardless, the 340 jets and metering plates have to be changed and the fuel distribution should be redone for a 60-ci change.

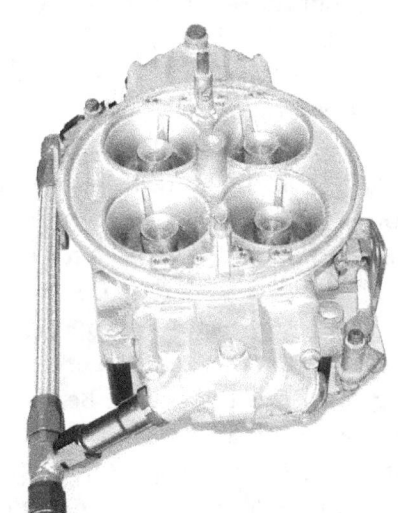

The Holley/Quick Fuel 4500 carburetor is the largest carburetor built and it flows giant amounts of air. The 4500s flow more air than many dual 4-barrel setups. They are rated at 1,100 cfm, 1,300 cfm, and more.

performance up. Edelbrock makes an adapter for this situation.

The other really great street package is the 6-barrel (carbs still available from Mopar and Holley). Recommended for all setups, it is the best street system until MPI (the Magnum engines). However, cost could be an issue; one intake manifold plus three carbs, linkage, and air cleaners can add up. With three carbs it is more complicated than a single 4-barrel. (All the tricks are in the tuning section in Chapter 10.)

There is no SP for the 6-barrel, so packages No. 4 and No. 5 might not be available and may need to be fabricated.

390 and 400: These big-inch engines demand a lot of airflow, so the 800-cfm Edelbrock AVS is the best 4-barrel carb; the 750-cfm vacuum secondary Holley is also a good choice. The 6-barrel is an excellent choice.

If you have cams bigger than .480 valve lift and heads that flow more air than 240/250 cfm, you might look at bigger carbs such as the 900/950-cfm Quick Fuel units or the Indy Heads intake with two 4-barrel carbs.

The 900/950-cfm units bolt to the standard carb pad but are double-pumpers. You can use a double-pumper, but you typically have to use more stall speed in the converter or more gear (axle ratio) or both.

420+: These engines can use more airflow, but the 750-cfm vacuum secondary Holley and the 800-cfm AVS are the baseline units. The 6-barrel is an option. The winner might be a 4500 carb (a small one at around 1,000 cfm) on a fabricated manifold or an 8-barrel on an Indy Heads manifold.

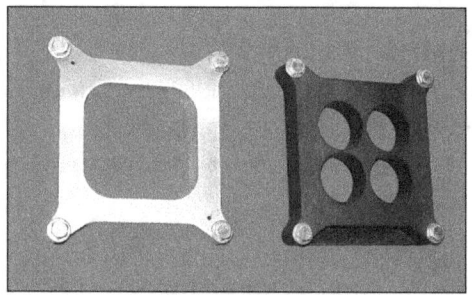

A carb spacer can be a good tool for tuning. You want one that is plastic or phenolic material. One-hole spacers (on left) and four-hole spacers (on right) are available, as well as 1/2-inch-thick spacers and 1-inch-thick spacers. Be mindful of hood clearance issues if you use carb spacers that are 1 or more inches tall.

The standard AFB or AVS 1/4-inch plastic carb spacer is on the right and the 3/8-inch-thick fiber ThermoQuad spacer is on the left. Fiber carb spacers are a good choice, if you can find them. If you have a choice, do not use metal carb spacers.

Carb Pad Gaskets

Most of the Holley and Carter/Edelbrock carburetor gaskets have been common so that both bolt patterns are in the gasket. I recommend using a plastic or phenolic spacer between the carburetor and the intake manifold with a gasket on each side. Edelbrock has a good selection of gaskets and spacers. Only a 1/4-inch is needed but 1/2- and 1-inch phenolic spacers are more common.

Throttle Body

Unlike the stock 2-barrel carburetor, the Magnum 2-barrel throttle body flows a fair amount of air, about as much as a small 4-barrel carburetor. When the Magnum MPI system was introduced, several companies offered modified throttle bodies (52 mm), but those options seem to have disappeared.

2-Barrel

All Magnum MPI systems use a 2-barrel throttle body. It has a 50-mm bore size (1.967 inches). Slightly larger throttle bodies do not seem to be commercially available. One possibility is to have your machine shop bore out the throttle body to a larger size and use larger throttle blades. Be cautious because the casting isn't that thick (around 52 mm, or 2.047 inches), but you can use 52-mm throttle blades or perhaps Edelbrock 2.00-inchers.

4-Barrel

Although there seems to be only one 2-barrel throttle body, many 4-barrel throttle bodies are made by many different manufacturers. The standard carb pad 4-barrel throttle body (1.75-inch bores) flows about 1,000 cfm. Companies such as Edelbrock, Indy Heads, and Wilson Manifolds offer aluminum 4-barrel throttle bodies in the 1,000- to 1,600-cfm area. Caution: Some of these big throttle bodies are made for the 4500 Holley carb pad (big carb pad) rather than the standard 4150 pad (square-bore pad for 1.75-throttle bores).

The 4-barrel throttle body flows lots of air but cannot be used on the 2-barrel intake manifolds. You must use the 4-barrel intake manifold with a 4-barrel throttle body. You can use the 2-barrel throttle body on the 4-barrel intake but not the other way around.

The smaller carb pad seems to gives airflow ratings in the 1,000- to 1,200-cfm range. The bigger numbers are based on the 4500 pad and 2-inch-and-larger bore sizes (1,600 cfm and up). For a street setup, the 1,000-cfm package is more than enough.

Fuel Pump

To convert a Magnum MPI engine to a mechanical fuel pump, swap the cam and front cover for the A-engine parts. The front cover also requires the water pump to be swapped to the A-engine version. The MPI electric fuel pump is located in the gas tank. The aftermarket has upgrades for electric fuel pumps for use with multi-point fuel injection (AEM). If you swap cams to the A-engine versions to gain the mechanical pump capability, remember that A-engine

INTAKE MANIFOLDS

tappets do *not* oil the valvetrain through the pushrods. Use Jeep V-8 (360, 390, 401) tappets to resolve this.

Fuel Injection

All Magnum engines were fuel injected (MPI) and most A-engines were carbureted. Once you have fuel injection, it is not one size fits all. The ECM receives input from about seven sensors to control the fuel and ignition systems. The intake manifold, the eight injectors, and the fuel rail are only the beginning. (These details are covered in Chapter 10.)

Nitrous

Nitrous kits come in many sizes based on how much horsepower you want to add: 100-hp kits, 250-hp kits, and others. You also have many ways to inject the nitrous into the engine, such as directly into the intake runner or at the carburetor flange, by using special plates (carb spacer) between the carb and the intake manifold.

The direct injector into the runner versions require the manifold to be modified for injectors, which sounds more expensive. The carb plate versions are much easier to install because they fit between the carb and the intake, don't require any machining, and have eight fewer injectors. (See Chapter 10 for more tips.)

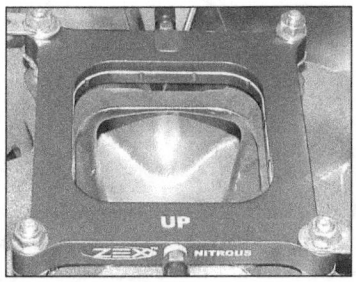

The nitrous plate kit inserts between the bottom of the carburetor or throttle body and the top of the intake manifold. The nitrous and fuel are injected into the manifold plenum from drilled holes around the outside. These systems are easy to install on an existing engine or intake manifold.

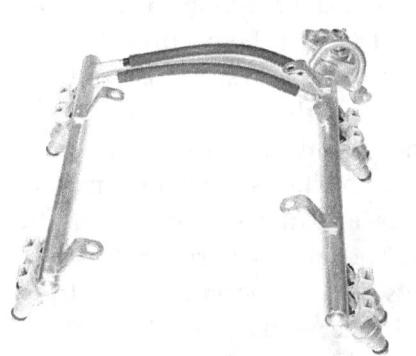

The Magnum fuel injectors' electrical connectors plug into the yellow square in the center or at the top of the injector housing (not shown). The fuel rail and the eight fuel injectors should be removed from the intake as a unit. Once removed, you can take each injector off individually by removing the clip and pulling the injector seal out of the fuel rail. As the engine's horsepower goes up, you may have to install larger injectors.

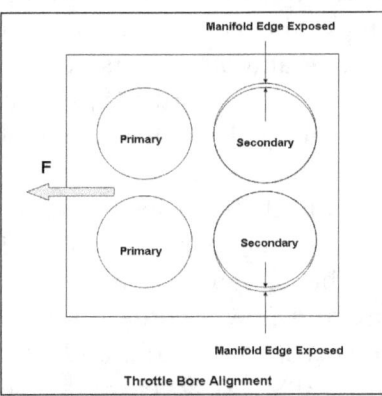

As you gather the hardware for the engine assembly, you want to check the carburetor (or throttle body) against the pad on the intake manifold. Install the carb without a gasket and then install the four screws finger tight. Next, open the throttles to wide-open position and look down the throttle bores to see if any part of the intake manifold pad is visible. This usually occurs on the secondary side and not on the primary side. If you can see the manifold, move the carb around on the screws and see if you can eliminate the overhang. If not, remove the carb, mark the exposed area, and take to the machine shop to be fixed.

Superchargers and Turbos

During the past few years all three major American auto manufacturers have introduced supercharged engines. Whether this OEM development is the cause or not, there seems to be a lot of aftermarket interest with superchargers and supercharging kits popping up on many projects. Indy Heads offers supercharger manifolds and many superchargers are available.

Supercharger manufacturers offer kits with all the necessary parts. Turbo manufacturers, which include Precision Turbo, Garrett, Turbonetics, and BorgWarner, make all the parts but don't put them together in kits.

On the other side, there are many turbocharger manufacturers but not many kit manufacturers. (More tips in Chapter 10.)

Final Installation and Prep

Intake manifolds are pretty much "buy it and bolt it on." The key item to check is the manifold fit/alignment and the port alignment.

The last thing to check on the manifold is how the throttle bores line up over the carburetor pad. It's generally not an issue with dual-plane intakes or with Magnum engines, but you need to check single-plane 4-barrels and the end carbs on a 6-barrel.

CHAPTER 8

OILING SYSTEM

The oiling system isn't as high profile or glamorous as heads, cams, and other parts. But as we all know, it plays a vital role in the performance and longevity of an engine. The oiling system touches all of those parts. Clearance is an issue for street cars and street/strip vehicles, so you have to make sure that the oil pan can't hit the ground. Also, make sure that the pan fits in the engine compartment, clearing the headers and steering linkage.

Although it may not be one of the leading topics at a bench-racing session, if the oiling system fails, you will have a catastrophic engine failure, which is very expensive. You need to bring the oiling system along as you develop power: improve the head, improve the oiling. When building a max-performance engine, you should upgrade the oiling system. Your first priority is to install a higher-capacity oil pan and a wet-sump oil pump for higher pressure and/or volume. The next priority is to add baffles to the pan (sump area) to control the oil.

The A-engine and Magnum engine bottom ends are very similar. The oil pump (not shown) mounts to the number-5 cap at the rear and the oil filter mounts directly to the outside of the block at the rear (shown at right).

Oiling Hardware

A-engines and Magnum engines use very similar oiling systems, especially in the short block. Valvetrain oiling, however, is different. The A-engine oils through drilled passages in the block and heads to the valvetrain; the Magnum oils the valvetrain through the pushrods.

The oiling system is actually involved with every part in the engine assembly. Many of the paths that the oil takes from one part to another are in the block and the crank. The oil also lubricates the cam, tappets, valves, rocker arms, pistons, rods. Rocker arms and valve tips are the most difficult parts to properly lubricate. Oil galleys drilled into the block move the oil from the pump to the bearings and other parts needing lubrication. These drilled passages must be plugged to direct the oil where it is needed.

The camshaft propels the oil pump drive, and that drives the oil pump. The oil pump puts out oil pressure and flow volume based on engine speed, low at idle and high at higher RPM. As a general guideline for oiling systems, you want the oil pump to deliver 10 psi per 1,000

OILING SYSTEM

The oil pump bolts to the number-5 main and the oil pick-up screws into the oil pump housing. Here, the pick-up's location is a function of the sump in the oil pan. (Photo Courtesy R. Koffel)

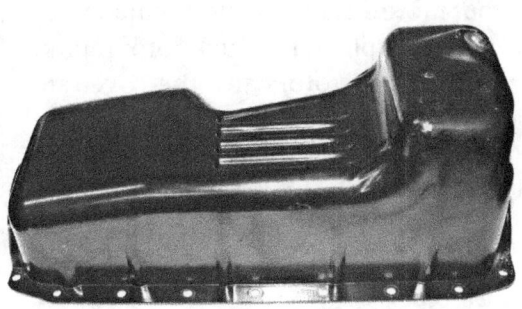

The oil pan has a sump that must be compatible with the engine compartment and vehicle chassis. The sump can be in the middle, at the rear (shown), or at the front, which is rare. Another component of an oil pan is the end seal radius. The 273, 318, and 340 share one set of radii and the 360 radius is smaller. These pans are not interchangeable.

rpm. Any internal oil leak(s) drops this number or makes it more difficult to obtain. Therefore, trying to control internal oil leaks is one of the key aspects of the oiling system but has little to do directly with the oiling system parts.

One of the first items to address is bearing clearances. Try to use new parts to get the bearing clearances back to the original numbers, which is especially true of the thrust bearing (number-3). Stock clearances are fine, but you don't want ones with .002 or .003 extra because you can't get any oil pressure with them.

The next internal oil leak is the rod side clearance. There are four of them. The specification is .006 to

Oil Path

Once filtered, the oil comes back into the block and up to the main oil galley on the passenger's side of the block. From the main oil galley it feeds all passenger-side tappets and the main journals starting at the rear: number-5 first, then -4, -3, -2, -1 in order. From the block's main bearings, it goes to the rod journals through drilled passages in the crank. At the same time, the oil goes from the top of the main bearing shell up to the cam bearings. The driver-side tappets are oiled after the front main bearings; the oil path crosses over at the front of the block.

Oiling the valvetrain is different in Magnum and A-engines. The Magnum engine oils the valvetrain through the pushrods. The oil pressure in the main oil galley forces oil through a small hole in the side and then into the tappets. It then goes into the hollow pushrod and to the rocker arm. The valve is oiled from the tip of the rocker.

The A-engine uses a different path. Oil that comes to the cam bearings (number-2 and -4) is routed around those journals (grooves) and/or through the number-2 and -4 journals (drilled holes) to a drilled hole in the head. The head has a drilled hole to match the one in the block and the oil comes up the pedestal and into the rocker shaft. The rocker shaft is hollow and distributes the oil to each rocker (drilled hole) and the rocker arm oils the pushrod end and the valve tip. From the cylinder heads, the cam and tappets, the crank and rods, the oil drains back into the pan and hence into the sump to start the cycle over again.

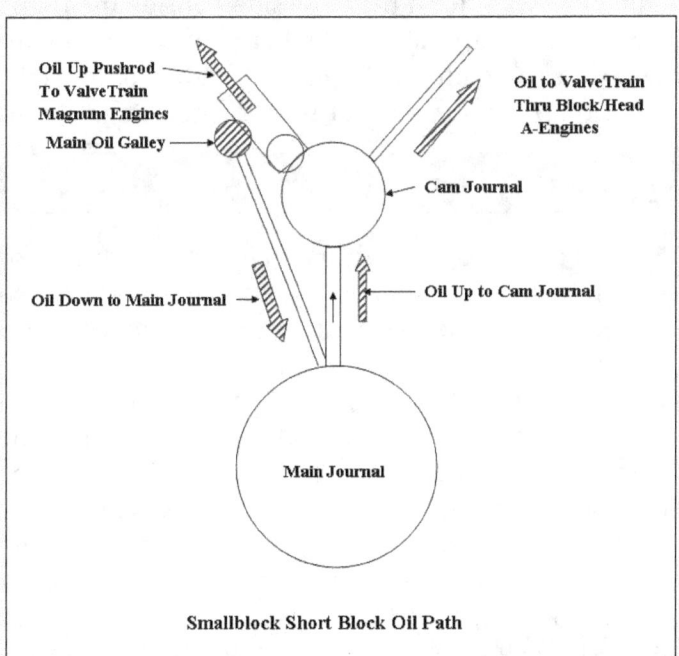

The oil path on the top left is the Magnum and the path on the top right is the A-engine. In both cases, the main oil galley feeds the crank's main journal, which then feeds up to the cam journal.

CHAPTER 8

A press-in plug goes into this oil passage at the rear of the block (see Chapter 1 for more details). The plug is about 2 1/8 to 2 5/16 inches up from the bottom of the block (without the cap) and 7 1/2 to 7 11/16 inches down from the china wall. The plug forces oil from the oil pump to the oil filter and then to the main oil galley.

Replacing the oil pressure relief spring inside the pump housing will increase the oil pump's output pressure. Note that the high-pressure spring increases the oil pressure by about 30 percent. The spring is behind the cotter pin and cap at the bottom of the housing.

.014 inch. In used engines, it could be as high as .020 inch. On a new engine, you want it on the close side (.006 to .010 inch), not on the high side (.012 to .014 inch or higher).

On the A-engine, do not restrict the oil to the heads or valvetrain. On the Magnum, the hydraulic tappet is installed with the oil hole away from the block wall (toward the center). (See Chapter 4.)

Oil Pump

The small-block oil pump sits inside the oil pan at the rear on the number-5 main cap. The oil pick-up threads directly into the oil pump housing. Both high-volume and high-pressure oil pumps are readily available for the Mopar small-block (Melling). I recommend upgrading to a high-volume pump if you are replacing the heads and cam.

To increase the volume of the stock-style oil pump, the rotors inside the pump are increased in thickness, which means that the pump pushes out more oil at the same engine speed. To accomplish this thick-rotor pump, both pump rotors and the cover are replaced. Kits for this conversion are no longer available. When building a high-performance street engine, always install a new oil pump.

Gerotor

Production small-block oil pumps are Gerotor designs (also spelled Ge-rotor) with four inner lobes and five outer lobes. Gerotor-style pumps are very efficient. Small-block pumps use a wide, rounded rotor lobe design; Milodon (performance oil pumps with Gerotor design) uses a similar four/five inner/outer rotor design but the lobes resemble a

Cut the Leaks

You do not want to reduce the amount of oil that the oil pump delivers to the engine for lubrication. What you want to do is reduce the loss of oil pressure/flow, which are actual internal leaks. All bearings are leaks but they are designed leaks that provide lubrication; you want to control them, not eliminate them. Control the clearance and control the amount of leakage. The main purpose of cutting down on internal leaks is to deliver more oil to the crank and bearings.

After the various clearances related to the crank and rods, the next most common internal oil leaks are associated with the tappets, 16 small leaks. The focus of this book is street performance and the vast majority of street performance engines are going to use hydraulic cams. Two solutions to the tappet leakage are available: sleeve the tappets or tube the passenger-side oil galley. The copper tube package (PN P4120603) is still available from Mopar but I do not recommend it because of hydraulic cam use. That leaves sleeving the tappet, which is a machine shop operation and may be expensive.

A sleeve in the tappet bore also cuts into the main oil galley and restricts it, which is not desired. To solve that problem, enlarge the passenger-side oil galley (to about 5/8 inch) past the tappets for cylinder number-8 and -6, or about halfway. You need to use one or two sizes larger than the stock main oil galley size (about 1/2 inch). Then tap the end with the bigger thread size and larger end plug. Finally, have the machine shop drill a small hole through the new sleeve and into the main oil galley again so the hydraulic tappets work.

Drilling out the passenger-side main oil galley past cylinders number-8 and -6 one or two drill sizes might be a good tip for any performance engine. ■

OILING SYSTEM

The Gerotor pump has four inner lobes and five outer lobes. It is difficult to describe the shape of the lobe but it is a good oil pump design.

pyramid. (The name Gerotor stands for generated rotor.)

Pressure

The universal guideline for oil pump pressure is 10 psi per 1,000 rpm. The typical stock pump probably puts out about 50 psi. The high-pressure relief spring is maybe 30 percent higher. Do not remove the oil pressure relief spring unless you have a new one *and* the press-in retainer cup in case the original is damaged during removal or use.

Oil viscosity has an effect on oil pressure. Engine/bearing clearances also have an effect on oil pressure; close clearances help, wide clearances hurt.

Clearances

The production small-block oil pump provides adequate performance for street use if it is not worn-out or damaged. The clearance between the outer rotor and the oil pump's main housing should be less than .014 inch. The clearance between the inner rotor's lobes and the outer rotor at the tip should be less than .010 inch. With the cover off, the clearance between a steel straightedge placed across the face and the rotors should be less than .004 inch.

The pump must turn freely once assembled. If it passes these tests, it can be reinstalled.

Pick-Up

The oil pick-up threads into the main pump housing of the oil pump, but where the inlet sits (the other end of the pick-up) is a function of the oil pan and the pan's sump location and depth. If you install a pan with a dropped sump (Milodon or Moroso), you must install a new pick-up from same manufacturer.

If you switch the sump location, you must have a new pick-up. The inlet for the oil pick-up should be just above the bottom of the pan/sump and toward the center/rear wall of the sump (passenger-side rear wall in a drag engine). Do not hand fabricate your oil pick-up; buy from oil system manufacturers such as Milodon or Moroso.

Breathers and the PCV

The breathers and the PCV (positive crankcase ventilation) valve are mounted in the valvecover (one on the driver's side and one on the passenger's side, typically) but should be considered part of the oiling system. Breathers and the PCV valve have been used with all production engines since the late 1960s.

The basic circulation system uses the breather in the valvecover to collect the exhaust gases that are in the valvecovers and the crankcase and returns them to the air cleaner. The PCV valve is designed to function with the breather (usually mounted on opposite valvecover). The PCV valve opens when there is a positive pressure in the crankcase, which indicates blow-by, and blow-by is not desired in any performance engine.

Oil

Adding oil to the engine is probably the last thing that you do in the engine assembly process; if you forget this step, you could be in some serious trouble. Because it is done last, you may not give the oil selection as much thought as you should. Today the oil replacement cycle (miles between oil changes) has increased from about 3,000 miles to 5,000 or even 10,000. Oils are better and engines are better. The last Magnum engine in 2002–2003 was probably not new enough for this trend (it started around 2010–2014).

The first choice for oil today is to use standard or synthetic. The next choice is which viscosity to use. Some of today's lower-weight synthetic oils offer thinner options for viscosity than used to be available ("O-" and "5-" weight oils).

Break-in Oil

As you begin to assemble the engine (when you install the camshaft into the block and when you install the tappets onto the cam and

---

ZDDP Oil for Cams

Mechanical cams have more aggressive profiles and higher spring loads and tend to have scuffing issues first. With all the latest technology, hydraulic cam manufacturers have pushed the aggressive scale. If you use these cams (mechanical or hydraulic) you should consider using high-zinc oils.

CHAPTER 8

into the tappet bores), you usually use an engine break-in oil or cam break-in oil. Chrysler/Mopar used Lubrizol oil for this purpose. Crane and Comp Cams have their own cam break-in lubes. In some cases, the cam manufacturer recommends a cam paste.

Any cam break-in oil requires that the oil be changed after a short break-in cycle.

Oil Filter

The regular oil filter attaches to the outside of the cylinder block on the passenger's side at the rear. It threads directly into the side of the block. It is very important to have a good oil filter on any street engine. Replace it frequently.

Right-Angle Adapter

The tricky part that relates to oil filters is the right-angle oil filter adapter, which is available from either Mopar Performance or Mancini Racing. The adapter bolts into the same location as the filter itself (a long bolt is included in the adapter kit). Then the filter threads into the adapter at 90 degrees to its original position and also rearward of its original position. The adapter kit is designed to move the oil filter for added exhaust header clearance. When installing the adapter, rotate it so that the oil filter is pointing rearward at the axle.

Windage Tray

The windage tray is a curved piece of sheet metal that attaches to the number-2 and -4 main cap bolts. These main cap bolts have special heads that accept a small screw, which actually attaches the windage tray. The windage tray fits inside of the oil pan, so for any modification or revision you must keep the oil pan in mind. Most aftermarket trays are designed for specific stock or aftermarket oil pans; the pan and the tray are a team, whether Milodon or Moroso.

The 340 and 360 high-performance engines are the only production engines that used a production windage tray. It clears the stock 3.31-inch stroke and the 3.58-inch stroke. It may have to be modified for long-stroke 4.00-inch

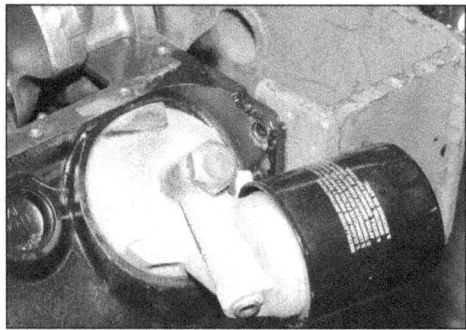
In many cases, the direct-mount oil filter is in the way for headers. If you need clearance in this area, use the right-angle oil filter adapter. It is aluminum and rotates the oil filter 90 degrees from its original position, which will help with header clearance.

The hollow bolt (bottom) goes into the center hole in the large round adapter and is used to hold the adapter to the side of the block. (Photo Courtesy R. Koffel)

The production 340 windage tray attaches to the number-2 and -4 main caps with special bolts. The tray is intended to help control the oil that is in the oil pan.

crank engines. In 1974 and newer engines, the tray attaching holes are slotted to fit the 340 and 360 main cap bolt widths.

The windage tray is designed to control the oil in the pan during acceleration and braking and control windage losses from the spinning crankshaft. For performance gains, I recommend using an aftermarket pan and baffle/scraper/tray. Milodon and Moroso offer many versions.

Oil Pan

Several versions of the production oil pan are available. The 273, 318, and 340 all use the same basic oil pan. The 360 pan is unique because the end radius is smaller on the 360

Milodon makes oil pans for the A-engine pan (shown) and Magnum. These have a wider sump than the basic pan. This side-bucket design allows the sump to hold extra oil without hurting the engine's basic ground clearance.

OILING SYSTEM

pan. They are not interchangeable. Magnum pans are similar (5.2L is unique from 5.9L), but the sump locations based on the vehicle tend to be unique.

Capacity

If you are building a high-performance street engine, you should increase the pan's capacity because more oil absorbs more heat and enhances performance. Most A-engine and Magnum engine oil pans hold 5 quarts, including the filter. You want to increase this to 6 quarts or more. Moroso offers a pan with an extra quart of capacity plus baffles in the sump for better oil control. Milodon offers a deeper pan, for more capacity, and a sump that is wider than the engine block and increases the pan's capacity without affecting ground clearance.

Milodon offers seven different levels of oil pans, which differ in volume and depth. The drag race pan and the off-road pan are too deep (more than 10 inches) for street/strip conditions. The stock replacement is just that, but it is nice to know that it is available if yours is damaged.

Also available from Milodon are the 8-quart Street/Strip pan, the 6- and 7-quart Pro Street pan, and the 6-quart Road Race pan. The Street/Strip pan is 8¾ inches deep; the other three are about 7- to 7¾-inches deep.

For most applications, the Street/Strip pan is my first choice. If the car has a very low front ride height, one of the 6-quart 7-inch-deep pans is a better choice.

Moroso also offers a too-deep drag pan but also has an 8-quart pan that is 8¼ inches deep, which is a good street/strip pan. A road race pan should work well if it fits your engine compartment requirements. Champ

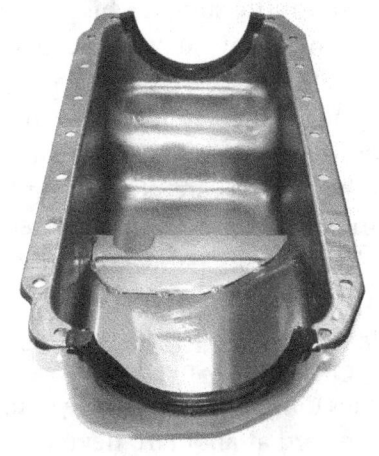

Inside the Milodon pan is a baffle added to the sump to help control the oil under heavy braking or acceleration, so it's suited to drags but not road racing. While this is easily said, another baffle may not allow installation of the pick-up into the sump. Milodon also has scrapers and trays for its oil pans; these help control the oil and cut windage losses to help make more power.

Pans and Canton Pans also offer pans that can be used on a street/strip engine.

High-horsepower and high-RPM engines should have one of these street/strip or better oil pans. The difficult part is where to draw the line. When a mechanical cam is added and/or the estimated power is more than 600 hp, you should upgrade to one of these pans.

The Sump

The oil pan's sump is the actual bottom of the pan (wet-sump style) and where the oil is collected after it has lubricated the engine's moving parts and is gathered for its next trip through the pump. The typical production sump is about as long as it is wide (almost square) and the width is out to the edge of the block minus the two rows of attaching bolts.

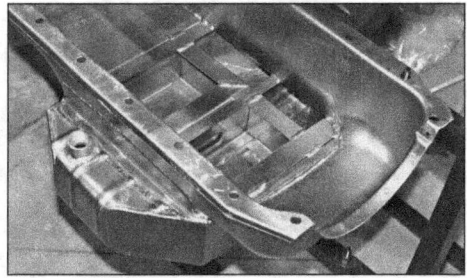

In some cases, the internal sump is very complicated with trap doors and special chambers. It is all designed to help control the oil in many different directions and to aid the oil pick-up.

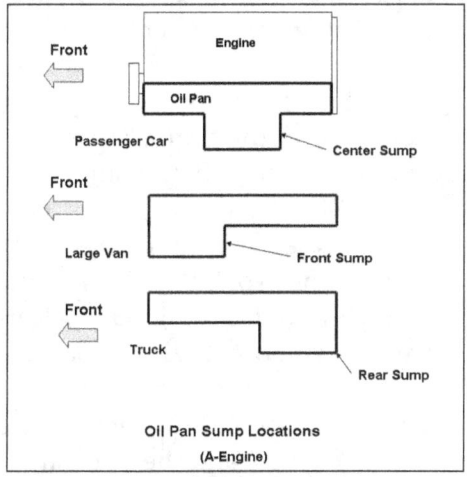

The A-engine oil pans are different for cars, trucks, and vans. The center sump is the most popular because it's an easy fit on more cars. Drag racers like to modify the truck pan's rear sump. The custom pan manufacturers, including Milodon, Moroso, Charlie's, and Champ, can put the sump wherever you want it to fit your application.

Sumps are a feature of wet-sump oiling systems.

In A-engine production pans, the sump could be located at the front of the pan (large van), in the middle of the pan (passenger car), or at the rear (trucks). Although Magnum engines in trucks and passenger cars use pans with different sumps, it isn't as neat as an A-engine.

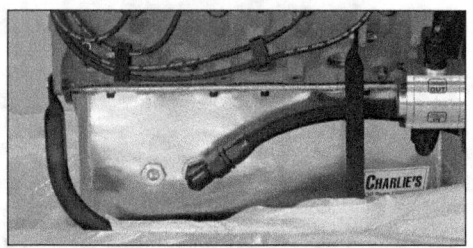

Custom pan fabricators, such as Charlie's (shown), can offer almost any configuration, including sump location, general size, and pick-up arrangement as well as dry-sump multiple pick-ups or wet sumps. These fabricated pans are generally welded aluminum. (Photo Courtesy L. Lawson)

To increase the oil pan's capacity, you can lower the sump. To do that, you need to cut off the sump and weld a 2-inch piece onto the pan. This increases the sump's capacity by a quart or two, but it also reduces the engine's effective ground clearance, and you don't want to damage or rupture the oil pan driving over a speed bump or driveway incline. The model or vehicle and the orientation of the engine in the engine compartment generally dictate the location of the pump.

Ground Clearance

Typically, other items on the bottom of the engine compartment hit the ground before the production oil pan or they hit at the same time. If the sump is lowered, it is the first to hit. You can weld a shield onto the bottom of the K-frame to help protect the sump or just be careful when driving on uneven pavement. Dropped sumps are popular in drag racing where the tracks are basically flat.

Baffles

Another performance tip (after increasing capacity) is to add baffles. The acceleration baffle is added across the rear of the sump as high as possible; it must stay below the crank. The rear baffle can be somewhat longer but the oil pick-up has to fit into the opening left between the baffles so you have to be careful. The rear baffle is angled downward at 20 degrees.

The braking baffle is added across the front of the sump at the same height as the front of the pan. The front baffle only needs to be about 2 inches long. The front baffle is angled downward at about 10 degrees.

If the pan has a rear sump, the rear baffle should be as close to the crank as possible. If the sump is in the middle, the baffle is at the top of the sump, even with the rear section of the pan.

Fabricated Pan

All of the above-mentioned pans and dropped sump pans are steel pans. In many cases, they are just the attaching flange with the sides and bottom welded on, but they are still steel. The fully fabricated oil pan has been around for many years. The Mopar small-block makes it much more difficult to fabricate the pan because of the front and rear large radiuses. Once you step into the fabricated pan arena, the manufacturer (Charlie's Oil Pans) can do almost anything, but typically these pans are used in racing. A wide-sump, close to stock height, aluminum pan with baffles is interesting for the street.

Custom pans, such as those offered by Charlie's, can offer features that you desire but may not be readily available for your engine as "shelf" items. For example, perhaps the desired pan is only available for the 318/340 block and you have a 360 block.

Another custom pan feature is having enough clearance for steering

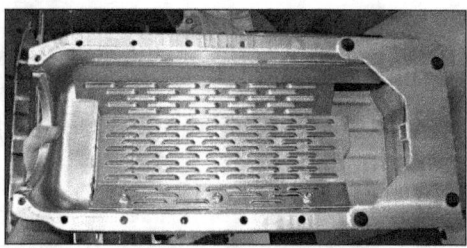

The Champ pan for the Chrysler/Mopar small-block has a wider sump than the basic pan. An interesting tray/scraper is added to the inside. It appears to attach to the pan rather than to the main caps.

and suspension components. A custom pan builder can address any of these issues. These custom pan builders also build big pans for drag race engines that focus on making more horsepower, but these pans are generally too deep for a street/strip vehicle.

Oil Pan Gaskets

The A-engine uses a four-piece oil pan gasket, two side gaskets and a front and a rear crossover gasket. Magnum engines use a one-piece gasket. Remember that the 318/340 and 5.2L gaskets are different from the 360 and 5.9L gaskets.

Oil Pump Drive

Another concern relates directly to the camshaft you use. If you plan on using a hydraulic roller cam or a mechanical roller cam in your engine, you should have an intermediate shaft, which uses a bronze gear or an aluminum-bronze gear. It is gold in color so it is very easy to determine if you have one. It should be pinned to the shaft. The problem is that these roller cams are made from steel and the production gear wears out very quickly when run against a steel gear. The bronze material solves this metallurgy problem.

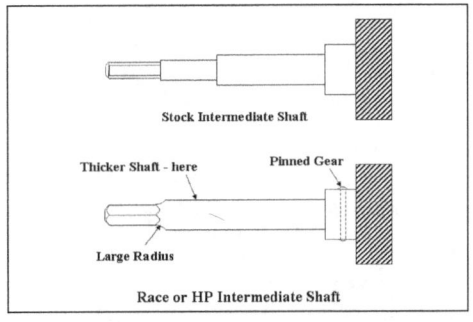

The stock part doesn't typically break by the gear. However, the gear is only pressed onto the shaft, so in high-performance applications, the gear (black or dark gray) can slip on the shaft. Moreover, the small end of the shaft just above the oil pump hex can fail. For performance engines, the first concern is to get an intermediate shaft that has the gear pinned to the shaft. These are available from Mopar Performance or Milodon; both use a heavy-duty shaft.

Magnum engines, which already have a hydraulic roller cam made from steel, are tricky. Chrysler engineers solved the steel problem by alloying and heat-treating the gear. My problem is that the finished production part looks just like the A-engine production part, which should not be used with roller cams. The Magnum part should work with all rollers, but you might talk to the cam experts (Comp Cams or Crane) to see if they have encountered any issues. If in doubt, use the Magnum shaft for the hydraulic cams and the bronze gear with the bigger cams.

If the engine is being built for the street and for durability (high mileage), you might consider the Milodon bronze gear, which claims premium material for better wear resistance.

Dry Sump

The dry-sump system allows a very low ride height for street or street/strip cars because it allows you to have very low front ends without having to worry about ground clearance for the bottom of the sump of the pan. In some custom cars, there is no room in the engine compartment for a wet-sump oil pan. A dry-sump system can help solve some of these issues. The dry sump provides a steady supply of oil under extreme operating temperatures in racing applications, but that's not an issue for the typical street/strip engine.

Everything discussed previously relates to the basic wet-sump oiling system. A dry-sump oiling system replaces most of the bottom-end hardware: pan, pump, and filter (maybe). Many dry-sump oiling system designs started with the early 354/392 Hemi and other big-blocks in Top Fuel dragsters and racing boats.

In the mid-1970s, the rules changed for NHRA Pro Stock, and big-blocks (426 Hemi) were allowed in small cars (Colt and Arrow). There was no room for a wet-sump pan in these small vehicles, so the dry sump jumped to the front of the class.

Much of the technology that is used today has its roots in this era. In this case the only parts that changed for the small-block use were the shallow pan and the front drive pulley. The typical dry-sump system has a very shallow oil pan and multiple oil pick-ups. The standard oil pump on the number-5 main is replaced with a separate four-, five-, or six-stage pump, which has one pressure stage and the rest are suction stages.

All suction stages pump oil to a remote oil storage tank, which holds the oil (8 to 12 quarts or more depending on the type of racing). The pressure stage draws oil from the bottom of the remote dry-sump tank and lubricates the engine similar to the wet-sump pump. The multi-stage oil pump is driven off the nose of the crank by a small Gilmer belt. The dry-sump pump (all stages) may be a Gerotor pump or a gear pump (the gear pumps are more popular). Typically the dry-sump pump is mounted on the lower driver's side of the engine block, but it may be switched to the opposite side.

My recommendation on dry-sump systems is to select one supplier for all dry-sump hardware and follow all recommendations for your application. Years ago, customers didn't use dry-sump systems because of expense. The biggest advantage of a dry-sump system is ground clearance, so that is very important to street applications.

Today, more and more "custom" street car owners want the look or style that comes with a dropped front end, and the dry-sump works in this environment. Do not mix and match your dry-sump parts. Moroso, Milodon, Dailey Engineering, and Barnes Dry Sump Systems are just a few manufacturers.

With a dry-sump system, the oil pump and evacuation pump are driven off the front nose of the crank, along with the crank trigger and an SFI dampener. The water pump is electric and does not require another belt. (Photo Courtesy L. Lawson)

CHAPTER 8

CHAPTER 9

Ignition System

Current aftermarket ignition systems and components offer significant benefits for A-engines. An A-engine needs to be converted from breaker point to electronic ignition system for any performance application. In essence, you optimize the ignition system so it effectively ignites the fuel charge in the combustion chamber. A max-performance engine typically intakes a larger fuel/air charge and you need an upgraded system that's correctly calibrated so the engine performs at its full potential.

The A-engine's original breaker point and coil pack system is woefully inadequate for today's max-performance engine. Therefore, you should convert to Mopar Performance, MSD, Accel, or another modern electronic ignition system.

Magnum engines are unique and the ignition is part of the computer. The ignition system is everything that is required to ignite the air/fuel mixture inside the combustion chambers of the engine. These ignition parts are distributor, spark plugs, plug wires, control box or ECU (electronic control unit), coil, ballast resistor, switches, wiring, battery, starter, ground straps, voltage regulator, and a few odds and ends.

With the introduction of fuel injection (MPI) with the 1992 Magnum 5.2L engine, an ECM replaced the ECU, and an additional six or seven sensors were added to the system.

All Chrysler/Mopar small-block engines have the ignition distributor at the rear of the engine. It sits vertically, a little left of center. Electronic ignition should be the standard ignition for any performance engine. The eight-point reluctor is in the center and the vacuum-pot is at the lower right.

Spark Advance

To make maximum torque and horsepower, the spark plug must fire at a specific moment relative to the crank and piston. A chart or graph of this event relative to engine speed is generally called a spark advance curve. Spark advance is much more critical on street engines or street/strip engines because they use the full range of engine speeds and loads; race engines tend to run at high speeds and a fixed advance.

In general the total spark advance curve has three phases: initial, centrifugal, and total. Initial advance is the number that you set with a timing light by rotating the distributor housing while the engine is idling at low speed.

The distributor has a mechanism inside the housing that provides centrifugal advance, which changes with the engine speed (RPM).

The sum of the initial advance and the centrifugal advance is called the total advance. For racing applications you set the total advance rather than the initial advance. If the spark advance is graphed or plotted against the engine speed or RPM, the resulting graph is called the spark advance curve.

IGNITION SYSTEM

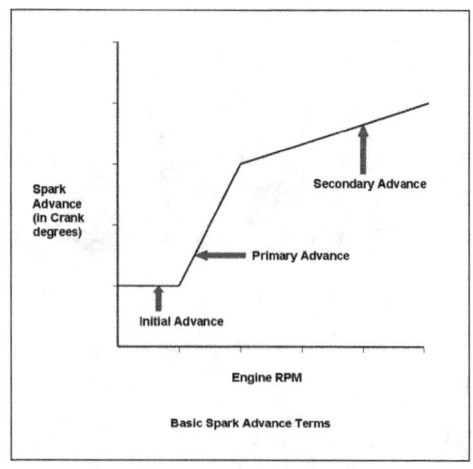

The basic spark advance in a standard ignition consists of three parts: the initial, the primary advance, and the secondary advance. The primary uses centrifugal force with a light springs and the secondary works with higher RPM; it uses a heavy spring with a loop in the end.

Another type of advance is vacuum advance, which is an add-on advance. A pot attached to the side of the distributor creates the vacuum advance. It is driven by engine vacuum, a small vacuum line runs to the end of the pot from the bottom of the carburetor. It is very important to a true street car but is often disconnected (plugged) for racing.

For example, assume that your distributor has 22 degrees of centrifugal advance built into the advance mechanism. If you set an initial advance of 10 degrees, you have a total advance of 32 degrees (10 + 22 = 32). If you increase the initial advance to 13 degrees, your total advance becomes 35 degrees (13 + 22 = 35).

Vacuum advance is an add-on, so if you have 15 inches of vacuum at cruising speed (freeway), total advance at this RPM (maybe 1,800 rpm) might be 25 degrees (13 initial plus about half of the centrifugal) plus the 15 degrees of vacuum advance for 40 degrees at cruising speed, which results in better fuel economy. If you go to wide-open-throttle, the vacuum drops to zero and the vacuum advance also drops to zero. It's back to 25 until the RPM changes.

But I'm getting ahead of myself. To discuss the ignition system for street and performance applications you have to know what spark advance is. The actual advance curve is controlled by the internals of the distributor (or the computer in Magnum engines).

When selecting an ignition system, the standard Chrysler electronic system offers the best bang-for-the-buck. Period. Once you have the basic electronic distributor you have many options. I favor Chrysler ignition boxes. The orange box is set up for the street and the chrome box is for the street/strip engine.

MSD 6 is probably the most popular option for the street/strip. MSD 7 is the race ignition and the high-RPM ignition (7,500 rpm and up), but it is not required for the street/strip application in most cases. For the street/strip engine, I favor an MSD Blaster coil.

Performance ignition manufacturers offer three kinds of conversion kits: one for the standard engines, aimed at general street engines (based around a vacuum-advance distributor), and one for racing engines that was based around a race distributor (faster advance, or fixed advance, maybe billet, and sometimes mechanical tach drive features in the distributor) and an upgraded race ECU (higher RPM and more energy).

Magnum engines have computer-controlled ignition, but some customers prefer to adjust the ignition themselves. If you want distributor adjustment in your Magnum engine, the solid-shaft distributor must be replaced. The electronic conversion kit (Mopar Performance) is the easiest way to get the hardware you need for the new electronic distributor.

Distributors

A-engines used rear distributors; Magnum engines used solid-shaft distributors with the advance hardware built into the computer or ECM. The exception is the Lean-Burn package

Mopar Performance introduced the capacitor discharge conversion kit that included the new electronic distributor, an ECU (electronic control unit), wiring harness, and ballast resistor. This made the switch from a points ignition to the new electronic ignition much easier and less expensive.

The electronic ignition distributor housing is aluminum. The vacuum pot for the vacuum advance is at the bottom. Two clips hold the cap on; one is at the top right and one is partially hidden at the bottom.

High Energy Electronic Ignition

The typical Chrysler/Mopar electronic ignition uses a high peak energy and a long spark duration time. However, the aftermarket's multi-fire ignition triggers the same spark plug to fire many times during each cycle. Although these multi-fire systems were designed for racing, they provide significant performance gains for street ignitions.

As the racing engines' RPM increase, less time is available to fire the spark plug so the newer race ignitions only fire the plug one or two times per cycle, especially at higher RPM. The current hardware is designed for very high energy, both in magnitude and time duration.

A typical engine takes about 30 millijoules of energy to ignite the typical fuel/air mixture in a cylinder's combustion chamber. Most ignitions systems exceed this at lower RPM ranges. As the load (more torque) and the RPM increase, the ignition system requires more energy. Ignition systems are rated by engine speed: street, maybe up to 6,000 rpm; race, up to 8,000 rpm; pro race, up to 9,500 rpm.

Remember that the ignition's coil is the source of energy for the system and it makes energy in direct proportion to the voltage that is available in the system. The amount of voltage is directly related to the voltage that is available in the battery and what the battery delivers to the ignition system (wiring, grounds, etc.). On a street car, if you have a charging system (alternator), the battery voltage and charge is less of a concern. ■

Ignition Specs

	273/318/340/360	5.2L/5.9L Magnum
Style	Point and Electronic*	ECM/Computer**
Firing Order	1-8-4-3-6-5-7-2	1-8-4-3-6-5-7-2
Distributor Rotation	Counterclockwise	Counterclockwise
Total Timing	35 degrees	35 degrees***

* The A-engine used point-ignition up to 1970 and electronic ignition from 1971 on. Some 1972–1973 and newer A-engines used Lean-Burn ignitions but typically upgraded to electronic for performance applications.

** All Magnum engines use the ECM ignition system. The distributor no longer has spark advance functions.

*** The total advance in these engines is built into the ECM and the distributor does not set it.

The electronic ignition's distributor is the trigger for the ignition's timing. The eight-point reluctor in the center is the trigger wheel and the magnetic sensor is at the top. The sensor does not touch the reluctor so there is no wear with mileage. Adjustments to the gap between the sensor and the reluctor are made by loosening the screw (lower left), then using a screwdriver in the V-slot (just below the screw) to gain the proper gap, and finally tightening the screw to hold the gap.

The Magnum distributor for the MPI system uses a solid shaft; the engine's advance curve is built into the computer. The distributor sends the spark to the various cylinders but is not the triggering mechanism. A sensor (the black disc and wire) is inside the housing and it helps the computer with timing.

built in the mid-1970s that also used a solid-shaft distributor.

Vacuum Advance for A-Engine

For many years the standard production A-engine distributor has been equipped with the vacuum-advance electronic hardware and also served as the basis for the standard performance distributor. The housing is made of aluminum so it is very lightweight. The vacuum-advance pot is mounted to the outside of the housing; it is the easiest way to identify one of these distributors.

There have been many versions over the years. Most are based on the advance curve, which is directly related to the springs in the advance mechanism. Production used two springs: one light and one heavy (with a loop in the end). Performance

IGNITION SYSTEM

distributors had one spring, or two light springs, and the performance advance curve was fully advanced by 2,000 rpm.

The vacuum-advance pot is on the outside of the housing and has an arm that reaches inside and attaches to the advance mechanism. The vacuum does nothing if the vacuum hose is not attached. The typical vacuum source is the carburetor. It is good for street engines because it is an add-on advance, which helps increase fuel economy in high-vacuum situations.

Billet Distributor

Most billet distributors are basically electronic distributors where the main housing is made by CNC-milling a block of aluminum. MSD now makes a billet distributor with the advance mechanism on top of the reluctor, which allows easy access. MSD has plotted out six different advance curves (slow to fast) based on color-coded springs and amounts of total centrifugal advance ranging from 18 to 28 degrees. Because it is just inside the cap, it is easy to make adjustments and doesn't require a distributor machine.

These MSD, Accel, and Crane billet distributors are nice but somewhat expensive. The standard electronic distributor is for the street/strip. One interesting approach is the new MSD adjustable mechanical-advance billet distributor. Another new possible solution is the MSD E-curve billet distributor, which has a program inside the distributor, easily accessed on the outside of the housing, that changes the advance curve.

Crank Trigger

On a V-8 engine, only four blips are needed because the crank rotates at twice the cam speed. Part of the system is a bracket that is added to the front of the engine designed to hold the triggering sensor(s). This bracket is designed with timing adjustment capability. Typically the system uses two pick-ups for a racing engine: one for starting and one for actual running.

Cap and Rotor

Vacuum-advance-style, mechanical tach/billets are built for the Chrysler electronic ignition distributors; the Magnum type fits only the newer Magnum computer distributors.

The vacuum-advance distributor has a notch in the bottom lip of the cap at the clip location. The mechanical tach version has a small tab that protrudes from the lower lip of the

The crank trigger's popularity seems to have returned in many small-block classes. With a crank trigger, the reluctor and sensor's basic trigger mechanism is moved from the distributor to the nose of the crankshaft. A large-diameter wheel is mounted on the front of the SFI dampener. This trigger wheel from MSD has four magnetic blips mounted in the outside diameter of the wheel.

cap, and the bracket that holds the cap on has points that the tab centers in.

The Magnum version is the easiest to spot because it has spark plug ends in the terminals and two small screws where the spring clips are normally located. The first two electronic distributors used two spring clips to hold the cap onto the main housing. The two caps are not interchangeable.

Accel services caps for both Chrysler electronic distributors. MSD services the caps for their distributors, which use Magnum-style terminals in the cap.

Manufacturers can offer almost any group of features and almost any advance curve with billet distributors. By the 1990s, performance ignition systems had upgraded to special tach takeoffs that were electrical, not mechanical. The tachs were compatible with the race ignition boxes; the mechanical tach takeoff was no longer required.

The trigger wheel of the crank trigger system mounts to the front of the engine, in front of the SFI dampener. The sensor bracket and sensor are mounted to the lower right of the trigger wheel. (Photo Courtesy L. Lawson)

CHAPTER 9

Aftermarket Ignition Systems

If you're running a mild street engine that does not rev above 5,500 rpm and runs less than 9:1 compression, a stock ignition performs well. If you're building a 500-hp or more powerful engine, you need an upgraded ignition system.

Most max-performance builds have large-port aluminum heads, aggressive cams, and intakes and carbs; the OEM ignition (electronic) system (the box) was not designed to keep pace, so upgrade the box (orange or chrome) followed by upgrades to the coil, plug wires, and plugs (colder). If you don't, your engine won't perform to its potential. In the final analysis, if your engine does not provide strong enough spark for the fuel charge, you're wasting potential performance.

Mopar Performance, MSD, Accel, and PerTronix offer complete high-performance ignition systems for A-engines, and they offer components for almost every application, whether it's street, street/strip, or race. When building a max-performance, you should select a complete aftermarket ignition system as a kit or select the components that complement one another. As such, you should buy a distributor, ignition box, coil pack, and spark plug wires from a single manufacturer that work as an integrated system. Although you can mix the components from various manufacturers, often there is no performance gain to be realized, and then you have to verify that all components are compatible.

PerTronix

PerTronix has long been one of the leading aftermarket manufacturers of high-performance ignition

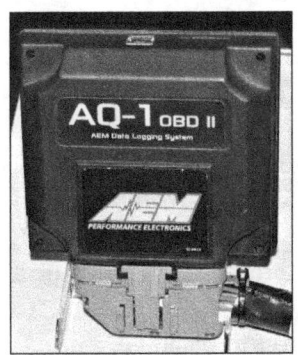
This is an AEM ignition box (OBD II or onboard diagnostics) for the Magnum. The OBD II is the federal government's mandated emissions test standard that all production engines and vehicles must meet. OBD II dates from about 1998. AEM has many versions of its ignition computers.

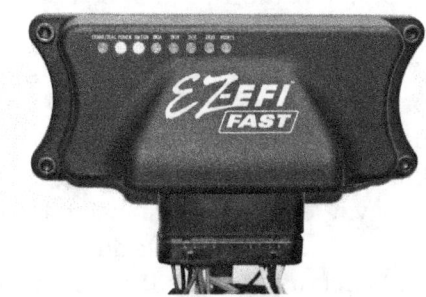
The FAST computer ignitions can be stand-alone or they can work with the computer that is in the vehicle. Many variations are available depending on what you start with and where you want it to go.

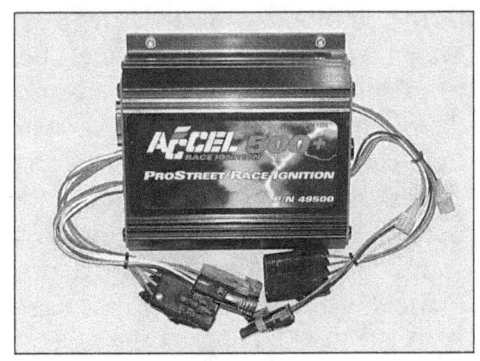
The Crane "FireBall" ignition is an extremely high-energy system. It is designed for use with the A-engine. Other versions work with the Magnum MPI family.

The AEM computer ignition box has two giant electrical plugs, which is fairly common in MPI systems. In some cases, the computer uses three large plugs. Each computer must receive inputs from 8 to 10 sensors.

This SCT computer is about the size of an old cell phone (about 3 by 6 inches). It plugs into the vehicle and works with the computer that is in the vehicle. It has many options for re-curving the ignition and fuel plots.

Accel has many ignition systems for many different applications. These are designed to work with the A-engine and can be used in "pro street" or racing engines. Other versions work with the Magnum MPI group.

IGNITION SYSTEM

systems. The company makes a wide range of distributors, digital CD boxes, coils, and wires that are suitable for A-engine small-blocks.

Made of CNC-machined 6061 T6 billet aluminum housing, the PerTronix Flame-Thrower II distributor simply slides through the manifold and into the block. Attach a few wires and it's ready to run; it works with any inductive ignition system coil, but high-RPM performance can be improved when it is used with the low-resistance (.6 ohm) Flame-Thrower II coil. You can use any multi-spark CD ignition box with the distributor.

The distributors can run up to 10,000 rpm, so they are tough. You need to select the coil that's suited to your particular application, so PerTronix offers coils with different voltages. The Flame-Thrower II produces 45,000 volts, the Flame-Thrower HV supplies 60,000 volts, the Flamethrower III 45,000, and the Flame-Thrower HC throws out 60,000 volts.

MSD

Many engine builders select the Pro-Billet distributor, MSD 6 box, and Blaster coil for high-horsepower street engines or for street/strip. The Pro-Billet distributor is made of 6061 T6 billet aluminum, which is similar to the PerTronix, and both of these tough distributors are less prone to deflection. This plug-and-play distributor simply slides into the distributor shaft hole and you clamp it into position. The distributor can operate through 10,000 rpm, and it has an adjustable mechanical advance assembly that allows you to accurately set timing. In addition, you can easily modify the advance curve to match your specific application.

The MSD 6-Series provides strong spark energy and precisely controls ignition actuation, so if you're building a max-performance engine of 500 hp or more, this box helps deliver strong throttle response and better overall performance. MSD offers several different versions of the MSD 6 box for almost any engine package.

Most engine builders start with the Digital 6AL box that's designed for aggressive driving and some form of racing rather than the MSD AL-2 box, which is suited for street/strip applications. This box has a programmable advance curve. The Extreme Duty 6 ALN is designed for racing applications. As with most engines, they are going to produce more power and high-ignition energy, greater combustion chamber temperature, and longer duration.

When using the billet distributor and the MSD 6 box, you should use the compatible MSD Blaster 2 coil. It puts out 45,000 volts compared to 15,000 from a stock coil.

Mopar Performance

The Mopar Performance electronic ignition kit (try Jeg's or Mancini Racing as a source) features an aluminum vacuum-advance distributor, orange-box ECU, wiring harness, and ballast resistor. It is designed for street engines that operate at less than 6,000 rpm. Most shops find it offers the best performance for the dollar. I suggest using the MSD Blaster coil (see above) with this package.

For the street/strip package, just upgrade to the chrome-box ECU for higher RPM engines (about 7,500 rpm). For higher RPM and/or racing, upgrade the ECU to the MSD 7 and its compatible coil.

Advance Curve

Two small springs and two pivoting weights control the distributor's advance curve. The two springs can be changed to change the curve, but this does not apply to the Magnum engines.

In general, the design functions by lighter springs allowing a faster advance curve. Re-curving the distributor (a popular performance trick) is basically changing the springs in the distributor. it is easy to change the springs, but it is more difficult to know what the new curve is, and a distributor machine spins the distributor up to speed and shows you what the new curve is. Distributor machines are difficult to find today; one source is Koffel's Place.

Ignition Timing

In most cases, Chrysler/Mopar small-block engines run best at 35-degrees total spark advance (the sum of the initial advance and the centrifugal advance). Because vacuum goes to zero at wide open throttle (WOT), it is not involved in this area of performance.

As a general guide, street performance distributors (vacuum) were fully advanced by 2,000 rpm; the race distributor was fully advanced by 1,500 rpm and also had a flat curve. The crank trigger was fully advanced after it started and also had a flat curve.

Magnum

Basically the Magnum needs the same advance curve as the A-engine. It also needs the same total advance except that it is accomplished in the computer and therefore the computer must be reprogrammed (by SCT,

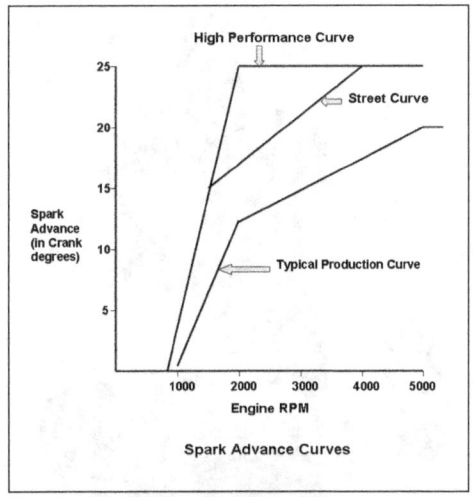

The production curve was just about fully advanced at 4,000 rpm. The generally recommended performance curve was fully advanced by 2,000 rpm. In the 1970s and 1980s, this was okay but it is too much spark advance too fast for the octane rating of today's gas. Actually, it isn't bad for racing at the track but you have to modify it for any street use. You want to try to reduce the amount of spark at 2,000 to 2,500 rpm; it requires a set of slightly heavy springs.

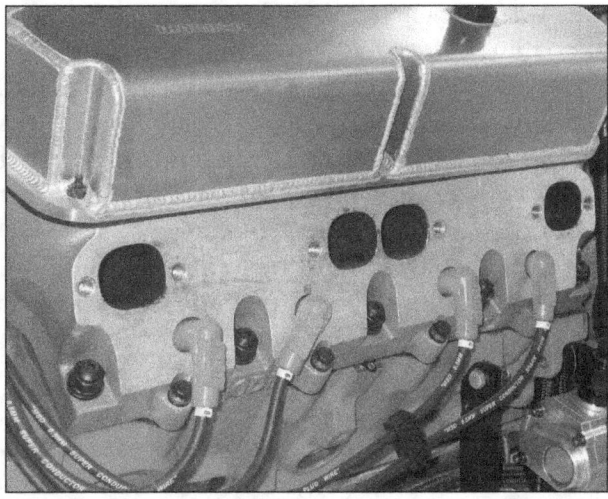

After the spark plug boot covers the plug, it is difficult to tell which way the plug is pointing. In Chapter 5 the combustion chambers showed that the W9 and B1-BA chambers have the plug pointing at the center of the exhaust valve and close to the exhaust valve's seat. Note how close the plug is to the exhaust port. (Photo Courtesy L. Lawson)

for example) or another computer added (such as from AEM or FAST). The HP A-engine has too much spark at 2,000 rpm, but it is not as big a concern on Magnum engines as long as the ECM is not "pushed" into the 2,000-rpm area. Six sensors help with fuel octane and load issues.

Spark Plugs

The job of the engine's spark plugs is to ignite the fuel/air mixture that is in the combustion chamber. This somewhat straightforward job becomes more difficult as the engine's output (torque and horsepower) and speed (RPM) increase. Production A-engines have had 3/4-inch-reach plugs for 2-barrel engines, 4-barrel engines, and high-performance engines, so the range is greater than you might expect. Magnums use one plug. In plug lingo, the A-engine used standard plugs and the Magnum used a resistor-type plug.

Gap

Magnum plugs use a gap of .040 inch. A-engine plugs use a basic gap of .035 inch. Wider gaps can be used with certain high-energy electronic ignition systems.

Mopar/Chrysler tested plug gaps with race ignitions as high as .050 to .060 inch. If the ignition is up to it, the wider gaps (maybe .040 for the A-engine and .045 for the Magnum) go faster, but the .035- to .040-inch gaps are more durable.

Street Plugs

The N12Y and the RC12LC4 plugs are a place to start in general. If more racing is expected, colder versions are recommended. I would also push the gap to .040 to .045 inch. Spark plug installation torque is as follows: cast-iron head, 26 to 30 ft-lbs; aluminum head, 18 to 22.

All Magnum engines use a heat shield around each plug. The shield can be removed with a pair of channel lock pliers. The gap in the heat shield should be pointing upward.

Plug Wires

Production A-engine and Magnum wires are 7 mm in diameter. Try to keep the cable that runs from the coil to the distributor as short as possible. The wires are not interchangeable between the two because the distributor caps use different terminals.

For street applications and higher-energy ignitions systems, I recommend 7.5-mm pre-made plug wires from Mopar, Accel, etc.

For the street/strip engine, I prefer the 7.5-mm pre-made plug wires offered by Mopar Performance or the 8-mm pre-made wires from Accel, Moroso, MSD, and Taylor.

For racing engines, consider 8 mm or higher. Moroso makes an 11-mm wire, Taylor makes a 10.4-mm wire, MSD and Accel offer 8.5-mm or larger wire. The large-diameter wires are designed for racing engines.

Suppression and solid-core spark plug wires are offered. Solid-core (metal) wires should only be used on race engines. Suppression wires provide protection from radio frequency emissions from the ignition system,

IGNITION SYSTEM

which may be more important with the computers and electronics that are found on today's cars.

Distributor Drive

The intermediate shaft drives the distributor, and it also drives the oil pump. The tab on the bottom of the distributor's main shaft fits into a slot in the top of the intermediate shaft (installation of the intermediate shaft is discussed in Chapter 9). For performance engines, I recommend the race shaft because it has a pinned gear and that feature is very important to the ignition.

The aluminum-block sprint car engine uses a special distributor/magneto that has the drive gear and pilot attached to the distributor (all one piece) because the aluminum block does not use an intermediate shaft. It is designed for use with a dry-sump oiling system; therefore the standard oil pump is not used and leads to the intermediate shaft going away.

If you have a new block, make sure that you have a distributor drive bushing pressed into the block. If it is a used block, assume that you should replace it. This bushing is the last place you want oil and it takes a beating in high-mileage applications. (Chapter 1 discusses how to measure bushing wear.)

Coil and Ballast Resistor

The ignition coil and the ballast resistor need to work as an integrated system. Although the standard production coil has adequate performance with a CD box, you have a much hotter spark when using it with a booster coil. It works fine if you switch from a points ignition to an electronic (coils are not generally included in electronic ignition kits). The production coil is fine for general street use but there are upgrades.

The ignition system is also a factor and must be considered part of the team. For a general street performance upgrade, use an MSD Blaster coil for your application. Some race ignitions, such as the MSD 7, require special coils; do not mix-and-match.

Of the many coil specifications, but voltage tends to be the most popular, ranging from 34,000 to 55,000 volts. Coils are also rated on amperage, which varies from 140 ma to 2.0 amps, and spark duration, which varies from 200 to 350 us.

The ECU/ECM

Electronic ignition offers many advantages over the basic points ignition. Here, I focus on electronic-style ignitions. These ignitions use a control box called the ECU. Magnum engines use a computer ignition controller called an ECM.

ECU for A-Engines

Mopar offers three levels of performance ECUs: orange (street), chrome (street/strip), and gold (race). The orange unit is good for about 6,000 rpm. The chrome units offer more performance with RPM up to 7,500. The gold box is good for more than 8,000 rpm. The black production unit is good for about 5,000 to 5,500 rpm.

ECM for Magnum Engines

The ECM (or PCM, power control module) is different for every model in each year. The two-wheel-drive unit is different from the four-wheel-drive unit, the 5.2L is different from the 5.9L, the automatic transmission is

The MSD Blaster coil is a good performance upgrade from the stock coils. Some coils are made for specific ECUs or ECMs (electronic control modules), so be careful when making your selection.

different from the manual transmission, and a 1994 is different from a 1996. It seems crazy and is very confusing.

The ECM controls all ignition systems, such as total spark advance, initial spark advance, advance curve, and any vacuum advance that may be part of the map. For any performance upgrade, the computer (directed by the ECM) must be reprogrammed. Mopar Performance offers a few high-performance ECMs, but models are very limited, so I do not recommend them.

Chrysler/Mopar Performance computers are great for street vehicles and fully compliant with CARB emissions standards, but they are difficult to find. Certain years can be reprogrammed.

You may also want an overlay computer by AEM, FAST, or SCT. This second computer modifies the

CHAPTER 9

The ECU is the standard ignition for use with an electronic distributor. The orange box on the right is the street ECU and the chrome box on the left is the higher-RPM, dual-purpose ECU.

MSD 6 is a popular ignition and MSD offers several versions of it. When you have the correct distributor, the ignition box doesn't care what engine it runs. It can be used on the street or strip. These ignition boxes do not work with the computer ignitions (MPI-style) or with Magnum engines.

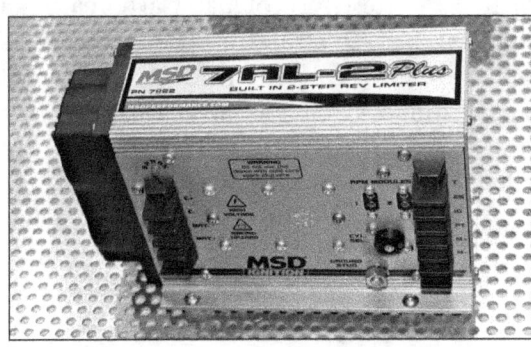

MSD 7 is the race ignition for the A-engine and it is very good. It has many features that are helpful in racing.

original program and also offers other options for more performance, but the production computer still operates the car's electronics. Although products continue to change and evolve, AEM, FAST, or SCT are the best sources for Magnums and A-engines.

Aftermarket performance ECMs filled the void, but the OEMs didn't want to give out their programming information, so each company solved the problem in their own way. The SCT original approach was to reprogram the Chrysler computer, basically the same as Mopar Performance did. Today, SCT offers reprogramming services but uses a supplemental hand-held device that reprograms the engine's ECM; the customer can select one of several curves for added performance.

The FAST people took a different route but have devices that work with the factory ECM and piggyback to adjust the performance curves. The MSD system appears similar to the FAST system.

The original AEM system (programmable ECM) basically replaced the original factory ECM. The new units seem to be moving toward the SCT approach where the new unit works with and overrides or reprograms the factory ECM.

The initial settings (centrifugal and vacuum) are the primary parts in typical electronic ignition system components. The ECM performs these functions on Magnum engines. The crank sensor is bolted to the back of the block and reads the engine's TDC position through slots (windows) in the flexplate, which is inside the bellhousing. The sensor then sends the signal to the ECM.

This means that the distributor no longer adjusts the engine's timing. If you try to advance the distributor by rotating it for more advance, the computer knows and resets the timing to what is in its program. That is why you have to have the computer reprogrammed if you want a performance upgrade.

For racing applications, an MSD 6 or MSD 7 is typically used (A-engine). Another option is one of the digital ignitions mentioned above. On the Magnum side, AEM or FAST are two of the most popular ignition systems for these engines.

Wiring

Most aftermarket ignition kits come with their own wiring, as did the electronic ignition kit. It was originally a five-wire harness, but that was updated to a four-wire harness.

CHAPTER 10

FUEL SYSTEM AND TUNING

Magnum engines use MPI, so the fuel system discussion has to address MPI and carburetion. (The Appendix discusses Holley and AFB/Carter carb tuning.) Most of the readily available carburetors are set up for a 340- to 360-ci engine from the manufacturer, but bigger cams, better heads, or more cubic inches can require adjustment.

Fuel system components are found from the gas tank to the carburetor inlet, including the electric fuel pump, filter, mechanical fuel pump, pressure regulator, and fuel lines, plus the fuel rail and injectors on the fuel-injected engines. Mechanical fuel injection systems have been available for many years from Hilborn and Kinsler. Electronic versions of these systems are also available from Kinsler. These are race systems and are popular on Sprint Cars.

4-Barrel Carb System

Holley/Quick Fuel or Carter/Edelbrock versions are suitable carbs. Most aftermarket intake manifolds have a dual attaching pattern so that it accepts both styles, but the production manifolds accept only the Carter/Edelbrock version. Vacuum secondaries are based on the AVS model and are preferable for street use because the secondary fuel pumps provide a steady supply of fuel over different operating ranges.

Mechanical secondaries (also called double-pumpers) work fine on manual transmissions. Double-pumpers can be installed on high-performance street cars with an automatic transmission, but you usually have to use more stall speed in the converter and/or more rear axle ratio.

The ThermoQuad Carter carb is a very good street carburetor but parts are not easy to find. The 6-barrel intake system is also a great street system but requires the intake and the three carburetors. The Holley 4500 is the biggest 4-barrel carburetor and requires its own mounting pad for both the wider spaced attaching bolts and the larger throttle bores. Holley and Quick Fuel make these carburetors, and they can flow 1,000 to more than 1,500 cfm each. These big carbs are generally used in racing, especially drag racing. In addition, there are now standard Holley-style carbs (small pad) that flow 950 cfm, but they are double-pumpers.

In the past few years, carb manufacturers have introduced smaller versions, in the 750-cfm area.

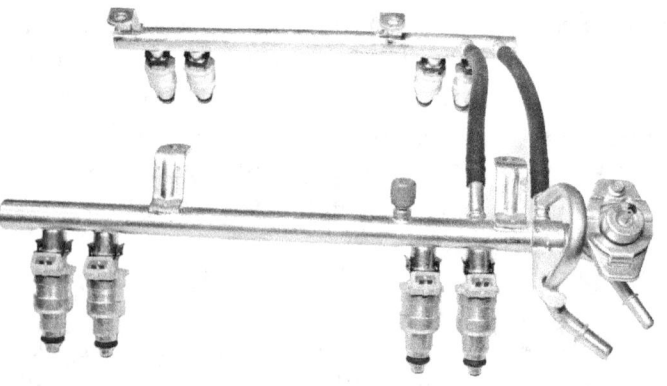

The engine's fuel system centers around eight injectors and two fuel rails (shown) or a carburetor. The fuel injectors require some electronics while a carb requires an ignition system. The driver-side and passenger-side fuel rails are similar on the production Magnum MPI system except for the fuel pressure regulator (lower right). The electrical wiring plugs into the yellow square opening at the top of each injector (wiring not shown).

CHAPTER 10

Throttle Body and Carb Selection

The Holley/Quick Fuel and the Carter/Edelbrock are the two main styles of 4-barrel carburetors. For street use, you want a vacuum secondary version of the Holley/Quick Fuel carburetor. With the Carter/Edelbrock, you want to use an AVS. For the Magnum MPI, Holley has offered the 52-mm throttle body. You don't really need the 4-barrel throttle body, but it is readily available and larger 2-barrel throttle bodies are not available (55 or 60 mm). Likewise, all carburetor sizes shown in the chart are not available in the AVS or vacuum secondary versions. ■

Engine Size	Carb Size (cfm)	Throttle Body Size (mm, cfm)	Optional Throttle Body Size (mm, cfm)
273/318 (5.2L)	500 to 650	2-barrel, 50	2-barrel, 52
340/360 (5.9L)	650 to 750	2-barrel, 50	2-barrel, 52
384/402 (6.3, 6.6L)	750 to 850	2-barrel, 52	4-barrel, 1,000
426/440 (7.0, 7.2L)	850 to 900	4-barrel, 1,000	4-barrel, 1,000

Note 1: The 4-barrel throttle body requires a 4-barrel intake manifold. The 2-barrel throttle body can be used on the 4-barrel intake manifold with an adapter, but it cannot be done with the 4-barrel on the 2-barrel intake.

Note 2: Throttle body size options are limited; 1,000 cfm is not required but is what is currently available.

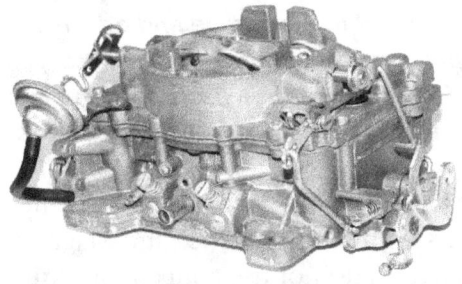

Several varieties of carburetor (Holley, Carter) and parts for them are readily available. Carburetors were used on the A-engines from its introduction in 1964 almost until its end in the late 1980s. Magnum engines were not produced with carbs.

Fuel Injection System

The Magnum MPI system for fuel injection is the best baseline to copy. Mopar Performance made a complete 340 to 360 MPI conversion kit (P5153590) designed for the crate engine, but it's not readily available.

AEM and FAST kits cover most electronics but require some hardware. (See Chapter 7.) The basic electronic fuel injector has to be sized for the amount of horsepower that the engine makes. AEM and FAST computers generally feature programmable fuel and spark maps, which can

Fuel Injector Selection

Fuel injectors used in an MPI system must be upgraded based on the engine's actual output. Each injector assembly must fit into the hole in the manifold, must fit into the fuel rail, and the electrical connection must match to the wiring harness being used. Using Chrysler injectors is the easiest solution for the first few packages.

The production Magnum fuel injectors from 1996 through 2003 flow about 23.2 pounds per hour for about 300 hp on the street; others allow you to achieve up to about 600 hp (45 pounds per hour) in several steps. The injector must fit into the intake manifold boss in the fuel rail; it must also have the correct electrical plug and compatibility with the computer. You have to reprogram the computer any time that you change the injector flow rates.

Baseline Chrysler Injectors

Part Number	Flow at 3.8 Bar (pounds/hour)	Flow at 3.0 Bar (pounds/hour)
Stock 5.2 and 5.9	23.2	20
P4452803	30.0	26
P4452804	38.0	32
P4529495	45.0	38

FUEL SYSTEM AND TUNING

One of the key sensors in an MPI system is the crank position sensor, which is located at the passenger-side rear, past the number-8 cylinder. Two screws that go in the holes by the bellhousing hold it in place.

be used on your personal computer at home.

Fuel

Most cars run on gas, but that is only one kind of fuel. In many parts of the country ethanol alcohol is mixed with gas at the pump; E85 is 85-percent ethanol. Most racing classes use gas, in some cases a specific blend, but methanol alcohol is popular in the categories where alcohol fuel is legal. The major carburetor manufacturers offer special versions of their carburetors that are designed for use with alcohol fuel. The jets and internal passages have to be changed to flow the proper amount of this new fuel for proper operation of the engine.

BSFC

The brake specific fuel consumption (BSFC) is the ratio of fuel consumed in pounds per hour to the horsepower produced. Most OEM or

The electric pump pushes the fuel up to the mechanical pump for hard launches. I recommend Carter 4594 or P4007038 electric pump (rated at 72 gallons per hour at 7 psi) because the pressure is compatible with the carburetor and the mechanical pump can pull through, which means that it doesn't have to be on all the time.

factory gasoline engines have a BSFC of about .50.

The very highly tuned normally aspirated race engine tends to operate in the area of .40 to .45.

Typical turbocharged or supercharged engines run in the .55 to .60 BSFC range.

For engines using methanol for fuel, the BSFC factor is doubled or 1.00 for naturally aspirated versions. The factor is 1.10 to 1.20 for supercharged engines on methanol.

Mechanical Fuel Pump

All A-engines are equipped with a mechanical fuel pump mounted on the passenger-side front of the engine. The pump has a long arm that rides

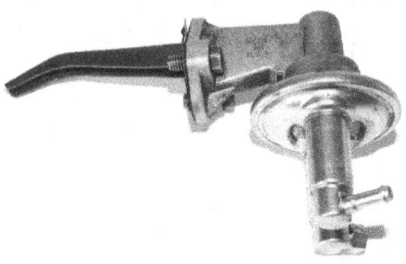

All A-engines used a mechanical fuel pump mounted on the passenger's side of the front cover, just ahead of the number-2 cylinder. You can identify the A-engine pump easily because it has a long arm to reach in and follow the eccentric on the cam.

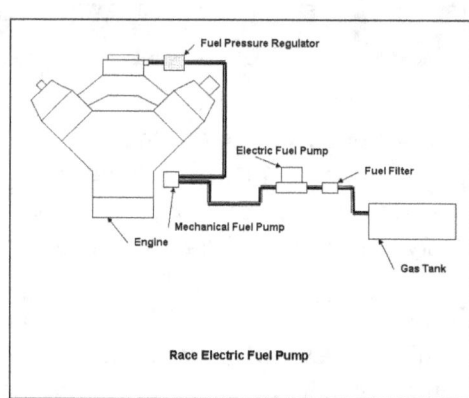

With any carbureted fuel system, you should have one or more fuel filters and an electric fuel pump, mounted in the rear ahead of the fuel tank. You also want to have a mechanical pump mounted to the engine and a fuel pressure regulator. In most cases, you don't need both the regulator and the mechanical pump; you only need one.

directly on the cam eccentric, which fits on the front of the cam. Magnum engines do not use a mechanical fuel pump. The front cover has no hole for the pump arm or bolt holes for attaching; the cam is shorter because the eccentric was removed.

The fuel pressure regulator is fairly small and is generally mounted just before the carburetor and is adjustable. Most electric fuel pumps pump fuel at a higher pressure than the carburetor's needle and seat mechanism can manage. Therefore, a regulator is necessary to moderate the flow and pressure to a level that the carb can handle.

Electric Fuel Pump

Most performance engines built for street use can use a single electric fuel pump. It should be mounted in the rear near the gas tank and away from the exhaust system. You want to use a mechanical fuel pump because it can act as a regulator for the fuel supply system.

If the mechanical fuel pump is removed, add a fuel pressure regulator. If this swap is made, the regulator should be mounted near the carburetor(s) and before the fuel line splits for multiple entries or multiple carburetors. Use the frame rail to help protect the electric pump.

Fuel Regulator

If one or two electric fuel pumps are added at the rear near the gas tank and the mechanical pump is removed, you must use a fuel pressure regulator. The regulator should be matched to the electric pump(s) that you plan on using. For example, an electric fuel injection system uses a fuel regulator that adjusts in the 25 to 40 psi range. A carburetor needs a delivery pressure of 5 to 7 psi, so the carbureted regulator should adjust in the 5- to 10-psi range.

Electric fuel pumps designed for racing are larger than the 4594 and can pump a lot more fuel at higher pressures. This is a plus for cars that accelerate hard but for most applications you will need to dial down with the regulator.

Injector Size Calculation

Injectors are rated by the amount of fuel that they flow. Injectors that are going to be used must be sized for the revised performance of the engine (horsepower). Most production Magnum engines (1996–2003) used the 23.2-pound/hour injector. The original 5.9L engine was rated at about 245 hp. To calculate the proper injector size for your engine you can use the following formula:

$$HP = FR \times N \times .8 \div BSFC$$

Where:
HP = horsepower potential of the engine
FR = flow rate of the injector at 3.8 Bar (pressure)
N = number of cylinders
.8 = a practical maximum injector flow rate for street use
BSFC = the brake specific fuel consumption for engines; .5 for a typical V-8 engine

For example, for the 5.9L engine using stock injectors (23.2), you can plug in the various numbers as follows: 23.2 x 8 x .8 / .5 = 297 hp.

You can rearrange the equation for FR, which becomes:

$$FR = HP \times BSFC \div (.8 \times N)$$

Years ago, race cars used two electric fuel pumps mounted in parallel, but the electric pumps pumped less than 100 gph. Most of the current electric fuel pumps designed for racing pump 150 to more than 300 gph and they are reliable. Don't forget the regulator with these high-volume pumps.

Magnum MPI

MPI is an easy system to work with if the factory installed it, as occurred with all Magnum V-8 engines. It can be very complicated if you are making a conversion or a custom installation.

Independent of the basic hardware, intake manifold, throttle body, fuel rail, the eight injectors, and electric pump in the tank, there are about eight sensors that must be puter to know what's happening so everything works properly.

The ECM controls both the fuel and the ignition in MPI systems. The ECM is very important to the fuel system (see discussed Chapter 9 for more details). When working on an MPI fuel system, remember that it has pressure in it even if the engine is not running. Exercise caution and follow the factory pressure release procedure before disconnecting the fuel line.

Fuel Injectors

A fuel injector is used for each cylinder in a V-8 engine. The injectors are mounted in the intake manifold port runners close to the mating line between the intake manifold and the cylinder head.

The injectors are basically electric solenoids. The fuel is delivered to the

FUEL SYSTEM AND TUNING

injectors under high pressure. The high pressure makes for a fine spray. The nozzle end of the injector fits into the machined boss in the intake manifold and the top end fits into the fuel rail. The engine's wiring harness connects to each injector, and each connector has a number tag for the correct injector, such as INJ1 and INJ2, etc.

The ECM controls the injector opening and, therefore, the amount of fuel it flows. Each injector is attached to the fuel rail with a special retaining clip and each one is sealed to the fuel rail with an O-ring. Remove the injector and fuel rail assembly from the intake manifold first. Next remove the clip and then the injector from the fuel rail.

Fuel Lines

Most A-engine vehicles were built with a 5/16-inch fuel line. For performance projects, I recommend upgrading to a 3/8-inch fuel line like those in the 426 Hemi and 440 big-blocks. On any vehicle that is 20 years old or older, I recommend replacing any rubber in the original fuel line.

Replace any fuel filter with a new one. Be sure that the filter matches the size of the fuel line being used.

Airflow

Ultimately, airflow controls the amount of horsepower that the engine delivers. The heads and cam allow air into and out of the combustion chamber and the intake flows the air into the intake ports. The throttle body or carburetor controls the airflow that goes into the intake manifold.

Carb Tuning

The Magnum and A-engine small-blocks were fitted with the Carter/Edelbrock AFB and AVS, the

The throttle body selection is extremely limited; the stock 2-barrel and a 4-barrel are the main choices. Because no fuel is in the MPI throttle body, the big 4-barrel isn't as much of a problem as it can be with carburetors. The standard 4-barrel throttle body uses 1.75-inch throttle bores and flows around 1,000 cfm. Edelbrock offers a 4500 carb base throttle body with 2-inch throttle bores that flows 1,600 cfm and another version with 2.25-inch throttles that flows 2,000 cfm.

The 4500 Holley–based carburetor is large and the carburetor pad is larger than the standard carb pad. The spacing on the large throttle bore used in the 4500 carb requires it. You want the carb best suited to your engine package. These flow 1,000 cfm to approximately 1,450 cfm. (Photo Courtesy L. Lawson)

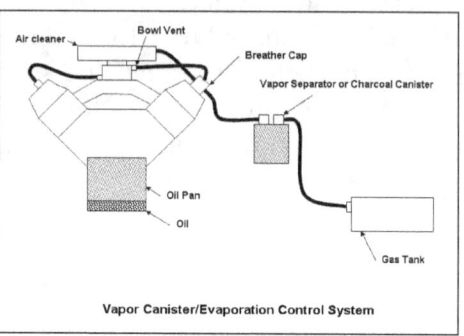

A charcoal canister is typically mounted to almost all cars built after about 1972. It is usually on the passenger-side fender shield. The engine's PCV and the breather are connected to the carburetor and the air cleaner, which is mounted on top of the carburetor, is then connected to the canister. The charcoal canister is vented or connected to the fuel tank. This is a nice way to vent the vapor separator filter. Remember that these lines are fuel lines; they should have fuel-line rated hoses.

The vapor separator is used to help keep high-performance engines from vapor locking. It has one outlet up to the carburetor (on top), one inlet from the gas tank (bottom middle), and one return to the gas tank or charcoal canister. The vapor separator should be mounted vertically after the mechanical pump. The inlet from the gas tank and the return are both on the bottom of the filter. The vapor separator can be very handy for hot weather racing or summer cruising. These are available from suppliers such as Mopar or Year One.

CHAPTER 10

The Carter ThermoQuad is probably the best street 4-barrel carburetor, but getting parts for them can be a challenge. Service kits are easier to find, but jets and metering rods can be difficult to locate. You can check with a company such as Summit for a rebuilt unit. If the ThermoQuad were readily available (as are the AFB and AVS), it would be my number-one choice for a 4-barrel package, followed by the vacuum secondary Holley or the Edelbrock AVS.

Many Holley-based carburetors have two float bowls and two fuel entrances. With this configuration, you should use a fuel line setup similar to this. Several kits are available for these Holleys that make the extra plumbing easy to organize.

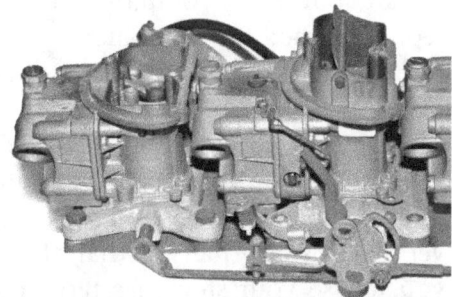

The 6-barrel (actually three 2-barrel carbs) is a great street induction system. When you are tuning the 6-barrel, just think of it as one 4-barrel carb with four secondaries.

Holley/Quick Fuel vacuum secondary 4-barrel, and other models. Aftermarket manufacturers generally shoot for the 340 to 360 engine size for the basic tune-up. (See the Appendix for detailed tuning tips on the Carter ThermoQuad 4-barrel carburetor and the 6-barrel Holley setups.) The AFB, AVS, TQ, and 6-barrel were all production packages on Chrysler cars.

Spacers

Spacers added between the carburetor and the intake manifold can be a useful tuning tool. I strongly recommend using a spacer of 3/8- or 1/2-inch minimum thickness. It can be made of plastic, phenolic, or canvas phenolic (Trans-Dapt). Also available are 1-inch spacers plus one-hole (open plenum) or four-hole options. You can find 2-inch versions, but that much extra thickness may cause hood clearance issues. I do not expect a spacer to be as effective on a throttle body application.

Magnum MPI Upgrade

When fuel injection tuning a Magnum MPI system, you must be careful of the order that you make adjustments for performance tuning. Because the computer controls almost everything, making performance improvements becomes a team effort. With a production computer (ECM), in many cases, you can install a few performance items on the stock program. If you add substantial things and make many changes, reprogram the computer to accommodate the new pieces. With MPI, newer vehicles are assumed to have a Magnum engine. (A-engine conversion to MPI is discussed in the section "MPI Conversion.")

Every engine-performance project is different, but the computer requires certain steps be performed in sequence, and there are lots of options. Here are the general steps that will help you accomplish your project:

Step 1: Install a cat-back exhaust system and install a cold-air air cleaner, which moves the air inlet from the top of the engine to low behind the radiator. The option (not required but offers increased performance) is to reprogram the production computer (more spark, more fuel).

Step 2: Reprogram ECM or install a computer upgrade from Mopar, if available.

Step 3: Install a set of headers (Tri-Ys if you have a choice). Keep the oxygen sensor and install a bigger cam (Crane grind number 2020 and PN 694111; because it has an E.O. number, it's legal in all states) along with better valvesprings (PN P5249464) and retainers (PN P4452032).

Step 4: Install a single-plane fuel-injected intake manifold (PN P5007398) along with an installation kit (PN P5007638), which makes the install go much smoother. Also install an MSD Blaster ignition coil designed for use with 1996–2003 Magnum hardware.

FUEL SYSTEM AND TUNING

Step 5: The aftermarket seems to offer few intake manifolds for upgrading the Magnum. Fuel-injected versions for the A-engine heads and carburetor versions for the Magnum are available, but the Mopar intakes are the only ones designed for an upgrade for the Magnum itself. Note that more fuel is needed, but the SCT computer reprogram should handle it.

Needing more fuel could mean a reprogram of the computer or an add-on computer (from SCT, FAST, AEM) that overrules the production computer.

Step 6: Install a deeper and/or wider oil pan (such as Milodon) with a scraper or tray designed to work with that pan.

Step 7: Install a bigger cam (valve lift about .450 to .500 inch). HP springs are okay.

A Few Options: At this point you could consider adding a new programmable ignition system from AEM or FAST. You can also consider a 4-barrel throttle body (about 1,000 cfm), which requires a 4-barrel intake manifold (PN P4876615) for the driver-side linkage common in passenger cars.

You will be exceeding the 300/350 hp level for the injectors, so you want to upgrade them. This is also where you might consider more cubic inches (such as a 4.00-inch crank) and/or better cylinder heads (such as Edelbrock aluminum or Indy Heads cast iron/aluminum or B1-BA aluminum).

A-Engine MPI Conversion

Converting an A-engine to an MPI system is similar to upgrading the Magnum, and you face the same challenges. Some of the many ways to do it are easier than others and some can be less expensive. Don't forget that all the parts must work together as a team.

Here are a few ways to accomplish your project:

Plan 1: For a 340/360 engine, install a complete kit (PN P5153590). Add an A-engine intake manifold for use with injectors (or switch to Magnum heads). Also add a Magnum flexplate (PN P4876706) for the windows.

Plan 2: Remove all the fuel injection hardware from a 1992–2003 production Magnum MPI engine. The computer must be the one used in the kit above. Any computer must be reprogrammed for stand-alone function. If you do not want to use the Magnum's gas tank and fuel pump, you can use an electric fuel pump (PN P5153688). Don't forget the flexplate.

Plan 3: Install an Edelbrock universal EFI sump fuel kit that allows you to use your stock gas tank and mechanical fuel pump and yet still have a high-pressure EFI system. You may integrate this kit with Plan 2 above.

Plan 4: Install an Edelbrock complete kit that includes manifold, 4-barrel throttle body, and everything else for an A-engine (318 to 360 engines). The kit is called Pro-Flo 2 and is rated for 450 hp (including 29-pound/hour injectors). The dyno test on a 340 showed 431 hp. You may have to upgrade to the 35-pound/hour injectors if you have a 400-incher.

Plan 5: Install an AEM or FAST programmable ignition system. This means installing a fuel-injected intake manifold for A-engine heads and a 4-barrel throttle body (about 1,000 cfm is typical). Well, you don't really need the 4-barrel; the 2-barrel is fine and it has three sensors attached.

Next, you need an electric fuel pump and a Magnum flexplate. If you have trouble finding a fuel-injected intake manifold for the A-engine heads, some Mopar A-engine carbureted intakes have the fuel-injection bosses cast-in, just not machined. Another option is to swap heads to the Magnum versions (Edelbrock, Indy, or B1-BA aluminum heads or Indy Heads cast iron).

Remove the mechanical pump and place a fuel pump cover over the hole. In most cases the ignition manufacturer (FAST or AEM) also offers hardware, including fuel rails and injectors, regulators that you need in addition to the electrical hardware.

Fuel Injection Conversion

Chrysler installed a throttle body fuel injection system on 1987 to 1992 A-engines. The small 2-barrel throttle body didn't perform very well in the horsepower and torque challenge. MSD has introduced the Atomic EFI system and it might change everyone's opinion. The self-contained unit looks like a Holley carburetor. It has four large injectors inside the basic housing. It has nozzles in the throttle bores like a carburetor. It is designed to support 525 hp with options. The throttle bores are 1.75 inches so it should flow around 750 cfm (my guess; it's not rated). MSD says that it also works with superchargers (up to 14 psi).

Nitrous Oxide

Nitrous systems come in all sizes, shapes, and configurations, including hidden systems, plate systems, and direct-port injection systems. My advice? Build your engine for nitrous or limit the amount that you use.

Performance gains of more than 500 hp have been claimed with some race systems. However, if you are using pump gas (92 octane), horsepower gains are about 100 or 200 hp. Using pump gas, street nitrous systems require less total spark advance by 2 to 4 degrees.

The baseline engine has the specifications for a naturally aspirated high-performance engine. With race-only nitrous systems this spark advance decrease can be as much as 12 degrees. In addition, street nitrous kits require colder spark plugs than the standard engine by one or two steps. For example, if you are currently using an 11 or 12 heat-range plug (based on Champion heat range numbers), you drop to a 9 or 10 heat-range plug with a street nitrous kit. In a race-only kit, this cold plug requirement increases even more.

With a nitrous system, you inject both nitrous and fuel (gas) at the same time. The direct-port injection, which requires eight nozzles, injects both the nitrous and the fuel through the same nozzle. The other style of nitrous system uses a central plate. Most off-the-shelf kits are based on 4-barrel carburetors.

A nitrous system has a lot of parts that are completely separate from the engine assembly's hardware. I strongly recommend a complete kit from a manufacturer such as ZEX, Nitrous Supply, Edelbrock, Nitrous Express, or Nitrous Oxide Systems.

Direct-port-injection nitrous systems are designed for serious competition and can offer horsepower increases up to 500, but they require modifications to the manifold and plumbing.

Supercharger

Your engine building plan should incorporate the installation

With a CNC-machine, carb spacers can get very fancy: one-hole spacer (left), large-pad 4500 Holley four-hole spacer (middle), and "blended" spacer (right).

of a supercharger, and accordingly, the compression ratio needs to be adjusted down; to 8:1, not 9 or 10:1. Because of the higher cylinder pressures, I recommend installing forged pistons. On a supercharger, dual 4-barrel carburetors are the most popular option.

An 8-barrel system could be rated at 1,200, 1,500, or 1,700 cfm or more, and it's suitable for many racing-based superchargers and perhaps even more street blowers.

With a street engine, you run pump gas, which has an octane of 92. This limits the supercharged engine's compression ratio to about 8:1 max.

The plate nitrous systems are probably the most popular and the easiest to install. They fit between the carburetor and the intake manifold and are about 3/8 to 1/2 inch thick. Nitrous goes in one side and fuel goes in the other. Plates systems can offer gains in the 100- to 200-hp range.

The supercharger's boost should be limited to 8-psi max.

As a general statement, the supercharger manufacturers try to match the supercharger size to the engine size (cubic inches). You do not want the same-size supercharger on a 318- and a 400-ci engine. The 340/360 engine might use a smaller blower (maybe 112 in one rating system) and the 400/440-ci engines, a 122 blower (same system).

The carburetor opening must be long enough for two carburetors in-line. Popular manufacturers are Magnuson, Whipple Industries, Eaton Performance Products, Spintex, and Weiand.

Most supercharger manufacturers offer many sizes of supercharger pulleys as a tuning aid for increasing the boost pressure. Edelbrock offers several diameters. Caution: most street blowers cause the engine to detonate if the boost pressure is increased; 8 psi seems to be a good max.

Edelbrock recommends using two PN 1405 Performer carburetors (600 cfm, manual choke, AFB) for supercharged engines. Edelbrock also recommends the following calibration for 340- to 440-ci engines: primary jets, .101 inch; secondary jets, .101 inch; metering rods .070 x .042 inch; step-up springs, 5 inches (orange); needle and seat assemblies, .110 inch.

CHAPTER 11

EXHAUST SYSTEM

The application of engine and engine internals determine the exhaust system requirements. Street, street/strip, road racing, drag racing, or any other particular application places the engine under different operating conditions. A street engine typically does not rev high, and strong torque is often the goal. On the other end of the spectrum, road racing engines rev high for nearly an entire race, so the engine and exhaust must produce the best performance at the upper end of the rev range. And, therefore, they require a much different exhaust system to run at their best.

In essence, an exhaust system must be tailored to a particular engine component package and use. In other words, when it comes to headers and exhaust, one type, design, or size does not fit all.

The exhaust system must physically fit in the particular vehicle, and because of that, tube length, size, and routing is constrained by the chassis. The manifold bolts to the head and lines up with the ports in the head and the head's attaching bolt pattern. However, much of the rest of the exhaust system (length, diameter, shape, and bend) can affect the engine's performance and its torque and horsepower curves. Because it affects the engine's performance, the complete system should be considered rather than only the manifold bolt pattern.

Objects in the engine compartment typically cause the header tubes to be routed in almost every direction.

Manifold

Most of us look at the header or exhaust manifold as a part that must fit the engine compartment. We often don't tend to give much thought to the rest of the exhaust system other than its basic fit to the body and its connection to the manifold.

Because the exhaust manifold or header bolts to the engine, you could consider it an accessory, but the exhaust system affects the engine's torque and power curves. This means that you need to select the proper hardware to work best with the rest of your engine package and for your application.

The only performance choice used to be a single exhaust or a dual exhaust, and the dual exhaust tended to come with big engines, with no real option for smaller engines. Early big-block exhaust development for the 1967 440 HP package (GTX and R/T models) led to the high-flow 340 exhaust manifold in 1968. The 340 manifolds were the standard for small-blocks for many years after 1968. From an engine performance standpoint, the 1968 340 exhaust manifolds are a giant gain over the 273/318 log manifolds, and they fit

CHAPTER 11

The 340 manifold has very smooth, rounded corners and reasonably equal lengths. The first cylinder, on the left, is long and the last cylinder on the right is short, but they are much better than the typical log manifold.

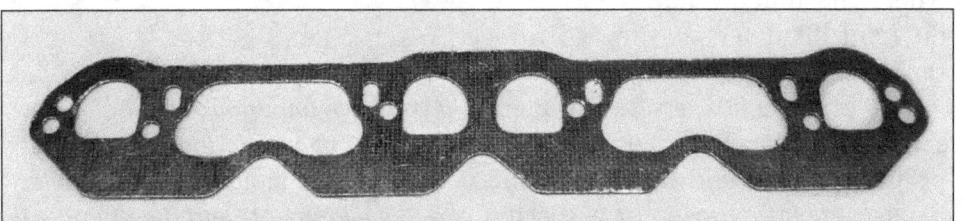

The original W2 exhaust pattern was changed to a wide-spaced pattern. The aftermarket gasket manufacturers put both the standard small-block pattern and the wide-spaced W2 pattern on the same gasket. Note that each set of exhaust ports has four attaching holes around it; the center two ports use common bolts. The standard bolt holes are the two holes, one on each side of the port(s), that are very close to the port opening. The W2 bolt holes are the other two holes that are farther from the port opening.

in the engine compartment, plus they are quiet and durable.

Steel Manifolds

For years, headers and exhaust systems were made of mild steel. Then some aftermarket manufacturers began offering stainless steel versions. Stainless offers durability advantages over mild steel. Typically stainless steel alloys contain at least 12-percent chromium and also have a very low percentage (less than .2 percent) of carbon. Some versions have high nickel content, which are popular in race cars and offer welding advantages. Low-nickel alloys are used in OEM production exhausts.

Cast-Iron Manifolds

Performance exhaust manifolds for small-blocks started with the 1968 340 engine package. These cast-iron exhaust manifolds are very good for performance. Because they were a compact design, they fit more body styles, but the less-swoopy design doesn't flow as much air. The 1970 and newer versions are not quite as good.

This remained the basic situation until the introduction of the 5.2L Magnum engines in 1992. The two sets of cast-iron manifolds provide about equal performance on the dyno. The 340 driver-side manifold is slightly better than the Magnum; the passenger-side Magnum manifold is slightly better than the 340. The 340 driver-side manifold is the most impressive looking in the engine compartment.

The A-engine and the Magnum engine share the same exhaust manifold bolt pattern. The W2 performance cylinder head used a wider-spaced bolt pattern when it was originally introduced. When the head was reintroduced in the late 1980s, the new W2 was machined with both bolt patterns. W2 heads used headers.

Header

Air enters the engine through the intake manifold and then flows through the cylinder head and engine. This airflow must be matched on the exhaust side to allow the increased airflow to exit the engine. This technology was originally used by Magnum engines from 1996 through 2003, but the aftermarket has advanced since then. The science isn't as important as availability. Street headers use small tube diameters and street/strip systems use slightly larger tubes. The big tubes are generally used on highly modified race engines only.

The four common tube sizes are 1½, 1⅝, 1¾, and 1⅞ inches. A 2-inch header tube is considered a race item.

Street headers usually have either 1½ or 1⅝ tubes. Street/strip headers usually use 1¾-inch tubes. The 400-inch engines usually use 1¾ tubes for the street and 1⅞-inchers for the street/strip. TTi step headers are good for both applications.

The typical shorty header or block-hugger header tends to be in the middle; it is an upgrade on the stock cast-iron manifold but not as good as an actual header.

Applications

A number of factors need to be considered when selecting a header for your particular engine package and application. Do not fall into the trap of thinking bigger is better. Instead, you need to embrace the idea of the correct-size header for the engine combination, so the trick is determining the best size and dimensions.

If you install a large 2-inch header on a mild or moderate street engine, your engine has little torque.

In such cases, the owner often blames the poor design of the header, but that's not true. Most of the time, a 1½- to 1⅝-inch pipe is an appropriate size for an engine that revs between 1,500 and 6,000 rpm.

Street versions have a small primary diameter (around 1⅝ inches) and are somewhat easier to install. A mid-level primary diameter on the collector is about 2¼ or 2½ inches. The racing versions usually have larger primary diameters (around 1¾ to 1⅞ inches) and a larger collector (2½ to 3 inches).

Equal-length primary tubes, desired in a race header, are very difficult to fit into a "street" engine compartment. The first cylinder's tube tends to be too long and the last tube tends to be too short. In some cases the solution to these problems was to run some tubes out through the fenderwell and back under the frame to gain the length. Fenderwell headers are generally the last choice because you have to cut up your car. The A-engine in the early A-Body (1966 and earlier models) is one package that fits into this last category.

Hedman, Hooker, and TTi offer headers for pre-2004 small-blocks; other manufacturers focus on newer cars built in the past 10 years of production. The street header with 1½- or 1⅝-inch tube diameter is the most popular. The larger 1¾- and 1⅞-inch (Hooker) are more difficult to find, but Hedman may make headers that are not shown in the catalog, such as a 1¾-inch four-into-one header. The TTi 1⅝ and 1¾ step header may work well in several packages.

Tri-Y headers commonly offer more torque and often provide a better fit in the engine compartment. The shorty header or block hugger was originally designed for street rods, but its use has spread to many other types of vehicles because it fits the engine compartments so much better than other styles of headers. The step header is the latest design and was developed for racing and is a special version of the four-into-one, where the four primaries have two different diameters as they go from the head to the collector.

All of these headers have dimensions such as tube diameters and primary lengths and these sizes and lengths are developed for a specific engine on the engine dyno. Tri-Y headers have been around forever, but they are difficult to find, and currently Doug Thorley shows a 1⅝ Tri-Y header (for trucks). Most super Stock engines (drag racing) use a custom-made version of the Tri-Y header.

Performance gains for headers and low-restriction exhaust systems vary because the stock systems range from log manifolds and single exhaust pipe, to 340 manifolds and dual exhaust. Generally 5 to 10 percent is a good baseline gain. As the engine becomes larger, a good exhaust system becomes more important. One caution: On the Magnum engines, because they are computer controlled, performance additions such as headers and a cat-back exhaust put the engine on the edge of being too lean. Another change from the stock system could cause an engine failure. When computer-controlled engines become too lean, they lose performance rather than gain it. At that point, you must have the ECM reprogrammed or a new computer installed.

The primary tube length of the header needs to be sized for the application and engine package. Some have heaped praise on equal-length headers, but once they

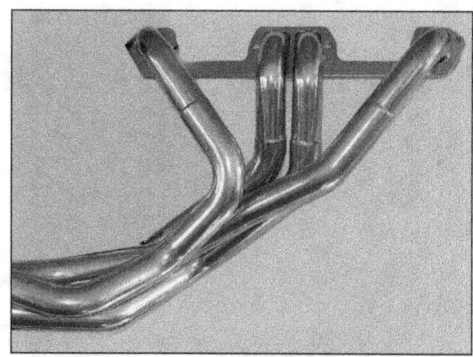

If you have enough room, the manufacturer can route the first and last tubes toward the center two (similar to this alignment) and then bundle the four tubes toward the collector.

are hooked up to a conventional exhaust system with mufflers, the performance gain is negated.

Shorty and mid-length headers have been proven to produce nearly as much horsepower as long-tube headers and are suitable for a street car. Shorty headers provide a performance improvement over OEM cast-iron manifolds, and for some cars and trucks, shorty headers are

Borla designed 4-into-1 headers with short primaries with all the tubes kept close to the side of the block. They were designed for street packages similar to a shorty header but offered added performance.

Calculating Header Cross Section

For all engine builders, maximizing volumetric efficiency is the ultimate goal because then the exhaust system and the engine as a whole perform at their best. High-performance legend Jim McFarland developed a simple formula for determining the optimum cross-sectional area of a header primary tube. This is particularly important for street engines because this formula helps identify the torque peak of the engine. By determining the optimal torque peak, you arrive at the most suitable primary pipe diameter, and peak power is usually no more than 1,500 to 1,750 rpm above the torque peak.

The connecting rod–to–stroke ratio influences the powerband spread between the torque peak and the power peak. When a constant stroke length is factored in, a longer connecting rod brings power and torque peaks closer to one another. A shorter rod typically increases the separation between the torque peak and the power peak.

When you've identified the torque peak, you can use the McFarland formula to determine the cross-sectional area of the primary pipe. Keep in mind that this formula is used to determine the cross-sectional area for a single cylinder.

$$\text{Cylinder Volume} = \text{displacement} \div \text{number of cylinders}$$
$$A_{c/s} = (\text{cylinder volume} \times \text{RPM}) \div 88{,}200$$
$$\text{Or, RPM} = (A_{c/s} \times 88{,}200) \div \text{cylinder volume}$$

Where:
$A_{c/s}$ = primary pipe cross-sectioned area
Cylinder volume = volume of a single cylinder
88,200 = mathematical constant
RPM = RPM at torque peak

When you know the cross-sectional area, you can calculate the corresponding primary pipe diameter to the closest pipe size available.

First, you need to determine the true inside diameter of a pipe for the purpose of calculating c/s area, using this formula:

Inside diameter = outside diameter − (2 × wall thickness)

Then, you need two more formulas:

$$A = D \times D \times .7854$$
$$\text{Pipe Size} = \sqrt{(A \times 1.273)}$$

Where:
A = cross-sectional area
D = inside diameter of pipe
.7854 = mathematical constant
1.273 = mathematical constant

These figures don't take catalytic converters and mufflers into account, which impact peak power. As a result, changing peak torque RPM to arrive at the correct header pipe size is more of a priority than trying to obtain peak power. Therefore, resist the temptation to always go up in size when it comes to the primary pipe because you want to maintain exhaust velocity and scavenging ability of the pipe and, therefore, peak torque. As a result, the formula for c/s area is based on engine speed, cylinder volume, and volumetric efficiency (VE).

For example, a 340 high-performance street engine (with a hydraulic cam) might make peak power at 5,500 rpm. One cylinder has 42.5 ci (340 ÷ 8 = 42.5). The peak torque is 3,750 (5,500 − 1,750).

Therefore, the cross-sectional area of the primary pipe is 1.81 square inches (42.5 × 3,750 = 159,375; A = 159,375 ÷ 88,200).

The pipe size is 1.52 inches ($\sqrt{1.81} \times 1.273$).

The actual pipe outside diameter is 1.60 inches (1.52 + 2 × .040).

Performance Trends offers computer programs that calculate all of this much more accurately and much easier than using the formulas. Unfortunately, the problem is that header manufacturers only offer certain header sizes: both primary tube diameters and lengths. So, if you find that your engine package makes peak power at 5,500 rpm (for example) and the header size is 1.50 inches, installing 2-inch headers is not going to make this same package peak at 6,500 rpm. And custom-made headers are a very high expense for a street/strip engine. ■

EXHAUST SYSTEM

the only option, so then it's simply a matter of determining the correct tube diameter.

As the most common headers, four primary tubes, varying in length from 24 to 36 inches, carry the exhaust gases from each cylinder to the collector.

Tri-Y Headers

The Tri-Y style of headers was one of the first designs. A Tri-Y header design starts at the head with four tubes matched to the four exhaust ports. After the four tubes come out of the flange, they are joined (merged) into two tubes. Then these two tubes are joined into one at the collector.

Originally the Tri-Y was noted for torque, while the four-into-one header was noted for horsepower. So over time, the Tri-Y header fell into obscurity. In the mid-1990s, SEMA asked the California Air Resources Board (CARB) to create a test program for performance parts so they could be sold for street use. Each part is tested and, if approved, assigned an emission exemption number.

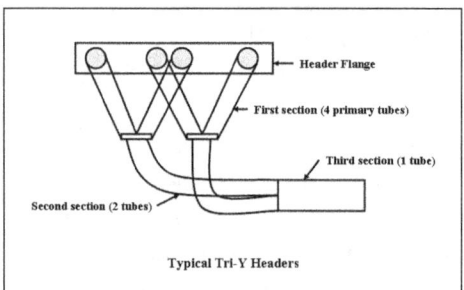

Typical Tri-Y Headers

The big advantage of Tri-Y headers was originally less tube in the engine compartment so they were easier to install and fit into tight engine compartments. Today, the Tri-Y header is used in race cars because it performs better across the full engine range; it has a wider, flatter torque curve. The name comes from the three sections and the Y-shape of the two halves.

Best Headers for an Application

In an effort to tie engine hardware into performance packages, I created five packages, which vary from 250 hp to more than 700 hp and all are intended for street/strip applications.

	Best Head	Header
Package No. 1	Bracket valve job (back-cut valves)	Street, 1½ or 1⅝ inches
Package No. 2	Edelbrock alum, Indy or B1-BA	Street, 1½ or 1⅝ inches
Package No. 3	No. 3 with bowl work	1¾ inches
Package No. 4	No. 3 with intermediate CNC-porting	1¾ inches
Package No. 5	Indy Heads or B1-BA fully CNC-ported	1⅞ inches

Note: Any one of these packages could use the TTi step headers. Larger displacements (400 ci and more) may need larger headers. Typically, 2-inch headers are designed for racing.

Street versus Race Headers

The typical four-into-one street header looks very similar to a race header. For small-block engines, race headers have somewhat larger primary tube diameters, such as 1¾ or 1⅞ inches, and have equal-length tubes. In addition, race headers usually use adjustable primary tubes and are more expensive.

Street headers use smaller tube diameters, such as 1⅝ inches, and have some tube-length variation. Smaller-diameter primaries allow for easier in-car installation and the length variation also helps ease installation.

During the mid-1990s, header manufacturers began making headers for the street that were emissions tested and approved. Many of these headers had thicker flanges (next to the head) and used thicker-gauge steel for the tubes. These headers are very good for the street, but they were made for production vehicles from 1995 on. You don't find this style of header for older cars/engines.

This is a short header but it is still a four-into-one design. It offers some of the advantages of fit and installation of the shorty-style header but still has the performance of the four-into-one header. This style is a good compromise for street use. A shorty header is technically a four-into-one–style header except that the primary tubes are very short, 6 inches to 1 foot. This style was first designed for street rods because the engine compartments are so small after the V-8 engine is installed. Shorty headers have grown in popularity because they are easy to install.

CHAPTER 11

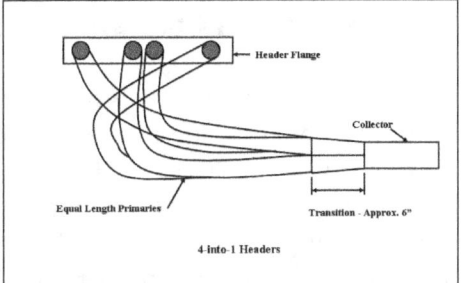

Street versions of four-into-one headers do not have the four primary tubes of equal length; the versions made for racing work very hard to gain equal length in the four primaries per side. The rear-most cylinder tends to be short and the front cylinder tends to be long so the manufacturer tries to loop one to gain length and direct-route the other to keep it short. The extra tube length fills the engine compartment and makes these much more difficult to install.

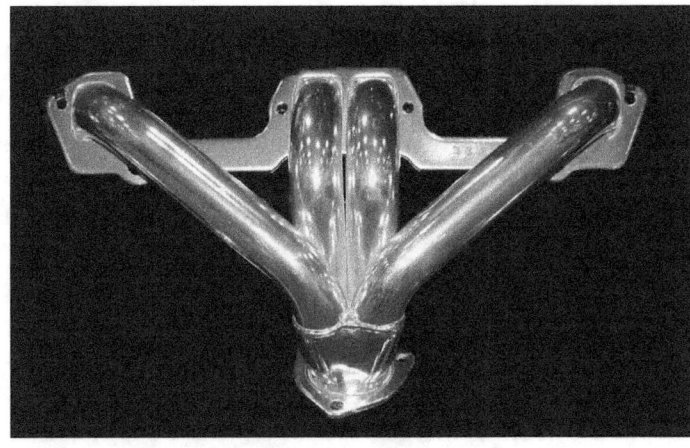

The shorty header can also be hooked back toward the block to gain more room and stay away from frame rails or steering linkage.

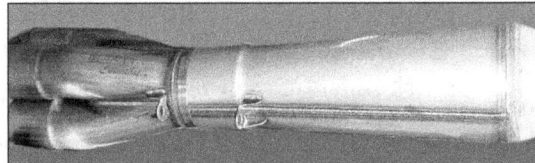

The merge collector joins the four tubes together (left) and tapers them down to a smaller size, and then it expands in size (right). The inside also tapers at the point where the four tubes are joined; standard collectors cut the tubes square at this point. The section to the right is called the megaphone.

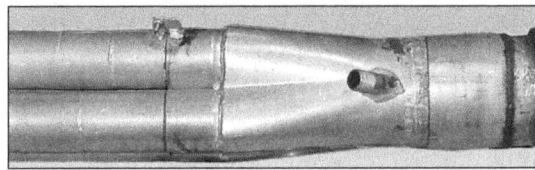

The typical standard collector is basically straight. The four tubes (two underneath not visible) on the left enter into the transition in the center; the straight collector is on the right. If these headers had been designed for use with an emissions engine, the oxygen sensor would be mounted in the transition/collector area, where the evac-fitting is currently located.

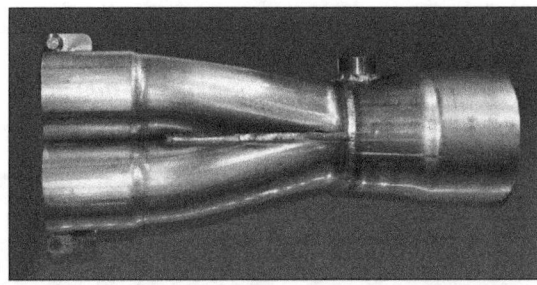

Both long and short merge collectors are available. The short versions do not use the megaphone. The four tubes enter at the left, are jointed and tapered down in size to the smaller diameter in the center, and then it expands going to the right.

Header manufacturers jumped at the chance to have street-legal exhaust products. They looked at various designs on the dyno, focusing on street vehicles and street use. They found that the Tri-Y design offered more torque and they could match or improve on the power of the four-into-one designs. The lengths of the primary and secondary tubes were different from the original designs and the tube sizes were changed, but the end result was that these Tri-Y headers made more torque and more power.

Shorty Headers

The shorty header is technically a four-into-one design, but instead of having 30-inch-length primaries, it has 6-inch primaries. It was originally made for street rods because enthusiasts tend to install big V-8 engines into small engine compartments that were designed for 4s and 6s. The shorty's biggest advantages related to ease of installation and fit into the engine compartment.

Step Headers

Technically step headers are another version of the four-into-one header. With a typical race header with all primaries designed at the same length, the tube size is constant. The primaries become larger and the length changes tuning for different performance characteristics, but the tube diameter stays the same for a given design.

With a step header, the primary tube changes size after 6 to 12 inches and may change size again before it reaches the collector. That diameter size change is called a step. These steps and the length of tube in each step are determined by extensive testing on an engine dynamometer. Each set of sizes and lengths is unique to the specific engine and RPM package.

The purpose of all this testing is to gain the best of both worlds: best torque while maintaining the best power. The typical step header is a race item that is custom-made based on lengthy dyno development. However, TTi offers an off-the-shelf step header that work well with all engine packages.

Flanges

The flange of a header bolts to the cylinder head and looks somewhat like a thick steel exhaust gasket. Each primary tube is welded into the flange. The exhaust openings in the flange are cut out. These ports in the flange come in several shapes, such as round, square, and D-shaped, plus others. Most small-blocks use the square shape except for the W2 heads, which use a D-shaped flange opening.

Merge Collectors

The typical exhaust header collector is a straight/round 2½- to 3-inch-diameter tube; the merge collector is tapered inside and out. Where the four tubes come together, the center point is extended and tapered to a point. The outer wall of the collector tapers slightly over a short distance. Then the collector expands until slightly larger than a standard collector. The length of the taper is changed for different tuning effects. Generally the high-flow and high-velocity exhaust gases in the merge collector try to increase the amount of torque and broaden the torque curve.

Oxygen Sensor

For 1980 and newer engines, the cast-iron manifolds use at least one oxygen sensor. They are also installed in the exhaust system ahead of the catalytic converter(s). Although not required on most A-engines, all Magnum engines have these sensors. If the exhaust manifolds are replaced with headers, the oxygen sensor should be reinstalled. This allows the ECM to function properly. The ECM controls both the amount of fuel and the amount of spark that the engine receives.

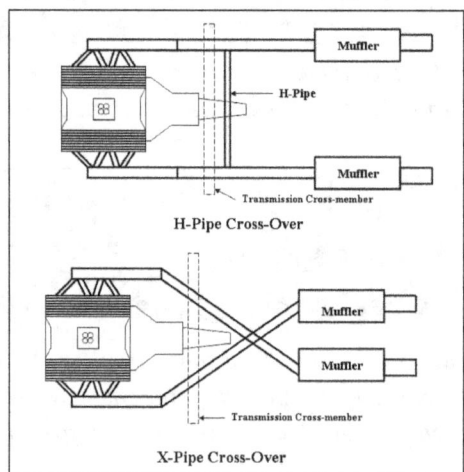

The H-pipe is used to increase engine performance while allowing a quieter exhaust. The actual H-pipe is a smaller-diameter pipe than the exhaust pipe; it connects the driver-side and passenger-side exhaust pipes. It is generally located behind the transmission crossmember.

The X-pipe crossover crosses the passenger-side exhaust pipe to the driver-side muffler and the driver-side exhaust pipe to the passenger-side muffler. They do not actually cross but are joined into an open box at the crossover point. The details of how the tubes enter the box vary but the box connects the two sides and performs the same function as the H-pipe.

Installation Clearance

The engine's oil filter is attached to the passenger's side of the engine toward the rear. Header tubes generally work toward the rear of the engine compartment as they begin to exit the engine compartment. One of the primary tubes of the headers often tries to hit the oil filter. The easy solution is to move the oil filter with the right-angle adapter (available from Mopar Performance, among others).

Coatings

Headers come with a variety of coatings, and these are applied mainly for appearance. Some are used as a form of heat shield or thermal barrier. Although some companies specialize in various coatings, most exhaust coatings are offered by the header or exhaust manufacturer. Coatings can be ceramic, polished ceramic, and nickel-chrome plated.

Manufacturers also offer thermal barriers that are applied inside the tubes. Although each type of coating offers unique features, the main focus of the heat barrier is to keep the

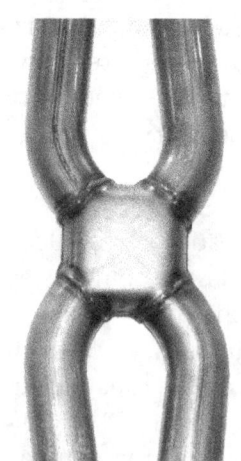

Exhaust manufacturers offer pre-made sections of the X-pipe for installation into your exhaust system. The top-to-bottom length is 2 to 3 feet. The mufflers are added at the bottom and the exhaust pipes are added at the top.

exhaust gas heat inside the tube and not allow it to heat up the engine compartment.

Pipe Crossovers

The H-pipe is a short tube that connects the driver-side and passenger-side exhaust pipes on any dual exhaust. The 340 and the bigger 360 engines can benefit from the H-pipe. Originally it was placed where you wanted the collector to end. So if the dyno testing showed that an 18-inch collector was the best package, you placed the H-pipe or crossover pipe at the end of the 18-inch collector.

Keep in mind that the floorpan design and transmission may not provide adequate clearance, so you have to verify that it fits the car. In most cases, the H-pipe crosses under the transmission crossmember or just to the rear of it, which puts it under the transmission output shaft/housing.

Manufacturers today produce H-pipe, maybe 3 feet long, with the crossover pipe welded together. These could be added to almost any exhaust system.

Similar to the H-pipe, the X-pipe connects the driver-side and passenger-side exhaust pipes to share the exhaust pulses. X-pipes are also made in about 3- to 4-foot sections, all welded together, and can be installed in almost any exhaust system.

In general, manufacturers produce X-pipe kits in 2½- and 3-inch pipe sizes so that it can match up to the exhaust system. This is a little tricky.

Flowmaster says there is no horsepower gain with either X or H crossover pipes. TTi says they provide a gain of more than 10 hp on a 400-hp engine package. Both crossovers are readily available from Flowmaster and TTi so I use one or the other; the crossover has always been good for performance. This hardware needs more investigation.

Mufflers and Catalytic Converters

At the beginning of performance small-block production, glass-packs and dual-exhaust conversions were common. As headers became popular, customers looked for better (lower restriction) mufflers. Early answers were the Street Hemi muffler (1966–1971) and the Imperial muffler. The Imperial was very good for performance, but it was larger than the Street Hemi and was difficult to fit into the smaller vehicles that carried the small-block. Another answer was the turbo Corvair, or the turbo muffler. It was smaller and easier to fit under cars.

Muffler manufacturers, such as Flowmaster, Borla, Magnaflow, TTi, and Dynomax, make suitable products for max-performance small-blocks. TTi and Dynomax Super Turbo mufflers are very compact and should fit most applications. The other three companies offer muffler bodies that are about 14 inches long and 18 to 19 inches long. But these may not fit all areas of the chassis.

Flowmaster and Dynomax offer a variety of inlet and outlet sizes; most are 2.5 or 3 inches. These mufflers can be positioned in the center, on the driver's side, or on the passenger's side, depending on length considerations.

Predicting sound level and tune is almost impossible, but that is one feature that manufacturers work hard to do. Back pressure is the key to performance. Short mufflers are probably the best option, but you should discuss the sound issue with the manufacturer or the local outlet or your local muffler shop.

Exhaust manufacturers are working on the exhaust tuning science on 2004 and newer vehicles and engines. On these vehicles, the catalytic converters are left on the vehicle and technicians tune what is ahead of them (headers) and what is behind them (mufflers and exhaust pipes). These mufflers are state-of-the-art hardware and the muffler may fit your application, but there is no install hardware so

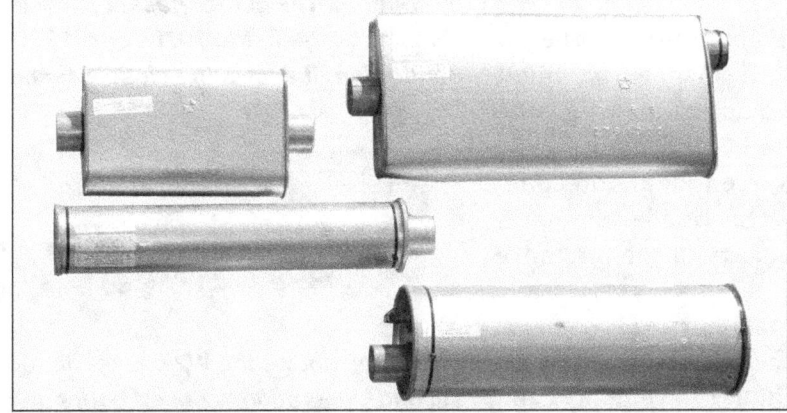

Many styles of mufflers are available. The short, flat muffler (upper left) is the easiest to fit. The large flat muffler (upper right) would be quiet but would be difficult to fit into some vehicles. The round muffler (lower right) would fit on some vehicles and not on others.

EXHAUST SYSTEM

it must be a custom install at your local muffler shop.

Many racetracks began requiring race cars to have mufflers in both drag racing and circle track racing. This restriction tended to be a local, rather than national, development. In the 1960s, manufacturers started looking for and developing low-restriction, lightweight, small, and easy-to-install mufflers. This led to better mufflers that actually lowered the engine's back pressure and still kept the noise at reasonable levels.

Today, these small mufflers are offered on a wide range of configurations with overall lengths of 13 to 20 inches. In most cases, the underside of the car dictates the specific style: center entrance, driver-side exit, or almost any other combination. These performance mufflers come in 2.25-, 2.5-, and 3-inch tube sizes to fit just about any exhaust system.

Cat-Back Systems

The "cat-back system" is a term that came about in the late 1990s to refer to exhaust systems that moved components behind the production catalytic converter. This typically means that the muffler and tailpipes are revised.

As the emissions testing era began in about 1995, the main enforcement agency (CARB) determined that the exhaust system behind the catalytic converter was free (open) and could be replaced. This made the term "cat-back exhaust" a performance standard.

Many manufacturers started making cat-back exhausts. Because the A-engine didn't have many catalytic converters in production, manufacturers didn't make these systems for the 1960s, 1970s, and 1980s cars. However, the technology works on new and old cars. Basically, on vehicles built after 1995, a cat-back system reduces the overall exhaust system's backpressure by 50 percent. Potentially this change can result in gains of 5 to 7 percent in power.

Tailpipes

Aftermarket tailpipes come in lengths of 2.25, 2.5, and 3.0 inches. I use the 2.25 version with up to 300-hp engine packages, the 2.5 version for up to 400 hp, and the 3.0 version for more than 400 hp. Caution: On new cars or trucks with MPI, a true dual exhaust (two pipes from the exhaust manifolds to the rear of the vehicle) should not be used unless you plan on reprogramming the ECM. Typically on these newer vehicles, the large drop in back pressure can confuse the sensors that input to the ECM and engine performance may suffer.

Gaskets

Sealing the exhaust manifold to the cylinder head can be a challenge. Cast-iron manifolds are easy, even with a thin gasket. Headers can be a problem. The header flange is not as stiff as the cast-iron exhaust manifold. In some cases, the header manufacturer designs in a small ridge around the port opening to help the gasket seal to the cylinder head. Using thicker gaskets (1/16 inch) also helps.

Today, some exhaust gaskets are made of a high-temperature material that is stronger and more resistant to leaks. A good tip is to apply some high-temperature silicone to both sides of the gasket before installation.

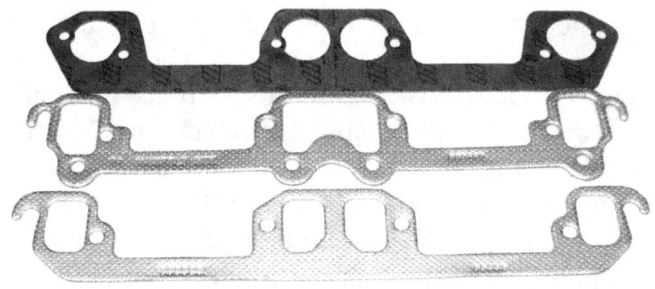

Exhaust gaskets are very important when using headers. The A-engine and the Magnum engine use the same exhaust bolt pattern. The standard gaskets are at the bottom. The center gasket is for use with air pumps; it was part of the emissions package in the 1970s and 1980s. The top gasket is for the W2, second generation; it shows the close attaching bolt holes.

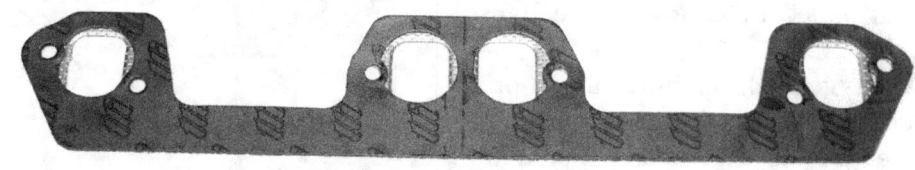

This setup shows the W2 gasket on top of the standard gasket. The second-generation W2 used both attaching bolt patterns so the bolt holes line up. Note that you can see the standard gasket inside the W2 port at the top and at each side. The W2 port is raised relative to the standard port and it is also wider.

SOURCE GUIDE

A-1 Technologies
7022 Alondra Blvd.
Paramont, CA 90723
a1technologies.com

Afco Racing Products
977 Hyrock Blvd.
Boonville, IN 47601
AFCOracing.com

Arias Pistons
13420 S. Normandie Ave.
Gardena, CA 90614
ariaspistons.com

ARP
1863 Eastman Ave.
Ventura, CA 93003
ARP-BOLTS.com

ATI Performance Products
6747 Whitestone Rd.
Baltimore, MD 21207

Autotronic Controls
1490 Henry Brennan Dr.
El Paso, TX 79936
msdignition.com

BHJ Dynamics
37530 Enterprise Ct.
Newark, CA 94560
harmonicdampers.com

Borla Performance
   Industries
5901 Edison Dr.
Oxnard, CA 93033
borla.com

Bouchillon Performance
937 Commerco Cir.
Hanahan, SC 29406
bouchillon
   performance.com

Bullet Cams
8785 Old Craft Rd.
Olive Branch, MS 38654

Burns Stainless
1013 West 18th St.
Costa Mesa, CA 92627

Canton Racing Products
232 Branford Rd.
North Branford,
   CT 06471
CantonRacing
   Products.com

Carrillo Industries
990 Calle Amanecer
San Clemente, CA 92673
carriloind.com

Charlie's Oil Pans
5281 S. Hametown Rd.
Norton, OH 44203

Clark Copper Head
   Gaskets
10510 Nassau St.
Blaine, MN 55449

Coan Engineering
1602 E. Havens St.
Kokomo, IN 46901
coanracing.com

Cometic Gasket
800-752-9850
cometic.com

Comp Cams
3406 Democrat Rd.
Memphis, TN 38118
compcams.com

CP Pistons
1902 McGaw
Irvine, CA 92614
cppistons.com

Crane Cams
530 Fentress Blvd.
Daytona Beach, FL 32114
cranecams.com

CSI Performance Products
16936 Cty. Rd. 252
McAlpin, FL 32062
csiperformance.com

Del West
28128 W. Livingston Ave.
Valencia, CA 91355
delwestusa.com

Diamond Racing Products
23003 Diamond Dr.
Clinton Twp, MI 48035
diamondracing.net

Dynatech
975 Hyrock Blvd.
Boonville, IN 47601
DynatechHeaders.com

Eagle Specialty Products
8530 Aaron Ln.
Southaven, MS 38671
summitracing.com/esp

Edelbrock Corp.
2700 California St.
Torrence, CA 90503
edelbrock.com

Gardner-Westcott
10110 Six Mile Rd.
Northville, MI 48168
HarlandSharp.com

Harland Sharp
19769 Progress Dr.
Strongsville, OH 44149
HarlandSharp.com

Hastings Piston Rings
325 N. Hanover St.
Hastings, MI 49058
hastingsmfg.com

Hedman Hedders
16410 Manning Way
Cerritos, CA 90703
hedman.com

Hogan's Racing Manifolds
303 N. Russell Ave.
Santa Maria, CA 93454
hogansracing
   manifolds.com

Imperial Services
PO Box 112
Frankenmuth, MI 48734
imperialservices.net

Indy Cylinder Head
8621 Southeastern Ave.
Indianapolis, IN 46239
indyheads.com

JE Pistons
15312 Connector Ln.
Huntington Beach,
   CA 92649
jepistons.com

Jesel
1985 Cedar Bridge Ave.
Lakewood, NJ 08701
jesel.com

Jomar Performance
211 N. Cass Ave.
Pontiac, MI 48342
jomarperformance.com

Kinsler Fuel Injection
1834 Thunderbird St.
Troy, MI 48084
kinsler.com

KB Performance Pistons
4909 Goni Rd.
Carson City, NV 89706
kb-silvolite.com

Koffel's Place
740 River Rd.
Huron, OH 44839
b1heads.com

Mancini Racing
P.O. Box 239
Roseville, MI 48066
manciniracing.com

Manley
1960 Swarthmore Ave.
Lakewood, NJ 08701
manleyperformance.com

Milodon Inc.
20716 Plummer St.
Chatsworth, CA 91311
milodon.com

Modern Cylinder Head
586-468-7914
moderncylinderhead.com

Moroso Performance
   Products
80 Carter Dr.
Guilford, CT 064437
moroso.com

Pro Gram Engineering
475 5th Street NE
Barbarton, OH 44203
pro-gram.com

Pro/Race Perforwmance
   Products
42295 Avenida Alvarado,
   Ste. 3
Temecula, CA 92590
pro-race.com

Quick Fuel Technology
129 Dishman Ln.
Bowling Green, KY 42101
quickfueltechnology.com

Schumacher Creative
   Services
2025 NE 123rd
Seattle, WA 98125
engine-swaps.com

Smith Brothers Pushrods
62958 Layton Ave., Ste. 4
Bend, OR 97701
pushrods.net

T & D Machine Products
4859 Convair Dr.
Carson City, NV 89706
tdmatch.com

TCI
151 Industrial Dr.
Ashland, MS 38603
tciauto.com

Total Flow Products
1197 Rochester Rd., Ste. N
Troy, MI 48083
totalflowproducts.com

Total Seal Piston Rings
22642 N. 15th Ave.
Phoenix, AZ 85027
totalseal.com

www.ingramcontent.com/pod-product-compliance
Lightning Source LLC
Chambersburg PA
CBHW080444090526
44586CB00047B/2310